DEEP TRIVEDI

Deep Trive
and maste
conducts
perspectiv
achieveme
he has led ....
success and happiness through his works.

In his voluminous works, Deep Trivedi has extensively explained Nature, its laws, its behaviour, its psychology and the effect it has on human life. No aspect of life and human psychology has been left untouched by him. He states that lack of psychological knowledge and understanding is the sole reason for all the sorrows and failures that pervade human life.

He has authored the bestsellers 'I am The Mind', 'I am Krishna', 'Everything is Psychology', '101 All Time Great Stories', 'The Black Book of Soul', '3 Easy Steps To Win At Life' and many more. His bestseller 'I am The Mind' has been published in several national and international languages. He has been awarded the Times Power Men Award 2018 for his immense contribution to society.

His command over the biggest psychologies of life can be gauged by the fact that he holds the record for 'Maximum Workshops on Human Life', 'Maximum Workshops on Psychological Aspects of Tao Te Ching', 'Maximum Workshops on Ashtavakra Gita' and 'Maximum Workshops on Bhagavad Gita', spanning 168 hours, 28 minutes, 50 seconds in 58 days in different National and International record books. He also holds the record for 'Maximum Number of Quotations on Human Life' (about 12038) on subjects such as Soul, Human Life, Psychology, Laws of Nature, Destiny and many more. He has also been awarded an Honorary Doctorate for his works on the psychology of Bhagavad Gita. His interactive workshops have brought about a revolutionary transformation in people's lives by addressing their day-to-day concerns. These workshops have been conducted in front of live audiences across India.

He is known for his special ability to touch upon the deepest aspects of life and explain them in a lucid language, leaving no scope for ambiguity. The distinct spiritual-psychological language and expression in his writings and workshops begin to have an instant effect on the mind of the reader or listener, which makes Deep Trivedi a pioneer in this field.

To know more about Deep Trivedi, visit www.deeptrivedi.com

First Edition: 2023

Price: ₹ 299/-

Printed in India

Concept, Illustration and Design:

AATMAN
INNOVATIONS PVT. LTD.

www.aatmaninnovations.com

Publisher: Aatman Innovations Pvt. Ltd.
Place of Publication: Mumbai

ISBN 978-93-84850-70-8

THE PSYCHOLOGY OF BHAGAVAD GITA
EXPLAINED LIKE NEVER BEFORE

I AM GITA

DEEP TRIVEDI

CONTENTS

Bhagavad Gita: An Introduction 01

Barriers to Comprehending and Assimilating Me 04

Grasp My Essence in Totality 11

Chapter 1 13

Chapter 2 24

Chapter 3 73

Chapter 4 90

Chapter 5 104

Chapter 6 112

Chapter 7 122

Chapter 8 131

Chapter 9 141

Chapter 10 155

Chapter 11 170

Chapter 12 185

Chapter 13 194

Chapter 14 210

Chapter 15 222

Chapter 16 235

Chapter 17 245

Chapter 18 259

Bhagavad Gita: An Introduction

I am the Bhagavad Gita, the eternal epitome of knowledge and wisdom. Who in the world is not aware of my existence? My glory is trumpeted across the world, for I am known to have stemmed forth from Krishna's consciousness, the only complete man in the known history of humankind. Indeed, it is a matter of great prestige for me that a historic being such as Krishna is my sire. And even more momentous is the fact that I have emanated from the supreme level of consciousness of a being as prodigious as Krishna; verily, this is what makes me the *Koh-i-noor* of all scriptures. It would not be erroneous to address me as the flowing river of truth, for all the mysteries of human life are ensconced within me. Indeed, the answer to every question pertaining to life is embedded within me. What is *karma*? What is the relation between *karma* and its fruits? What is the principle of birth and rebirth? What is the purpose of human life? What is *Parmaatma*, the Supreme Soul? What are the maxims to lead a happy and successful life? I hold the answers to all these and many other such questions concerning human life and existence, including the principles of creation and annihilation of the world.

Indeed, when such a vast reservoir of knowledge is encapsulated within me, there can be nothing more significant than reading and comprehending me. For, once you have read and grasped me – the Gita itself, sorrows and setbacks will disappear from your life, never to be found again. However, history bears testimony to the fact that "human

I am
Gita...
Grasp my
essence
and you will
not
need
any
knowledge
thereafter

life has been nothing save sorrows and failures since time immemorial". This reality has remained unchanged despite the presence of a great scripture like me! However, this does not imply a lack of effort on the part of people to read and comprehend me, for I am ranked amongst the most read scriptures of the world. Unfortunately, although I have been read extensively, my true essence has not been grasped (as yet). When, in fact, it is comprehension that is vital, not reading; and even more important is to imbibe and implement that which is comprehended. Nevertheless, for reasons unknown, people have miserably failed at grasping as well as elucidating my essence, and in turn, labelled me as complicated in order to mask their incompetence. Pray tell me, emanated as I have from the consciousness of a simple being like Krishna, how can I be complicated? If you endeavour to read and comprehend me with a mindset fraught with assumptions and presumptions, how am I or my creator to be blamed for it?

However, I'm aware of my significance and I very well know that having grasped my essence, the human being can scale the pinnacle of joy and success. As a matter of fact, I have been brought into existence with the sole objective of Arjuna's betterment and progress. And who in this world is not similar to Arjuna? Who doesn't need to read and fathom the mysteries enshrouded in me? But as you have labelled me complicated and difficult to fathom, today, I have myself come forward to shed light on all the mysteries enswathed in me. For, come what may, Krishna's compassion to lead human beings on the path of upliftment must not go in vain. And I am not only sanguine but also certain that my endeavour will forever disperse the clouds of misery and failure hovering menacingly over human life, thus ushering a golden era in which every home will have a Krishna – in various forms.

Bolstered by this hope, I have appeared before you today, nearly five millennia after my genesis.

Your very own,
Bhagavad Gita

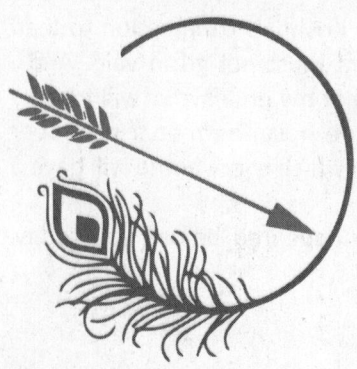

Barriers to Comprehending and Assimilating Me

Comprehension is a must, but there are four key barriers to grasping me in the truest sense. And before we proceed any further, let us steer clear of them.

1) Preconceived Notions about Me

It has been five thousand years since I stemmed forth from Krishna's consciousness. And although millions of people have read me since then, only a few were able to fathom my essence. Have you ever wondered why? That is because most people read me with preconceived notions such as 'Krishna is God', 'Gita is the truth' and so on. Well, if you are already in awe and hold such a strong preconceived notion about a scripture, how will you be able to comprehend it? The Gita is simply a discussion between two people who are at variance with each other. All you need to do is, keep your mind open and comprehend the arguments put forth by both of them, and at each point of discussion, try to grasp who between the two is right. But if you are already prejudiced in favour of Krishna and against Arjuna, then how will you comprehend? If you have already determined what is right and what is wrong even before grasping the essence of the discussion, then how can you possibly arrive at the right decision? How will you grasp the profundity of these matters? How will you discern the changes in the levels of their arguments and counter-arguments? Besides, if you have already made up your mind, then what is the point in reading or listening to their conversation at all? Hence, essentially, all you need to comprehend is that I am a scripture in which two people are debating over which is the better course of action, "to fight or not to fight." And it is you who has to decide who is right or wrong. And since you have to arrive at this decision, you must scrupulously comprehend the import of each and every argument they put forth. That is all.

2) Wrong Definition of Truth

This is the second impediment to comprehending me. It is generally assumed that since Krishna has enunciated the Gita, every word of it is true, and there is absolutely no need to contemplate over it or question it. One simply needs to follow whatever one is able to grasp and to any extent. When Krishna says "I am gambling", then it does not require questioning; one must simply sit down to gamble on the occasion of *Janmashtami*[1]. This is sheer disgrace, not only of a noble scripture like me, but also of a historical legend like Krishna. Indeed, everything Krishna has stated is true, but it is so in different contexts based on the Three Dimensional Theory. The Three Dimensional Theory pervades the entire universe; and even truth is no exception to it and is accordingly distinguished into three types. Nothing; no *karma*, thought or word is free of the Three Dimensional Theory of the world. However, a person ignorant about it cannot even understand the commonplace truths of the world, forget about comprehending me. That being said, I was explaining to you the Three Dimensional Theory with respect to truth. So, even though it is a fact that Gita holds the truth, even the truths stated in the Gita are segregated into three categories based on the Three Dimensional Theory of the world.

a) Eternal Truth

Eternal truths are principles applicable equally to all human beings of all times, without any exception or discrimination; for instance, the laws of *karma* and its fruits and the principles of birth and rebirth.

b) Truth of Time

These truths are spoken in accordance with the era one is in, and time and again, Krishna resorts to the prevailing scriptures and traditions of that era to help Arjuna realise the truth. Krishna does not need the support of scriptures to validate his words, but it is Arjuna who cannot do without them. Hence, Krishna refers to the scriptures of that time only to establish a better dialogue, but as they are mere references, they also change with the change of era and that of the scriptures.

---

1   *Janmashtami -* Krishna's birthday celebrated as a festival in India.

Unfortunately, human beings in every era have always been giving more credence to these very 'truths of time' cited in the Gita. And this too is a barrier in assimilating my essence.

c) Person-Specific Truth

It is imperative to bear in mind that Krishna, throughout the Gita, is addressing Arjuna; hence, all his statements have been made in view of Arjuna's state of mind at that moment. In modern parlance, you can term this a psycho-treatment that Krishna administered to Arjuna. Moreover, it is essential for you to grasp that all those statements were directed at Arjuna, not at you, and those verses can be of use to you only when your mindset resembles that of Arjuna. If not, you have to assimilate Krishna's words according to your own mindset. And the Gita can benefit you only when you successfully adopt Krishna's words to align with your psychology. Let me explain this to you with the help of an example of another great being, Gautama Buddha. One evening, Buddha was giving a discourse to his disciples... when suddenly, an emaciated man came doddering to seek knowledge from Buddha. Buddha looked at him from head to toe... and then spoke compassionately, "You shall surely attain knowledge, but to that end, you will first have to eat and drink to your heart's content and gain physical strength and become strong."

"As you say, my lord!" replied the man and walked away. After a while, there came a portly man with an enormous paunch, making it difficult for him to even walk. He too had come in hopes of acquiring knowledge from Buddha. Buddha ran his eyes closely over him, and then letting out a laugh, he declared, "Gaining knowledge is no big deal, it will happen in the blink of an eye. But in order to attain it, you must first lose half your weight through rigorous fasting and exercise." "As my lord desires," replied the man, and he too went on his way.

Meanwhile, Buddha's disciple, Ananda, who was sitting right beside him, was perplexed by these two instances. Unable to contain himself, he promptly asked Buddha, "This is incredible! You instruct one to feast on food and the other to fast. Kindly tell me, which path should I adopt to attain knowledge?"

Buddha chuckled and said, "Ananda! Were any of my words directed at you? No; right? So, why do you pay heed to what I advise others? Those were person-specific truths applicable only to them; they have nothing whatsoever to do with you." With the example stated here, I hope it is clear what person-specific truths are.

3) Gita – An Interminable Scripture

Many a time, I have seen people trying to fathom and expound upon individual *shlokas* or verses in isolation. However, in my case, this method of comprehension is wrong, for not only does every *shloka* have its own background but is also a part of a series of dialogues between two individuals. None of the *shlokas* can be analysed independently in isolation (of one another). These verses are not a monologue, but a continual colloquy registered in seven hundred *shlokas*, exquisitely encased in eighteen chapters. Throughout the Gita, Krishna responds to Arjuna's questions, and Arjuna in turn raises questions from the answers provided by Krishna, picking up the conversation from where Krishna leaves it. Hence, I cannot possibly be deciphered in bits and pieces; I must be comprehended in entirety in a sequential order. In fact, I have appeared before you today with the very purpose of helping you comprehend me sequentially...so that every human being can grasp my true essence.

4) The Three Dimensions of an Activity

As mentioned earlier, no particle or thought, no *karma*, activity or emotion in this world is exempt from the Three Dimensional Theory of the universe. And as the flow of my *shlokas* is also an activity, it has its very own three dimensions, namely Krishna, Arjuna and the battle of Mahabharata. Had any one of these three been missing, I would not have come into existence. Hence, it is imperative to understand the background of these three if you wish to comprehend my essence.

a) Krishna

An all-knowing being anchored in complete *Brahmacharya,*[2] Krishna never interfered in this great *leela* of Nature, or the divine play of Nature. This is why before the Gita came into existence, neither did he ever ask anyone to do anything, nor did he stop anyone from doing anything. And to comprehend the essence of the Gita, it is imperative to etch Krishna's *Brahmacharya* in your mind forever. Another significant aspect of Krishna's personality is that his entire life was dedicated to the greater good; and as he had anticipated this Epic

2   *Brahmacharya* - Conduct like *Brahm* i.e. to conduct oneself like Nature.

War called Mahabharata two decades before the actual battle, he had exhausted every effort, straining every nerve of his body to avert this colossal destruction. But when the war became inevitable, I came into existence by virtue of all that he said "to convince Arjuna to fight when the latter refused to fight".

b) Arjuna

Arjuna has been harbouring animosity towards the Kauravas for more than four decades, propelled by his desire to attain the kingdom that was snatched away from him. And now, after stoking his familial strife to the point that it has reached the brink of war, he is suddenly refusing to fight.

c) Mahabharata

Most kings of that era were hostile towards each other and suffered from the affliction of high ambitions. The fervent participation of a host of kings in the war is a fulmination of their bitter animosity and unquenchable ambition. Thus, this war reflects not only the mentality of the Kauravas and the Pandavas, but the collective mentality of that era as well.

Now that I have explained these barriers, mull over them and make a concerted effort to eliminate them. Once you have overcome the four barriers that act as stumbling blocks in comprehending me, you shall be ready to assimilate my essence.

Practical Application – 1

Write down your notions and beliefs about the Gita and Krishna.

A) ....
....
....
....

B) ....
....
....
....

C) ....
....
....
....
....

D) ....
....
....
....

E) ....
....
....
....
....

Now, make a pledge by repeating these words, "I hereby discard all my preconceived notions pertaining to the Gita and Krishna. With a fresh mind, I will now read and comprehend this Gita as if I were reading it for the very first time."

Practical Application – 2

The Gita has generally been beyond people's comprehension and the reasons for it have been explained here. However, before we proceed further with comprehending the Gita, it is important to thoroughly understand these reasons, because only then will the Gita be able to transform your life. Hence, in order to derive maximum benefit from the Gita, answer this question: As per your understanding, what are the barriers in comprehending the Gita? Write your answer in detail to ensure there remains no hindrance in grasping this life-changing wisdom.

....
....
....
....
....
....
....
....
....
....
....
....
....
....
....
....
....
....
....
....
....
....

Grasp My Essence in Totality

As stated earlier, secrets, supremely profound, are ensconced within me. All that is significant as regards the human mind, life and universe has been comprehensively discussed within my pages. And we shall, indeed, grasp the essence of all seven hundred *shlokas* in this book, chapter-wise, through the medium of Arjuna and Krishna. However, I would request you to not stop here but rather, consider the essence expounded by me as a guide. For, I hold such a vast ocean of knowledge within me that even if a hundred books are penned on me, they would not suffice. Furthermore, Krishna is a supreme being anchored at the pinnacle of truth. And truth has but one specialty; till the time it is not experienced deep within, it serves no purpose. Man cannot make even an iota of progress were he to rely on truth that is hypothetical and empty. Thus, once you have comprehended the essence of each chapter, deciphering its *shlokas* will not pose much difficulty to you. Simply contemplate on Arjuna's changing mindset reflected through his words and also strive to experience the entire gamut of truths, of every manner and kind, through the words of Krishna. Make this endeavour a daily practice. Upon doing so, truth will permeate deep within you. Believe me, one can have no better friend, well-wisher and guide than me. Just remember, every proclamation of Krishna is made from the zenith of truth. So, do not weigh his words on the scales of the prevalent scriptures or your own opinions and thoughts, else, you will go astray. Krishna is above and beyond all that is said in the world.

He is proclaiming the truth, direct and forthright. Ergo, the majority of his declarations are unique and novel. Thus, you too must study all the *shlokas* with the very objective of experiencing them deep within. Once those *shlokas* take root within you, you will be freed from all the ludicrous notions you have ever encountered. You will then become one with the truth. With the fervent hope that this propitious union comes into being, I dedicate this book to you.

Chapter 1

A vast and picturesque field of Kurukshetra has been turned into a battlefield. Scores of grim-faced kings and their regiments stand face to face, ready to kill or be killed. Bloodlust has everyone in its vicious grip. Each face is eager and expectant, prepared to unleash carnage and partake in the gruesome dance of death. The thunderous boom of drums and kettledrums reverberates through the battlefield, in expectation of the battle, as if to herald the beginning of some glorious event.

The pertinent point to understand here is that this battlefield of Kurukshetra does not exist externally. This *samsara* – this world is every human being's very own Kurukshetra. Each and every human being is engaged in a conflict with the world; when in fact, no battle of life lies outside. The root cause of all the struggles of life is within. All three principal characters of the Mahabharata verily dwell within every human being. Arjuna symbolises the brain, Duryodhana, the ego, and Krishna, the witness; and all three of them dwell within every human being, at all times. And every human being's Arjuna and Duryodhana, that is, his brain and ego, are constantly in disagreement with Krishna, that is, his witness. And all the external struggles of life are simply an outcome of this internal struggle. But the one who becomes a witness like Krishna has no struggle within; there is no conflict between his mind, brain and ego. And when there is no struggle within, he can

No battle of life lies **outside;** the **root cause** of all the **struggles** of life lies **within**

never be a part of any war externally. Ergo, there are two perspectives to view life; one is to look from the outside, which is called *Maya*, an illusion. And the other is a spiritual perspective, which teaches one to look within. And this spiritual perspective is the only true way to perceive life. So, if you wish to comprehend your very own Bhagavad Gita's essence, then do not look for this battle outside; rather seek it within yourself. Here, you must reflect upon the question: would this Epic War have been possible on the outside if the animosity between the Kauravas and the Pandavas had not grown roots deep within? In other words, if Arjuna is standing in the battlefield at present, then it is the result of an internal conflict between his mind, brain and ego. It is the result of a conflict between the 'Arjuna' and 'Duryodhana' dwelling within him. In short, all the reasons, the whys and wherefores, lie within you; what manifests on the outside is simply its reflection, its consequence. If there is no internal conflict between your mind, brain and ego, then there will never be a conflict in your life on the outside either. And to live a conflict-free, seamlessly flowing life is verily human life at its best. And 'Gita' for you is the greatest scripture ever enunciated to establish harmony between your mind and brain within. Once they are in sync with each other, there will be no struggle in life whatsoever. In short, the Gita is an unparalleled scripture that will transform you from Arjuna and Duryodhana into Krishna. Indeed, its purpose is to subdue the

Arjuna and Duryodhana within you and transform you into a witness, calm and composed. Once you become a witness, there will be no scope for struggle. Verily, even though Krishna is standing in the battlefield of Kurukshetra, he is not struggling; he is absolutely calm and composed within.

Returning to Kurukshetra, the cacophony of the kettledrums and drums is growing louder and louder, making the very ground beneath tremble. Any moment now, the sonorous note of the bugle will pierce through every other noise on the battlefield, declaring the start of the battle. That very moment, the blind father of the Kauravas, Dhritarashtra, sitting anxiously in his palace, asks Sanjaya, seated beside him, to apprise him of the scenario at the battlefield. And Sanjaya, who can see events occurring at a faraway distance, observes the battlefield carefully and prepares himself to satiate Dhritarashtra's curiosity. Here, do not assume the ability to see events occurring at a faraway distance as an extraordinary phenomenon or make-believe. No, it is quite commonplace. This is exactly what you need to comprehend; the human being is able to utilise merely a fraction of his faculties, be it his eyes, ears, or for that matter, his brain. And this is the very reason underlying his wretched and failed life. Otherwise, the human being has the ultimate potential to achieve just about anything. And this is what we must comprehend; if Krishna could anticipate this battle of Mahabharata twenty years before the battle becoming a reality, then why not others? In fact, the human being has such a remarkable power of intuition hidden within him that he can very well reckon that which is going to transpire in the future! Moreover, he can well discern the thoughts running through a person's mind, sitting right in the comfort of his house; he can catch the frequency of every place and person. In fact, I, your beloved Bhagavad Gita, am an incredible composition that can hone all of these astounding capabilities.

Concurrently, we must also understand why Dhritarashtra is asking 'Sanjaya' to apprise him of the events transpiring at the battlefield. It is because he is blind. And those who are blind are always inquisitive, whether they are blind by sight, brain or knowledge. And I do not want you to go around asking all and sundry "what is going on, or what will come to pass". I want you to increase your innate power to a level from where you yourself are cognisant of "what is happening today and what will befall on the morrow".

Meanwhile, as Sanjaya paints a vivid picture of the battlefield for Dhritarashtra, he says, "The vast battlefield of Kurukshetra is host to thousands of mighty warriors, all willing to fight to death. Countless warriors stand regally under the waving flag of the Kauravas, while a great many soldiers have pledged their troth to the Pandavas. It is difficult to assess which side is more formidable. But mind you, no face at the battlefield is creased with apprehension; in fact, the entire battlefield is bursting with fervent enthusiasm, as any moment now, the battle is about to begin."

But wait a moment... What is this? All of a sudden, Arjuna asks his charioteer Krishna, 'Steer my chariot forward and place it between the two armies. I want to have a closer look at the enemy front, to see which kings are supporting the evil-minded Duryodhana.' In response, Krishna nods and immediately steers the chariot in the middle of the two armies. Now, even this trifling incident contains many points worthy of our observation. Firstly, Krishna is Arjuna's charioteer in the battlefield, and to ride the chariot at the behest of the warrior is verily the duty of the charioteer. What you need to comprehend here is that Krishna is a charioteer not only in the battlefield but even in reality, as he, in the form of a "witness", is every human being's charioteer. But unfortunately, every person in this world has forsaken his witness, which should ideally be his charioteer in life, and opted for his "brain-ego" as the guiding force of his life. That is why, Krishna, one's charioteer for life, dwelling within him in the form of his witness, leads his life wherever his brain and ego direct it to. It is a law that only one force can hold the reins of life. If a human being so wishes, he can make either his "witness" the charioteer of his life or his brain and ego; the choice is his and it is completely at his discretion. But since most people have made their brain and ego the charioteer of their lives, they cannot blame their "witness" for the vicissitudes in their life. Secondly, just as Krishna holds the reins of the chariot in the battlefield, everyone should hand over the reins of their lives to their very own "Krishna, dwelling within them in the form of witness". You must comprehend that as long as the reins of your life lie in the hands of Arjuna or Duryodhana, that is, if they are in control of your brain and ego, you will find the chariot of your life placed in the battle of Mahabharata over and over again. Furthermore, Arjuna's wish to scan the enemy front establishes the fact that a human being's brain is superior to his ego. This makes it easier to understand the difference between the brain and the ego. The brain reckons that if one has to engage in a battle, then firstly, it is imperative to rightly gauge the enemy's strength; whereas the ego, as is its wont, leaps in the dark without a second thought. And this is why, time and again, it is smashed to smithereens.

Well, as soon as the chariot is placed between the two armies, Arjuna sweeps his gaze over the Kaurava front. He can, indeed, espy his own cousins, friends and relatives standing in this vast army of the Kauravas. Taking in the sight before him, all of a sudden, Arjuna is overwhelmed with sorrow. Submerged in that sorrowful state, he then looks at Krishna and speaks in a voice throbbing with emotion, "Espying my near and dear ones standing at war with me, my limbs are losing strength, my mouth is running dry and shivers are coursing through my body. Krishna, I cannot even begin to describe the state of my mind; the bow is slipping from my nerveless hands, my skin feels like it's on fire and my mind is becoming deluded. O Krishna, everything appears tumultuous and catastrophic to me. And even if it is not so, I still cannot see how slaying my kith and kin will lead to my well-being. Krishna, to tell you the truth, seeing all this, I wish for neither victory nor kingdom. O Krishna! Even if we do attain the kingdom by obliterating them all, what good is such royal comfort and such a worthless existence?"

"O Krishna! The enemy legion in front of me has my teachers, uncles, cousins, nephews, grandsires, brothers-in-law and countless other relatives. To speak the truth, Krishna, I do not wish to kill them even to attain the three worlds; hence, killing them for a petty kingdom is simply out of the question. I cannot commit this heinous deed even if I were to be killed. Besides, what will we gain by slaying them? On the contrary, we will only incur sin. Pray tell me, how can we possibly experience joy after killing our own family? These people are naïve; these greed-stricken Kauravas have no inkling of this grave sin, but we are aware of it all. Therefore, O Krishna, why shouldn't we deliberate upon this in order to avert this deadly sin?"

"Krishna, the scriptures state that slaying one's kith and kin defiles the women of the house and causes obliteration of the clan. The scriptures also state that on committing such a horrendous crime, one will have to languish in hell for an indefinite period of time. What astounds me, Krishna, is how did we acquiesce to this deadly sin in spite of our prudence? Therefore, come what may, I am relinquishing my weapons. I cannot commit this grave sin. Hereafter, even if they kill me, I am ready to die, but I am not prepared to commit this deadly sin." Speaking thus, Arjuna, utterly dejected and dispirited, casts his bow aside and slumps down in the rear end of the chariot.

With Arjuna putting down his weapons, the first chapter of the Gita comes to an end. I would now request you to pore over Arjuna's words again and again, and look within yourself to see if you are in agreement with him. Because, your journey ahead in the Gita depends solely on the extent to which your thoughts align with those of Arjuna's. Close your eyes and think, what would you have done had you been in Arjuna's place in the battlefield? What would you have said to Krishna? Would you, like Duryodhana, have been raring to begin fighting without really thinking of the consequences? You must ascertain whether your thoughts align more with Arjuna or Duryodhana. You must also determine which faculty is more powerful in your case—your brain or your ego. Grasp these points and introspect upon them, and then in the next chapter, we will see, to what extent Krishna concurs with Arjuna.

In life, we are constantly embroiled in innumerable problems, simultaneously grappling with a host of struggles. And the very essence of the first chapter of the Gita is, the root cause of all the struggles on the outside lies within us. Therefore, the struggles on the outside will not cease to exist until we identify their root causes and weed them out. And you are well aware that every struggle not only consumes your precious time and energy but also distresses your mind. So, mitigate the struggles of life because only then will you be able to accomplish something of consequence. And for this purpose, fill out the chart below, as it will help you alleviate your struggles.

Note:
Life can undoubtedly be mired in a multitude of struggles, but in this application, write in detail about the five most prominent struggles afflicting your life. This will provide clarity about which 'enemies' you need to decimate first. Thereafter, identify the root causes of those five struggles and list them down. Importantly, contemplate deeply on the root causes and then begin to enlist them. For, most external struggles in a person's life are caused by desire, expectation, fear, obduracy, ego, servile mentality, beliefs, resolves, principles, jealousy and so on. So, in order to free yourself of a struggle, eliminate its root cause within, and the struggle outside will automatically disappear. Besides, once you have eliminated the root cause within, the struggle on the outside will definitely stop distressing you, whether it is fully averted or not.

Write in detail about the five prominent struggles that exist in your life at present. Identify the root cause of each of these struggles within and write it below. Try to vanquish the root cause within. Once you have done so, put a tick ✓ in the box below.

A) Struggle

....
....
....

— **The root cause of the struggle** —

....
....
....
....

☐ **I have vanquished the root cause within**

B) Struggle

....
....
....

— **The root cause of the struggle** —

....
....
....
....

☐ **I have vanquished the root cause within**

C — Struggle

....
....
....
....
....

The root cause of the struggle

....
....
....
....
....

☐ **I have vanquished the root cause within**

D — Struggle

....
....
....
....
....

The root cause of the struggle

....
....
....
....
....
....

☐ **I have vanquished the root cause within**

....

....

....

....

....

The root cause of the struggle

....

....

....

....

....

☐ **I have vanquished the root cause within**

 Practical Application – 4

The first chapter of the Gita teaches us that every human being is grappling with his own battle of Mahabharata; this battle verily exists within him and simply manifests on the outside. And when the Mahabharata war exists within, then surely, its three principal characters, Krishna, Arjuna and Duryodhana are also present within us. Hence, recognise the Krishna, Arjuna and Duryodhana that dwell within you, for, they are invariably present in each and every person in varying degrees. I shall describe the qualities of all three, based on which write the percentage of each one of these three characters of the Mahabharata that are present within you.

Krishna

Krishna is a witness. He arrives at decisions after correctly assessing the circumstances. He performs deeds in the interest of the greater good, and never out of self-interest. And as he knows what ought to be done, must be done, he does not get deluded by external influences in this regard.

Percentage of Krishna in you ☐ %

Arjuna

Arjuna is intelligent and clever. He is easily perturbed by external influences, and is always mired in confusion. Though he is extremely talented, he is unable to perform when the time demands. He lends greater importance to logic than to truth and wisdom.

Percentage of Arjuna in you ☐ %

Duryodhana

Duryodhana is gullible, and is fond of amassing power and might. With utter disregard for good-bad or right-wrong, he creates trouble for himself and others. Stubborn that he is, he does not heed the voice of reason. Most of his decisions are detrimental to himself and to those around him.

Percentage of Duryodhana in you ☐ %

In the above chart, you have written, to what extent each of these three characters are present within you. Now, on a daily basis, weaken the tendencies in you that symbolise Arjuna and Duryodhana, while embracing the qualities that represent Krishna. I promise, this exercise will continue to change your life for the better the more you keep up with it.

Chapter 2

Furnishing numerous reasons to avoid fighting, Arjuna relinquishes his bow and arrows. Under these circumstances, the only pertinent question that needs an answer is, to what extent does Krishna concur with Arjuna? If Krishna agrees with Arjuna, then the basic argument would be put to rest and the Gita would end right here. However, this is not the case; instead of agreeing with him, Krishna asks the dejected Arjuna with great surprise, "O Arjuna! How has this delusion overcome you at this untimely moment?" And this statement alone is enough to display the profundity of Krishna's knowledge of psychology. This is the first statement uttered by Krishna in the Gita, but it is so succinct and precise that one cannot help but salute his knowledge of psychology time and again. Here, 'untimely' implies 'at the wrong time'. In essence, Krishna implies, "Arjuna, if you really wished to avert this war with the Kauravas, you had countless opportunities to do so in the past forty years. I had always wanted to avert this war; had you also agreed and supported my stance, we would never have had to see this day. But today, when the battle is about to begin any moment, your thinking is not in sync with the need of the hour. For, this war has now become inevitable. And a human being has no option but to accept that which is unavoidable, that which cannot be changed. Moreover, even if you want to desert the battlefield today, who will let you do so? Nobody will allow you to flee. Thus, your present thinking of not fighting the war is nothing save a delusion."

Further, Krishna says, "Irrespective of your reasons and rationale behind uttering such lofty words, or the logical arguments put forth by you to not engage in the battle, understand clearly that "getting mired in such an untimely delusion" is not the mark of noble men." And with this remark, Krishna has proven yet again that he is the master of human psychology. And it is imperative for each and every human being to assimilate this truth. This veritable psychological grasp of Krishna is what makes me, the Gita, absolutely invaluable and the greatest of all scriptures. To acquire a thorough understanding of this statement of Krishna, you must first learn about the composition of human beings and their mechanism of functioning. A human being possesses three great powers. First is the ego, which thinks of its own interest and then rigidly holds on to it. Next is the brain which cloaks even the ego, errant and wrong, in shrouds of fine words and thoughts. And last but not the least is the mind, which is close to Nature and flows unbridled and unrestrained. And the human being expresses everything that is going on at the level of these three powers through three mediums; first, through his eyes; second, his words, and third, his expressions... If a person is transparent about his thoughts and emotions, that is, if he displays on the outside what he is feeling within, then there is perfect harmony amongst these three powers; in other words, there is no contradiction amongst these three powers. That is why, a person, when he is lying, does not look you in the eye. And by all means, there is no need to explain any of this to Krishna. He is, after all, the ace master of this entire dynamics.

Indeed, Krishna has listened carefully to each and every word of Arjuna, while observing his facial expressions and the rapid blinking of his eyes. And he knows there is no consensus or harmony between Arjuna's words, eyes and expressions. In other words, what he is exhibiting outside is completely at variance with what he is feeling within. Understand this clearly: Krishna might have even agreed with Arjuna for once had Arjuna's words echoed his feelings within. But Arjuna is cunning; the thoughts racing through his mind are a far cry from the lofty words emanating from his lips... And this is simply not acceptable to Krishna. This is what you too must grasp thoroughly. For, I am extremely useful in learning the psychology of day-to-day life. You have to deal with thousands of people in your life, and you will notice that in the majority of them, there is no parity between their thoughts and their expressions. And, you well know that it is not that which is exhibited outside but that which lies within that holds significance. Therefore, although you have read what Arjuna is stating externally, it is far more important to fathom what he is actually feeling within. For, similar to Arjuna, almost everybody in this world makes grand pronouncements morning, noon and night. But those who are well versed in psychology do not fall for their bombastic rhetoric. That being the case, there is no question of Krishna, the master of psychology, falling for Arjuna's words. Now, we will try to comprehend why Krishna did not get influenced by Arjuna's impressive words and logical reasoning. And in order to unravel this baffling mystery, it is imperative to have a profound understanding of psychology. In fact, it would be more accurate to state that in order to gain any knowledge of psychology, it is imperative to grasp the Gita, that is, me. For, no other scripture has grasped "human psychology" in such great depth. It has been more than five millennia since my genesis, and I have witnessed human beings making tremendous progress in this period of time. But as far as psychology is concerned, they are still in the dark. The truth is, human life is nothing but a psychology, and only those with a deep grasp of psychology have led a happy and successful life. If viewed from this perspective, I can also be called the "magnum opus to help human beings attain happiness and success". And for you to comprehend this monumental work, it is vital that I speak in the scientific parlance relevant to your times. Ergo, I will employ contemporary words and prevalent principles in order to elaborate wherever necessary.

In order to comprehend the explanations that follow, you must first fathom the workings of Nature along with a few key principles of psychology. Clearly, something has changed within Arjuna, and he is also displaying this change on the outside, in his own way. This is nothing out of the ordinary. What is important is to comprehend the "principles of psychology" that are at work behind this change.

For, it is psychology which governs Nature. Therefore, in order to fathom this principle of psychology, firstly, you must grasp that "on the basis of the principles of time and space", two worlds simultaneously exist here. First is the outside world, called 'space' in today's scientific parlance, which is exclusively the world of outcomes. And second is the world within, termed 'time' in today's lexicon. It is imperative to comprehend here that all the 'reasons' for the events occurring in the outside world lie hidden in this internal world. And it is a law that no change can occur on the outside without a change occurring within. To rephrase this law in the lexicon of the twenty-first century, no change takes place in space, that is, outside, without a change in time, that is, inside. Therefore, time and its principles are extremely important. All in all, this implies that some change has occurred within Arjuna which is being manifested outside in the form of his refusal to fight the war. But the external change is of no consequence, for its root cause lies hidden within. And in order to grasp any of the subsequent points, it is vital to comprehend "what change has occurred within Arjuna and why". It is for this very purpose that knowledge of psychology is required, which I, your very own "Bhagavad Gita", am trying to impart.

Another pertinent point to note is that there are no separate laws for human beings in Nature. The laws of Nature are so profound that they are equally applicable to everything, right from the minutest atom to

> **O Arjuna,** these **changing** circumstances are **illusory** and **untrue;** whereas you are the **truth,** having the **capability** of **persevering** under any **circumstances**

the entire length and breadth of human life. And one of these laws applies to all the changes occurring in Nature, whether it is the change in speed occurring in inanimate objects or in the mind of human beings; and that law is the law of motion, discovered by the great scientist of your time, Sir Isaac Newton, who can also be called a great philosopher of the present aeon. Now, kindly recall Newton's Law of Motion; the law states that an object at rest remains at rest, and an object in motion remains in motion at a constant speed and in a straight line unless acted upon by an external force. And this external force can, indeed, be applied in two ways; if the force is applied in the same direction as that of the speed of the object in motion, then the speed in that direction will accelerate, and if it is exerted in the opposite direction, then the speed will slacken.

We shall now dissect Arjuna's situation with the help of this principle. For more than four decades, Arjuna had been harbouring animosity towards the Kauravas; and with the passage of time, his enmity towards them had only intensified. Just moments before expressing his inability to fight, he had zealously said to Krishna, "Place my chariot between the two armies. I want to see all those who are standing in support of the evil-minded Duryodhana. I want to correctly assess the might of the warriors I have to fight in the battle." That is to say, just moments before refusing to fight, he was raring to confront the enemy. Referring to Duryodhana as evil-minded clearly shows that just moments before he decided not to fight, Arjuna was furious with the Kauravas. So, how could a change that had not taken place in the past forty years, suddenly occur in a matter of moments? If comprehended on the basis of the Law of Motion, a change in speed is not possible without a new occurrence, or a new force applied to it. It is also apparent that the change that occurred in Arjuna is tremendous. For, the very same Arjuna who was craving war for the past forty years is now refusing to fight. This implies, the change has definitely occurred in the opposite direction. In other words, the pressure has been exerted in the reverse direction. This gives rise to the question, how did this happen so suddenly? What change occurred on the outside? What external pressure reversed the steadfastness that Arjuna was living with for the past four decades?

Well, what Arjuna saw on the outside was the vast army of the Kauravas which also included his kinsmen. With this, you must have realised that the sight of the Kaurava army has brought this sudden change in Arjuna's stance. You must have also discerned that instead of stoking Arjuna's raging desire for war, this sight, on the contrary, acted as an impediment to it. As mentioned earlier, this world is encompassed by the Three Dimensional Theory; therefore, not even a single change that occurs in this world can escape the influence of this Three Dimensional Theory. It is certain that a change has occurred in Arjuna, but there are not one but three possible reasons for this change. First, it is possible that Arjuna has embraced non-violence and to gain anything by means of destroying life and property may not seem appropriate to him anymore. Second, his heart might have suddenly been overcome with love for the Kauravas, as he might be thinking, 'What difference does it make whether it is we or the Kauravas who enjoy the kingdom? They are cousins, after all. Why fight with one's own cousins for a mere kingdom?' And third, it is possible that the sight of the mammoth army of the Kauravas has terrified him. And it is crucial to understand which of these three reasons is responsible for effecting such a drastic change in Arjuna. What exactly could have occurred that Arjuna, who was thirsting to shed blood moments ago, is suddenly refusing to fight? And there is absolutely no question of Krishna failing to discern the reason behind Arjuna's refusal to fight. Had Arjuna really attained the mental state of non-violence, then the Gita would have ended right here. Without wasting a moment, Krishna would have declared, 'O Arjuna! What you are saying is true indeed; leave this war and walk away.' Had love for the Kauravas really kindled in Arjuna's heart, Krishna would have perhaps looked into the possibility of holding a meeting between the Pandavas and the Kauravas without any delay. Even then, it would have been impossible, for, the Pandavas would have had to first sort the matter amongst themselves, in which case, it was certain that their wife, Draupadi would have had the final word on it. And as far as Draupadi was concerned, she would not have settled for anything less than the blood of Duryodhana and Dushasana. Similarly, it would have also become essential to convince the Kauravas to stop the war, which was unlikely, as there was no possibility of Duryodhana's gigantic ego agreeing to such a proposal. Most importantly, there was no time for any of these deliberations and engagements, as the sonorous sound of the bugle of battle could declare the war at any moment. Even so, had Arjuna's new-sprung love for his Kaurava brothers been genuine, Krishna would have definitely made one last attempt. Admittedly, Arjuna's love for his Kaurava brothers had been stirred to some extent, but Krishna certainly had no time to appreciate his familial love at the moment; he had no option but to disregard "Arjuna's fraternal love". Because, most importantly, the abject fear that Arjuna felt upon witnessing "the mighty army of the Kauravas and its fine archers like Karna, Bhishma and Drona" was far more intense than the stirrings of fraternal love in his heart. But as Arjuna was a man driven by his brain, on one hand, he was trying to cunningly hide his fear with his rhetoric of non-violence, and on the other, he was making an attempt to cloak the fear rising within him "in the garb of love for the Kauravas". In other words, he was striving to overplay the "compassion" that had kindled within him for the Kauravas. Now, he could have hoodwinked anyone in the world with such an attempt, but not the master of psychology, Krishna.

To comprehend further how Arjuna is cloaking his fear with the veil of non-violence and love for the Kauravas, you must meticulously review every word uttered by Arjuna. I have already stated that truth can never be concealed. The human being certainly makes vain attempts to do so, but the truth invariably manifests through his eyes, words and expressions. All one needs is the 'knowledge of psychology'. So, without further ado, let us begin analysing Arjuna's statements. On espying the massive army of the Kauravas, he says that his limbs are giving way, his mouth is becoming parched and his body is trembling, as he beholds his near and dear ones. Now tell me, do limbs give way at the sight of one's family and friends? Does the mouth run dry? Does one start trembling? These are all natural reactions when one faces a formidable foe. There is evidently no harmony between Arjuna's eyes, words and expressions. He might be calling these people his kinsmen but deep within, his mind is still beset with animosity for the Kauravas. Besides, the Kauravas had done nothing new in the past few moments to trigger such an outpouring of love from Arjuna's heart for them. And as mentioned earlier, no change can take place within until something new occurs on the outside. Further, he says that his skin is burning, the bow is slipping from his hands, his mind is getting deluded and he is no longer able to even stand properly. Needless to mention, these are all characteristics of a person gripped by abject fear. Curiously, just a year prior to this battle, the same Arjuna, with the assistance of King Virata's army, had made Drona, Bhishma and Karna bite the dust. Well, Arjuna is undoubtedly a fine warrior; but he well knows that the circumstances then were drastically different. Back then, Duryodhana had set out in search of Arjuna with only a small army in tow, and traversing a long distance, the army was undeniably weary. Moreover, they had anticipated clashing with a lone Arjuna sans any support, so finding the huge army of the Matsya kingdom standing shoulder to shoulder with Arjuna was a nasty surprise for them. And you all know how significant the element of surprise is in a battle; it is indubitably the most formidable weapon in any battle of life. Of course, there was yet another reason behind Arjuna's conquest over Duryodhana's army. True, the Kauravas were putting up a fight, but at that time, they were not even certain whether the warrior they were fighting against was really Arjuna or not. They had fought the entire battle in a state of quandary. For, the Pandavas were in *agyaatvaas* [3] so naturally they were not in their usual appearance. Hence, taking all these factors into consideration, the analytical warrior that he is, Arjuna currently harbours no doubt

3   *Agyaatvaas* - Living incognito, in disguise.

whatsoever that winning that battle was vastly different from emerging victorious in the present battle. Looking at the Kauravas' army, he can very well sense that triumphing in this war will not be easy. And despite his best efforts, he is unable to hide this very apprehensiveness. In his next statement itself, he remarks, "O Krishna, I can see only evil omens. Nothing appears agreeable upon seeing the vast army of the Kauravas." However, he immediately regains his composure and says, "Besides, O Krishna, I cannot see any good ensuing from slaying our kinsmen. Meaning, on one hand, I can see the possibility of our defeat looming large on the horizon, while on the other, even if I were to attain victory, I will be contending with the immense grief of killing my kinsmen. To tell you the truth, O Krishna, I want neither kingdom nor victory. What will I gain by slaying my teachers, grandsires and uncles? I do not wish to fight them even if I were to attain the three worlds, let alone this earth." But Arjuna seems to be forgetting that neither is anybody giving him the three worlds if he emerges victorious, nor this earth. The battle is strictly confined to gaining control over the throne of Hastinapur. And bear this in mind, the moment one loses, or if even the possibility of defeat looms overhead, then one begins rambling, "We have come into this world empty-handed and we will depart empty-handed too." As soon as they experience a few setbacks in life, everything appears "illusory" to them. But this is *shamshaan vairagya*[4] and not the true state of mind. And the stark truth of Arjuna's mind is that on one hand, he is frightened, and on the other, he does not see the prospect of gaining much benefit from slaying his kinsmen.

As for Arjuna, he is not done speaking yet; he still has a few arrows left in his verbal repository. Crossing all limits in his attempt to influence and delude Krishna, he now resorts to the scriptures and asserts that even they do not permit killing one's kith and kin. He says, "O Krishna, these men are ignoramuses but it is surprising that you and I, despite being scholars in scriptures, have acquiesced to committing this grave sin." Meaning, he is now preaching to Krishna! He is forewarning Krishna, "I am explaining all this to you in order to save you from a grave sin and open your eyes to the truth. We should be wary of deliberately opening the doors of hell for ourselves." And in the end, he says, "You are responsible for your own actions, you can

4   *Shamshaan Vairagya* - Detachment that occurs temporarily, but does not last long; for example, on the death of a loved one.

partake in this grave sin if you so desire, but I have decided that I will not fight in this war." Speaking thus, he casts aside his bow and arrows and slumps down in the chariot.

Having delivered such a persuasive and beguiling speech, he must have certainly expected Krishna to laud him and say, 'Arjuna, verily, you have opened my eyes. You have, indeed, saved me from committing a grave sin.' But Krishna is the master of psychology. From the very first statement uttered by Arjuna, Krishna had discerned that he had become frightened. In fact, the law of change states that if a change has to occur, it occurs right when an impediment is encountered. If a vehicle has to stop, it does so the instant you apply the brakes, not the next day! Similarly, Arjuna has not read the scriptures for the first time today. If they had to produce an effect on him, it would have taken place long ago. Likewise, Arjuna, since childhood, is well acquainted with the fact that the Kauravas are his cousins. So, if kinship were so valuable to him so as to influence him, it would have produced an effect a long time ago. The reason behind today's encumbrance is certainly something else; it is the fear in Arjuna's mind that deems vanquishing the mammoth army of the Kauravas to be an impossible task. You should also observe this tendency in day-to-day psychology. A person warms up to the enemy only when the foe appears more formidable than him. Man takes refuge in lofty principles of religion only when he suffers setbacks in life. For, nobody in this world is willing to admit that he has failed or is frightened. Here, everyone is busy concealing their defeat behind exalted thoughts and principles, day in and day out. For, having the word of their ruin broadcasted everywhere is a greater cause for concern for people than the actual ruination. And this is the very significance of your dear Bhagavad Gita. It begins by talking about day-to-day psychology and in the process, it touches upon all the profundities of truth.

However, returning to the present, most importantly, if Arjuna had surprised Krishna by refusing to fight, then the latter too had shocked Arjuna by not getting swayed by his words. In fact, in his very first statement, Krishna says, "Stop rambling and apprehend clearly that you are entertaining an untimely delusion. O Arjuna, you are trying to prove your greatness by taking refuge in sundry scriptures and asserting your love for the Kauravas. But know this with certainty, noble men do not conduct themselves in the manner you are behaving at present."

Further, you must comprehend two more points in order to decipher what the rest of the Gita says. Had it been an ordinary situation, then perhaps, Krishna would have closed the discussion at this point and held his peace. Because he knows that every human being in this world is free, and one shall reap what one sows. In truth, nobody can force anybody in any manner in this grand, perpetual *leela* of life transpiring between Nature and the human being. However, this is with regard to one's personal life. Otherwise, the truth is that as long as there is life, everybody has to live, whether it is Krishna, Buddha, Christ or any other wise being. So, if not on a personal front, at least collectively, everybody is living for the welfare and progress of humankind. This serves as the rationale as well as the purpose for their life. Similarly, at present, for the sake of the greater good, Krishna has become bound to the task of convincing Arjuna to fight. Because, if Arjuna does not fight, then the victory of the Kauravas would be ascertained; and if this became a reality, it would set a wrong precedent. And in the coming ages, the dignity of women would be put at stake even more brazenly and fearlessly. In short, the battle has become inevitable! Whatever destruction of life and property has to happen, will happen. Such being the case, it is better that the Pandavas emerged victorious, for this will at least compel people to think twice before perpetrating any vile act in the future. Looking at the disastrous end of the Kauravas, man will steer clear of evildoings. Krishna had been relentless in his pursuit to avert the war for as long as it was possible. In fact, he had devoted several years of his life only to the mission of trying to avert the war between the Kauravas and the Pandavas. So, do not erroneously presume that Krishna wants the Pandavas to win the war owing to his familial relation or friendship with Arjuna. No, this is not the case, because even Duryodhana is a relative of Krishna.[5] Ergo, do not view Krishna through the lens of any relation, else it will be a grave fallacy, and you will simply fail to grasp my essence. As mentioned earlier, Krishna, Arjuna and the Mahabharata serve as the foundation of my being. Hence, it is imperative to understand these three players in order to comprehend

5   Krishna's son, Saamb, had married Duryodhana's daughter, Laxmana.

me. And Krishna's mind is so evolved and elevated that the concept of friend or foe doesn't exist for him. His mind is concerned only with the greater good. And in this inevitable war, the greater good lies in the victory of the Pandavas. Because, when the present destruction is inevitable, then naturally, Krishna is focusing on setting an example for the future. Please do not presume that the Pandavas are virtuous and the Kauravas are sinners. Truth is always bitter; and the bitter truth about the Pandavas is that virtuous men never compromise the dignity of a woman by apportioning her amongst five brothers on the pretext of obeying their mother's command. It is also true that men who put their own wife at stake in a game of dice can never be called noble. Therefore, in essence, Krishna's sole interest is centred on helping the Pandavas win the war, bearing the greater good in mind. And to that end, it is crucial that Arjuna fights with his heart and soul. However, this by no means denotes any prejudice on Krishna's part, for he is compelled to act in this manner purely for the sake of the greater good. Going forward, comprehension of this point is important to grasp my true essence; because many people are of the opinion that even though Arjuna had embraced the path of non-violence, it was Krishna who was adamant and incited the former to fight. However, Krishna has no personal agenda whatsoever. It was Arjuna who had always hankered after war, be it in the past or on the present day. As for Krishna, he had endeavoured to avert this war even in the past for the sake of the greater good and even today, he is bound to convince Arjuna to fight in everybody's best interest. Indeed, Krishna had always been against combat between two armies. He had always attacked the root cause of the problem, instead of resorting to a battle between two armies. And in keeping with this approach, he had slayed countless evil-doers. But no innocent person had ever been hurt in the process. To accuse such a compassionate being of inciting violence displays the human being's ignorance. The truth is, history has never witnessed the birth of a more compassionate being than Krishna. And verily, when my creator himself is the wondrous Krishna, anchored at the zenith of compassion, then I, the Bhagavad Gita, am bound to be overflowing with compassion too. In fact, it is my utmost compassion that compels me to elucidate all this for you, in order to help you grasp my true import. Because, who can know better than me, how imperative it is for you to have a thorough understanding of Krishna for your own betterment and progress?

All in all, remember, at this juncture, Krishna's consciousness is fully centred on convincing Arjuna to fight the war. And when can he succeed in his objective? When he demolishes all three arguments furnished by Arjuna to not fight the war. Now, kindly recall those three reasons; first and foremost, Arjuna is resorting to quoting the virtues and sins mentioned in the scriptures to justify his desire to flee from the battlefield. Secondly, he is asserting his fraternal love for his cousins in order to desert the battlefield. And he is offering both these reasons just to delude Krishna, when in fact, neither of these two is the actual reason for his present condition. Ergo, in order to convince Arjuna to fight, Krishna has to prove that these two reasons that Arjuna has given to avoid fighting are merely his delusions. In other words, Krishna has to first establish the futility of Arjuna's knowledge of the scriptures. Only then can the door that Arjuna is trying to inch towards in order to evade the war by "resorting to the scriptures" be closed! Likewise, Krishna also has to prove that Arjuna's love for the Kauravas is a delusion. Only then can Arjuna's plea to run away from the war on account of his fraternal love be overridden. And then remains the task of finding an antidote to Arjuna's fear. For, as long as fear is present within, Arjuna will never be ready to fight the war on the outside, that is, in the battlefield. And even if he agrees to fight, he cannot win the battle if he fights half-heartedly with such a spiritless mind. Indeed, Krishna's task does not conclude with simply convincing Arjuna to fight. For the greater good, it is imperative that Arjuna wins the war as well.

Hence, at present, Krishna is determined to ensure the victory of the Pandavas for the sake of the greater good. And this is possible only when Arjuna fights with conviction, pouring all his heart and soul into the war. And for that purpose, Krishna needs to pay attention to three key points. One, he has to liberate Arjuna from the bondage of scriptures; two, he has to prove Arjuna's fraternal love to be a delusion, and three, he has to convert Arjuna's deep-seated fear into confidence. Now, moving forward, anything that Krishna enunciates in this book shall revolve only around these three main points, as this is the sole objective of Krishna. Etch this in your mind, Krishna is not interested in imparting knowledge to Arjuna; he only wants to convince him to fight the war. As I have already mentioned earlier, Krishna is a being completely anchored in *Brahmacharya*. He does not interfere the least bit in this divine play of Nature. For this reason, wise beings also call him the only complete *avatar*.[6] So, never presume that Krishna wants to impart knowledge to Arjuna. Else, not only will you demean Krishna but you will also fail to comprehend my true essence.

However, let us return to Krishna's very first remark. He says, "O Arjuna, from where has this untimely delusion overcome you?" In other words, he attacks Arjuna's fraternal love. Krishna is chastising him by saying, "Is this the time to display fraternal love?" Secondly, he is saying, "Noble men are not overwhelmed by such ill-timed delusion." In other words, he is telling Arjuna, 'You are deeming yourself noble by brandishing your knowledge of the scriptures, but you must know that nobody becomes great by resorting to the scriptures. The truth is, "great men flow with the time." And thirdly, Krishna says, "This delusion of yours will certainly not bestow glory unto you." This statement of Krishna must be grasped well. Here, Krishna is using Arjuna's fame to counteract his fear. Remember, psychologically, there are only two ways to expunge fear. One is to give a strong assurance, and the other is to thrust an even bigger fear upon the fearful person. If there is ample time to drive away the fear, then assurance is effective. But when there is paucity of time and eliminating the fear is the

O Arjuna, I will **bestow** upon you the **knowledge** that will **rid you** of all **delusions**

6   *Avatar* - In Hinduism, an *avatar* means the material appearance or incarnation of a deity on earth.

need of the hour, then only one solution remains, to induce a new fear quickly. And since Arjuna is a renowned personality, having attained fame as a brave warrior, Krishna is using the fear of that selfsame "fame" on him. He is reminding Arjuna, 'You are a celebrated archer; hence, if you flee the battlefield, your reputation will be tarnished.' Thus, in his very first statement, Krishna launches a powerful attack on the very root of Arjuna's three reasons to flee the battlefield. That is why I pronounce Krishna as the ace master of psychology, impossible to be hoodwinked.

Having grasped the points discussed so far, you must also comprehend the meaning of psychology in day-to-day life. Psychology is the stream of knowledge through which you can discern what a human being is feeling at any time in its entirety. And psycho-treatment is an art through which you can mould a person's mind as per your wish. And, at present, that is exactly what Krishna is doing; administering psycho-treatment to Arjuna to convince him to fight the war. Now, all that remains to be seen is, whether Arjuna manages to find an antidote to this psycho-treatment, or whether Krishna succeeds in transforming his mind. Here, you also need to remember that all subsequent events depend entirely upon the intensity of Arjuna's fear. For, it is fear which is the root cause of his adamant refusal to fight. He is taking refuge in scriptures and fraternal love only to conceal his fear. Thus, no sooner is his fear expunged than he will himself let go of these two excuses in which he has taken refuge. It is also possible that his fear may weaken under Krishna's persistent attack on his fraternal love and scriptural knowledge. This, in turn, implies that Krishna would, indeed, have to relentlessly attack Arjuna's "three reasons to not fight" in order to persuade him to wield his weapons. Who knows which argument might work and convince Arjuna to fight!

So, without further ado, let us hark back to this interesting exchange unfolding between Krishna and Arjuna. In his very first statement, Krishna has attacked Arjuna's fear, fraternal love and knowledge of the scriptures. But it was impossible for Arjuna to forsake his delusions with this slight persuasion. Hence, Krishna had to take the conversation forward; for, not resting until the accomplishment of a task undertaken for the greater good was an integral part of Krishna's being. Thus, until Arjuna is convinced to fight, the question of Krishna relenting and abandoning the task does not arise at all. And all things considered, it is Arjuna's three delusions that Krishna needs to chip away at in order to persuade him to fight. And, as the root cause of these delusions is fear, Krishna immediately states in no uncertain terms, "O Arjuna, do not succumb to cowardice. It is unbecoming of a mighty warrior like you. Ergo, abandon the petty frailties of the heart, gird your loins and get ready to fight. Do not make attempts to delude me with your lofty statements, stating that you have embraced non-violence or that fraternal love has kindled in your heart. I can clearly discern that you have yielded to unmanliness." Indeed, with his "candid declaration that Arjuna has succumbed to unmanliness", Krishna on his part has ruled out Arjuna's useless arguments pertaining to scriptural knowledge and fraternal love. He makes it amply clear as he states, 'Even if you present any such arguments further ahead, I will plainly see it for what it really is...your fear.'

Verily, Arjuna is left with no choice. So, he poses a direct question to Krishna, "How shall I fight Bhishma and Dronacharya?" Examine Arjuna's words carefully. He is asking, "How?" He is not questioning why he should fight them. However, Arjuna is a man driven by his brain. His fear has been exposed once, but he quickly regains control of the conversation and says, "O Krishna, what I mean to say is, both are deeply revered." Then, he continues, "I would prefer a life spent begging alms than killing these noble men. Because, in the end, what would I achieve even after slaying them? Kingdom, riches and glory! O Krishna! Besides, we do not even know what the outcome of this war will be. Who will win?" In other words, Arjuna manages to conceal his fear for a brief moment, but can a man hide the emotions running amok within him forever? That too, especially when a person like Krishna is standing before him? For, Krishna has candidly called Arjuna a coward, and it has also produced the desired effect on Arjuna. In the first chapter, Arjuna had employed flowery speech, replete with embellishments, and made lofty declarations to hide his fear, but his words immediately lost their sparkle and flourish the moment Krishna called him a "coward". Now, every once in a while, he is also evincing his fear. And his final statement is a part of that same sequence. The words, after all, slip from his lips, when he says, "Krishna, mainly, we do not know who will win this war." In other words, if he is certain of victory, then what is stated in the scriptures is of no consequence to him. If winning is a foregone conclusion, then there is no question of upholding fraternal love either. This is exactly what the common man also does in his day-to-day life. Etch this in your mind; most often, it is timidity that cowers behind lofty, grandiose words. If there is no dread and no fear of vanquishment, then there is no need to employ lofty words either. However, Arjuna is not done speaking yet. Brilliant that he is, he has already contemplated his next move, as he says, "Alright, Krishna! Even if we do win this war, what will we gain? What is the use of attaining the kingdom sans Kauravas? We verily need to snatch away the kingdom from them while they are still alive. If they themselves are not alive and present, in whose hearts will we strike awe with our royal airs?" What Arjuna is saying at the moment is also a part of the day-to-day psychology of common people. In this world, nobody wants victory for victory's sake; everybody desires victory to rouse the envy of their friends and foes; especially, to make their friends and well-wishers jealous. If one does not get to flaunt one's success in front of them to their consternation and envy, then success loses its charm. And this is psychology, the very truth hidden within every human being; just peep within yourself and others, everything will become crystal clear in an instant.

Coming back to the colloquy between Krishna and Arjuna, Krishna employs the word 'coward' with such effect that it becomes clear to Arjuna that it would not be easy to hoodwink Krishna. At the very least, he realises that the person standing before him is extremely intelligent. Indeed, had there been anyone else in place of Krishna, then Arjuna would have perhaps succeeded in deceiving him. But that is exactly why he is the inimitable Krishna! And this verily is my pride and honour that my progenitor 'Krishna' is the ace master of psychology. And I am not stating this in vain; just behold the impact my sire makes! He has made only two statements so far and Arjuna is already beginning to steer towards the right path. Leaving aside all acts and attempts to delude Krishna, he has begun speaking his mind. Further, he openly admits to Krishna, "You are right. I have succumbed to cowardice. So,

I will not beat around the bush any longer and straightaway ask for your suggestion: what is the most advantageous course of action for me at the moment?" In short, he is implying, 'Tell me only that which is decidedly good for me. In other words, do not give me advice which will prove detrimental to me. And while advising, keep in mind that nothing untoward should befall me.' This implies that Arjuna's fear is still intact. Presently, he is extremely worried for himself. And, after being called a coward by Krishna, he is even admitting that he is terrified. Psychologically, 'fear' is an extremely dangerous emotion. And it is not easy to expunge fear, especially when it has made such deep inroads in a person. Arjuna's statement, in which he says, "O Krishna! Show me the path which will be decidedly good for me," makes everything crystal clear. Krishna has also gauged that now, Arjuna will not be easily convinced to fight. Indeed, if Arjuna senses the slightest danger in any advice given to him, he will not concur with it.

All in all, Arjuna is, indeed, asking Krishna for advice, but subject to conditions. He is saying, 'No harm should befall me. In other words, whatever advice you give me, I will first deliberate over it and only if it seems "decidedly to my advantage", will I abide by it.' Well, you cannot even begin to imagine how deluded a terrified person can get. And revealing the same deluded state of mind, Arjuna further says to Krishna, "I am your disciple and I perceive a guru in you, O wise one. I will take refuge in you." Now, just think; how can these two aspects, taking refuge in someone and stating a condition or stipulation, go hand in hand? But this is exactly how every fear-stricken person talks. Observe this phenomenon in your day-to-day life; you will find everybody seeking advice from others, but subject to conditions. Nobody follows the advice as prescribed. Each person analyses the advice received, and acts on it only if it bodes well for him or suits his convenience. Yet, just like Arjuna, he pretends to have taken refuge in you, seeking your advice and promising to abide by it. However, the moment you give your opinion, he exclaims, 'No, what you are saying doesn't seem appropriate.' And herein lies my significance; I begin with the psychology of day-to-day life, which if grasped well, will lead to the comprehension of the higher psychology of life and Nature as we progress. Well, returning to Arjuna, he continues, "Krishna, you must

O Arjuna, it does not befit you to hide your cowardice using the scriptures as a shield

understand my quandary. I am hopelessly trapped. Whether I attain the kingdom of Hastinapur or the throne of the gods, even these temptations are not able to provide me the impetus to fight the war at present." Well, what can Krishna say? For, Arjuna is clearly stating, 'I will pay heed to anything you say, but kindly do not ask me to fight. I will certainly not fight. For, even the greatest temptations are incapable of alleviating "the grief which has gripped me at present".' And this is verily Arjuna's current predicament. Till now, he has engaged in numerous fights and skirmishes in his greed to attain the kingdom, but today, he is not able to bring himself to fight. This begets the question, what has changed today? In the past, he was so overcome by greed that he didn't care for his life. Today, he is so concerned for his life that he is not willing to fight, irrespective of the immense gains the war might lead to. There are two important points to note here; first, Arjuna is conceding that he is gripped by fear, and second, he is analysing his mind correctly. And now, we will proceed in tandem with Arjuna's changing state of mind, for, Krishna's entire conversation is addressed to Arjuna's current state of mind. In place of Arjuna, had Bhima refused to fight, then I would have come to exist in a different form. And had Duryodhana refused to fight, I would have been markedly different. You must also grasp that had Buddha or Christ been in Krishna's place, then too, my form would have been radically different. Perhaps then, Arjuna would not have accepted his cowardice so soon either. It is also likely that anyone in Krishna's place would not have been able to sense Arjuna's timidity. Quite possibly, they would have fallen for Arjuna's intricate web of words and eventually agreed with his reasoning. So, I owe my immense value only to "Krishna's keen insight and grasp of psychology". And for this sole reason, I am of service in every sphere of life, right from the matters of day-to-day life to ascending the pinnacles of joy and success. However, returning to Arjuna, having said everything he could possibly think of, he now tells Krishna directly, "I will do whatever you ask of me. But bear in mind, I will certainly not fight." Well, what can Krishna say? He is, indeed, in a quandary. But Krishna is, after all, the ace master of psychology. No dilemma or deviousness of man can bind or blind him.

Listening to such perplexing words uttered by Arjuna, Krishna observes him carefully for a brief moment. But seeing his brows furrowed in confusion, Krishna cannot help but guffaw. He cannot help it, because Arjuna's words are so ludicrous that anyone would burst out laughing. On one hand, Arjuna is seeking advice from Krishna, and on the other, he is informing Krishna of his decision not to fight. While on one side, he is terrified, on the other, he is brandishing his knowledge of the scriptures. So, Krishna, with amusement dancing in his eyes, says, "O Arjuna! You are, indeed, speaking like the wise, but you are behaving just like an ignoramus. One who is truly wise does not lament either the living or the dead. O Arjuna! Presently, all your remarks are hovering around death. Deep within, you are terrified of your death, while on the outside, you are evincing distress over the probable deaths of your uncles, teachers and other near and dear ones. When, in fact, the truth is, there is no such thing as death in this world. Ergo, your sorrow, at present, is not over death, but it stems from your ignorance concerning death. The truth is, there never was a time when I did not exist or you or all these kings. Nor in the future shall any of us cease to be. O Arjuna! You must clearly grasp this simple truth; just as a person's body passes through the stages of childhood, youth and old age, it also passes through life and death. That is, with death, the human being attains a new body. Therefore, wise men who are patient and forbearing are not in the least affected by "this ongoing cycle of life and death"."

"O Arjuna! Bear in mind, the contacts between the senses and the objects, which make us experience the feelings of heat and cold, happiness and sorrow are (by nature) constantly surging and ebbing. As long as there is life, this play will continue. For instance, overwhelmed by the senses, you are miserable today, having clashed with the mighty army of the Kauravas. Similarly, you were grieving yesterday, because you were not seated on the royal throne of Hastinapur. In the past, you were lamenting about the fact that your beloved Draupadi was apportioned among five brothers. So, on the outside, we will keep encountering ever new situations. But all these situations are subject to change; they are transitory in nature. A wise man does not get perturbed by these ever-altering circumstances. Indeed, only the person who neither rejoices nor grieves within, irrespective of whether the situation on the outside is good or bad, is worthy of *moksha*— liberation from the cycle of birth-rebirth. Because, O Arjuna, these changing circumstances are illusory; they are untrue; whereas you are the reality, the truth, having the capability of remaining unchanged under any circumstances. So, let the untruths outside keep changing, but you must become steadfast yourself. Mark my words, O Arjuna! Nobody is capable of destroying such a steadfast human being.

O Arjuna! You are indestructible and eternal. You are not the body, you are the soul. This body is perishable; so, as long as it exists, the circumstances on the outside will keep changing. Therefore, stop worrying about both, the changing circumstances as well as the body. For, you are entirely separate from them. Your sorrow does not stem from the fear of war or death; instead, it stems from your ignorance of not knowing that you are but a soul. Behold me, there have been countless upheavals in my life; why, I was even born in captivity and brought up in the shadow of death. That is not all; my entire life has been spent with the ominous clouds of death hovering over me. And even today, here I stand between two opposing armies! But tell me, did you ever see me unhappy? Certainly not! Why? For, I am aware that I am not Krishna; I am a soul. And a soul neither slays, nor does it get slayed. The soul is unborn and eternal. It just is. Thus, O Arjuna, know this with certainty—you too are nothing but a 'soul'. Concurrently, you must also realise that all these kings are also nothing but souls. And then you will yourself comprehend that nobody can slay or be slayed. But until and unless this realisation dawns upon you, violence and non-violence will continue to exist for you. In fact, these concepts dominate the lives of all such ignorant beings. And until this realisation dawns upon the human being, he will continue to fear death and pride himself on killing. Until such time, he is deluded about his life, and even fears hurting the smallest of beings such as ants. Verily, all such delusions stem from ignorance regarding the soul.

O Arjuna! Imagine you are watching a play where one character is killing someone, and another is saving someone's life. Now, will the character who acted the part of the slayer grieve and wring his hands in anguish after the play is over? Will the character who acted as the saviour feel proud once the curtains fall? No! If someone were to behave in this manner, everyone would think that he has taken leave of his senses. Likewise, apply this metaphor to your life and try to perceive it from the level of my consciousness. For, I am seated at the supreme peak of consciousness. I am nothing but a soul, pure and enlightened. Ergo, anything that has become inevitable is nothing but a play to me. O Arjuna! I have found even those lofty people who make great claims about knowledge, mired in delusion when it comes to this matter. But my friend, you must save yourself from getting deluded. Trust me, everyone in this world, including you, is nothing but a pure and pristine soul. And for the soul, all these physical bodies are mere changing raiment. Yes, I agree that the body is precious too, but once its death becomes a certainty, to grieve over it or be terrified about its imminent end is a fallacy. The truth is, just as the human being garbs himself in new raiment, discarding the old one, this soul assumes new bodies, casting off the old ones. The human being's soul cannot be slayed by a weapon nor can it be burned by fire or dried by wind. It is everlasting, all-pervading, immovable and eternal. Thus, you should apprehend this truth and vanquish all your sorrows. You should immediately do away with both, the sorrow of dying and the delusion of killing. Arjuna! Even if you cannot instantly experience the immortality and greatness of this soul, and you believe that it is subject to birth and death, then too there is no cause for you to grieve. Because, even according to this belief, one who is born is certain to meet death. And the one who dies is certain to be born again. Thus, whichever way you look at it, you should not nurse the fear of dying and the delusion of killing at all. Why do you not comprehend this simple truth that everybody in this world was unmanifest before birth and will become unmanifest again upon dying? That is, everybody in this world is manifest only for a short while, in the interim period between birth and death. So, why lament for this body which is manifest only for a little while?

However, you will not comprehend my words so easily. For, the problem is, there are countless discussions over religion but none about the soul. Only one in many great human beings looks upon the soul in wonder, only one in millions describes its essence and only one in billions expresses an interest in fathoming it. Ordinarily, discussions in the name of religion just skim the surface. This is the reason why even religion abounds with delusions of violence and non-violence. But Arjuna, you must pay heed to the truth and anchor yourself in it. Without doing so, the predicament you presently find yourself in will not dissipate. Not only you, without anchoring oneself in truth, no human being's sorrow and misery, be it of any kind, will ever be dispelled. Till then, the human being will remain entangled in the "dual clutches, that is, the duality of attachment and delusion". So, trust me, in order to banish your sorrow, you must grasp that this "soul" dwelling within every physical body has always been indestructible. It cannot be slayed by anyone. Once you comprehend this truth, you will never grieve over anything. For then, there shall be no scope for any delusion to prevail either.

Further, if you are unable to fathom the ultimate truth, then I too will have to descend to your level in order to have an effective conversation, as it is imperative for you to comprehend my words. So, if you do not consider your soul to be your *dharma*, your duty, then consider your *Kshatriyata*[7] as your duty. And it is common for a *Kshatriya* to fight for his kingdom and his people. As a woman cooks meals for the family; likewise, a businessman cannot object to earn nor can a *Shudra*[8] decline to wash and clean for any reason. And there is no denying the fact that you are a *Kshatriya*. And for a *Kshatriya*, there is no task nobler than fighting a righteous war. And that exalted task now lies in front of you in the form of this war, so fight and be

---

victorious! And upon emerging victorious, ensure the progress of the kingdom of Hastinapur and its populace, as this is your primary duty as a *Kshatriya*. You cannot put the bright future of Hastinapur at stake in order to save your own life. You cannot let the reins of Hastinapur fall into the hands of the evil Duryodhana again. Nor can you put the lives of your brothers, sons, Draupadi and your army at stake by refusing to fight. You are the finest archer in this army, so if you run away from the battlefield, then all these people will die for no reason at the hands of brutes like Karna, Bhishma and Drona. Wallowing in your own anxiety, you cannot turn a blind eye to the woes of your brothers and sons. Owing to your predicament, you cannot put at stake the lives of the warriors who are standing on the battlefield in your support. Why don't you comprehend that defeat is certain if you desert this war? The death of your brothers and sons is inevitable if you flee the battlefield! And in such a situation, the dignity of Draupadi could be put at stake once again. As a *Kshatriya*, you certainly cannot turn your back on all these responsibilities merely to save your own self."

So far, you have comprehended the tale quite well; now read the rest of the discussion through the words of Krishna and Arjuna themselves. This will give you an insight into "their expressed and unexpressed emotions" as well. Henceforth, I will become the "witness" and hand over the reins of the conversation to Krishna and Arjuna.

Krishna:

I had employed my best means to convince Arjuna, using all the arguments I could think of, to help him see sense. But (to my utter dismay) even after such earnest efforts of explaining and convincing on my part, Arjuna did not budge from his stance of refusing to fight. Indeed, how could he pick up arms when his fear ran so deep that he wasn't worried about his own brothers, sons or even Draupadi! I was well and truly trapped. For, at least in my presence, what ought to happen, must definitely happen. And from that standpoint, Arjuna should definitely fight. But the question is, how do I convince such a terrified and deluded person to fight? Had Arjuna perceived the matter from the level of the ultimate truth, this discussion would have ended long ago. For then, he would have instantly fathomed that this battle is inevitable, the soul is eternal, and thus, the act of slaying and being slayed is nothing but an illusion. However, as even the wisest of human beings fail to fathom this truth, how could one expect Arjuna to act differently? If even those with profound knowledge are embroiled in one illusion or the other, how could Arjuna forsake his delusion? Let him not, but fight the battle he must! To that effect, I even tried to rouse his *Kshatriyata*—the virtue of (being) a warrior. Besides, at the moment, he is but a *Kshatriya*. For, even at present, the desire to attain the kingdom lies deeply embedded in him, and even today, he bears enmity towards the Kauravas. It is just that all of this has been shrouded by the fear that has him in a vice-like grip at present. But unfortunately, I was not able to kindle his *Kshatriyata* either. Even so, what ought to happen must definitely happen. How can I be called Krishna if I were to accept defeat? After all, it is for a reason that I am hailed as "Jai Shri Krishna". I am not called the only complete *avatar* for no reason. I can descend to any level, from truth and *swadharma*[9] to self-interest and make anyone do my bidding. For, the soul has only one principle, "that which ought to happen must happen; and that which should not, must not happen at any cost". In other words, if Arjuna is required to fight the war, then by all means, he must fight; and under ordinary circumstances, he wouldn't have objected to it either. He had, indeed, arrived at the battlefield, keen and thirsting to fight, for then, he was anchored in his *swadharma* of *Kshatriyata*. So, at present, one thing is clear, if I have to convince him to pick up arms again, I will have to nullify the factor that has triggered this change of heart. And you must comprehend that even in day-to-day psychology, there are only three ways to change a person's mind. The simplest and ultimate method is to make him realise the truth. And I have already tried that method by explaining to Arjuna the immortality of the soul. But it did not work. Thereafter, I had endeavoured to kindle his *swadharma*, but unfortunately, his sense of duty as a *Kshatriya* was not roused either. Here, you must also grasp that if one's mind is transformed by truth, then that change is permanent. If his mind is transformed with *swadharma*, then he performs every task with his heart and soul. But when both these solutions fail, then there remains only one way to alter a person's mind—to rouse his self-interest. And needless to say, everyone understands matters of self-interest very well. Likewise,

9   *Swadharma* - Duties towards oneself.

everyone is well familiar with the language of self-interest, that is, the language of fear and greed. But this is the language of depravity. Although the mind changes by this method, the change is only temporary. Moreover, this method has another drawback, and that is, a person afflicted by fear and greed cannot perform any task wholeheartedly.

Even so, what other recourse did I have at the moment? So, without wasting time, I decided to wield the dual weapons of fear and greed upon Arjuna. To begin with, rousing his greed, I said, "O Arjuna! Only the fortunate *Kshatriyas* are accorded the chance to fight such a righteous war. This war shall open the doors to heaven. Hence, do not lose out on this golden opportunity. Moreover, bear in mind, Arjuna! If you run away from this war, you will lose all the fame you have earned so far. Do not be under the impression that on deserting the war, people will perceive you as having embraced non-violence or renunciation. No, everybody will perceive this as an act of escapism, thinking that you fled the battlefield out of fear and fear alone. Undoubtedly, your reputation will be besmirched. Then, wherever you go, whomever you meet... you will only face humiliation. It is better to die than to live a life of such ignomiy. Till now, Arjuna, you have received only acclaim and adulation, but if you flee from the battlefield, you will be met with disgrace. It is better to fight than to live such a life of humiliation; for, it at least grants you the opportunity to emerge victorious and enjoy the kingdom. So, you must realise,

O Arjuna, that which is the **best**, wherever and whatever it may be, is essentially **a form** of **mine** my friend, that there is everything to gain and nothing to lose in fighting this war. If you emerge victorious, you will gain fame and kingdom. If you die, you will find instant release and go to heaven. However, if you flee the battlefield, you will lament your entire life. On one hand, people will disparage you, and on the other, the grief of the death of your kith and kin will haunt you for the rest of your life. So, do not apply your brain. Grasp my words by means of truth or *swadharma*, or perceive it through the lens of self-interest, the choice is yours. But ultimately, you have no option but to fight. Furthermore, bear in mind that time is ticking. The battle is about to begin at any moment and we do not have much time to converse. Besides, nobody will let you flee from the battle, and you will needlessly die on making any such vain attempt. The Kauravas will get what they want without expending any effort. So, act sensibly and without further ado, prepare yourself to fight."

With this, I concluded the Gita. Arjuna certainly should have agreed to fight now. But his expressions and demeanour bespoke otherwise. That being the case, I could not afford to drop the reins of the conversation, so I began to convince him yet again. I reckoned that when he could not be persuaded even through the weapons of fear and greed, it is better to raise the standard of the conversation, as Arjuna had a standard of his own. So, I thought it wise to convince him by 'centring the conversation on truth and *swadharma*' instead of gain and loss. Hence,

I posed a direct question to Arjuna, 'Pray tell me, what really worries you? It is the outcome of the war, isn't it? So, let whatever is about to happen, happen. Why are you concerned? You simply need to maintain your equanimity and prepare yourself to fight considering victory and defeat, gain and loss, and sorrow and happiness as one. In so doing, you will not incur sin. In fact, a person who makes no distinction between these dualities can do anything and never incur an iota of sin. For, if there is anything sinful, it is self-interest. One craves victory, not defeat; desires gain, not loss; one hankers after happiness, not sorrow. O Arjuna! One ought to relinquish these dualities from all actions. Focus on performing at least one action, setting aside all these dualities. Look at me for instance; what do I stand to gain from this war? Whoever wins or loses, how does it make any difference to me personally? Yet, here I am, standing with you. I never accord importance to victory or defeat, or loss or gain, in anything I do. On the other hand, an ordinary human being, without considering these factors, would not be able to move even an inch. This is the very difference between me and everyone else, and essentially, this is the distance between me and them which they all have to traverse and ultimately bring themselves to the same level as me. This is the veritable mystery of life which everyone needs to fathom. Every human being has to comprehend that joy lies above happiness and sorrow; contentment reigns supreme over gain or loss; duty comes before victory or defeat, and *karma* is a human being's duty performed to attain joy and contentment. Moreover, although duty and righteousness are much discussed, Arjuna, let me tell you the clear distinction between righteousness and unrighteousness today. If you perform any *karma*, considering it a duty to attain joy and contentment, then it is righteous, else, it is unrighteous. It is not a question of war or renunciation; it is the intention or the reason behind performing the action that matters. If you fight in order to gain a kingdom, then it is unrighteous. If you wage a battle, nursing enmity for the Kauravas, even then it is unrighteous. But if you want to fight for the well-being of the inhabitants of Hastinapur, then it is righteous; if you wish to fight in order to safeguard the dignity of women, then it is righteous. And if you are thinking of fleeing the war, then it is nothing but an illusion. For, the war is inevitable now. And to turn your face away from the truth and reality is the ultimate debasement of a human being. Thus, forsake your worry about "what will happen" and fight the battle considering it a *raas* dance. For, as a *Kshatriya*, it is your duty to establish the best and most just rule over the people of Hastinapur and to safeguard the dignity of women.'

With this, I drew the Gita to a close once again. In my opinion, there was no scope for any doubt or misgiving now. Indeed, I hoped that Arjuna would now agree to fight, sporting a cheerful smile. In a way, Gita has reached its conclusion for everyone at this point. For, the answer to the question of what one ought to do and not do, has become crystal clear. But it is an old habit to mull over victory and vanquishment or gain and loss; and old habits die hard. Likewise, Arjuna, suffering from the same predicament, still did not agree to fight. Well, so let me start afresh! Do I have any other recourse except convincing him to fight?

Thus, taking the conversation forward, I said, "O Arjuna, I tried to explain 'what you should and shouldn't do' through the course of Jnana Yoga, the path of knowledge. But you are a *Kshatriya*, who understands the language of *karma* better. Ergo, you may grasp the same point through the course of Karma Yoga, the path of selfless action. Once you grasp this knowledge, you will be freed from the bondage of *karma*. For, your predicament at present does not concern *karma* but the fruits of *karma*. You have no objection to fighting; what troubles you is the possible outcome of this battle. So, listen to me carefully; you may just overcome your anxiety over the outcome of the war and fight the battle with your heart and soul. Mark my words, O Arjuna! Whether you grasp the point through Jnana Yoga or Karma Yoga, the bottom line is that you have to fight this war wholeheartedly. Because, duty plainly implies, "what should happen must happen and that which shouldn't, must not happen at any cost". And thus, you have no alternative but to fight wholeheartedly. In fact, the plain truth is that in this world, no human being ever has the option to choose between "what to do and what not to do". Everyone here is bound by Nature's great *leela* which states, "what should happen, must happen". And a person who lives in adherence to this never drifts away from Nature, irrespective of what he does. But unfortunately, nobody in this world lives with the determination to follow this sole principle. Here, everybody has divided their intellect amongst countless resolves, owing to which they keep searching for options in anything and everything. You too are acting no different at present, O Arjuna. And there are two key reasons behind this tendency; one is, hankering after the fruits of *karma* and the other is an overabundance of knowledge. Influenced by these two factors, people become inclined towards scriptures and rituals. They believe nothing can be better than attaining heaven. Their interest well lies in all those rites and rituals which assure them gain and profit, and pursue those activities which suggest ways to prevent losses. People with such deluded minds are unable to anchor themselves in the one Supreme Soul; in other words, they fail to stand firmly and determinedly for "what ought to happen". And know this well, O Arjuna, all the scriptures of the world that have established *karma's* connection with gain, have created confusion and weakened the human being's singular resolve. Then, it doesn't matter who penned or enunciated such scriptures, or which religion they belong to. O Arjuna, it is not a question of what you are doing and not doing but whether you are living with a single resolve or countless ones. I am asking you to fight with one firm resolve, but you are hell-bent on dividing your resolves by dragging the scriptures into the conversation. You are explaining the import of virtue and sin to me. But etch this in your mind: having a singular resolve is virtuous and getting mired in delusion is a sin. And misled by the scriptures, you have presently become deluded. So, set the scriptures aside and become one with an equipoised mind. Let your inner consciousness guide you for what you should do. For, the inner consciousness is every human being's very own scripture; in fact, it is his sole scripture. As for the world, it is rife with a deluge of scriptures, and the actions suggested in them are at variance with each other. If one advocates performing a certain action, the other condemns it and suggests a contrary action. So, why should you be concerned with them? Simply establish a connection with the Supreme Soul dwelling within you – the only one who is cognisant of the truth of this moment. Know this, O Arjuna, the one who heeds the voice of his soul within, abounds with an overflowing reservoir of energy. He finds himself attaining supreme knowledge. Such a being has only as much use for all the scriptures and doctrines of the world, as he has for small water bodies upon discovering a vast and boundless reservoir. Why do you wish to gather deluded knowledge given in bits and pieces, forsaking the river of knowledge ever-flowing within you? And as for knowledge (of the former kind), the human being has absolutely no need for it. For, the soul in every human being is well and truly replete with knowledge of every kind. I too am not imparting knowledge to you here; in fact, I am only inspiring you to listen to your soul. Just listen to its voice, pay heed to it and you will agree to fight the battle wholeheartedly. Thereafter, you will not talk of fleeing from the battlefield, alluding uselessly to the scriptures.

Yet another astonishing behaviour on your part is that you want to flee the battle supposedly on the grounds of uncertainty over its outcome. But the truth is that "you have a right over your *karma* but never to the fruits thereof". O Arjuna, this one statement encompasses everything. Man should focus only on his *karma* and not on the reasons for performing or not performing those *karmas*. However, you are acting otherwise. You had come to the battlefield armed with countless reasons to wage a war. But now that you are here, you are citing thousands of reasons to not fight. But look at me; since I have no reason for being on the battlefield, I am not giving reasons to run away from here either. In fact, there is just one reason behind all my actions and that is, what ought to happen, must happen. Thereafter, I do not worry about the outcome, and instead welcome whatever fruits my actions may bring in their wake. This is not only the right and true way of living one's life and performing *karma*, but it is also Nature's great *leela*. That being the case, why should I become an obstacle in "the flowing stream of life and Nature's great *leela*"? Thus, you too must let go of all the reasons to fight or not fight in this war and become a part of this grand *leela* of Nature. Let life flow in whichever direction it flows. And whatever happens in due course, just let it happen.

In short, anchor yourself in *samatva*, in equanimity. Be equipoised not only in victory and defeat but also in accomplishment and non-accomplishment. Focus your attention solely on the task before you. Stop focusing on the fruits of action, and stop pondering over the reasons. In so doing, you will behold nothing but the battle, and you will be able to fight wholeheartedly with a smile on your face. And only then will you be able to perform to the best of your potential in the battle. Then and only then, will you be favoured with the best possible outcome of the battle. But if you mull over the fruits of the action or divide yourself amongst several reasons, you will never be able to put in your best performance in the battle. For, the outcome will be produced by virtue of action, not by your thinking. Thus, consider this maxim I have imparted unto you as the ultimate maxim to ascend the pinnacles of joy and success. All my life, I have focused only on the task at hand, and just see, I have traversed the formidable journey from being an ordinary cowherd to becoming the illustrious *Dwarkadheesh*, the King of Dwarka, never losing any battle of life. So, set aside everything else and know that we have a right only over *karma*, and not its fruits. With this maxim firmly entrenched in mind, fight with every ounce of your being, and leave all else in the hands of the one who controls everything."

However, it is not easy to give up the expectation of the outcome and ponder over its reasons. And Arjuna was also facing the same predicament. Although he was comprehending my words, he was unable to act upon them. Therefore, in an attempt to explain this very point in greater detail, I stated: ""*Samatva buddhi*" or an equipoised state of mind is the supreme state of being. To deliberate upon victory and vanquishment or gain and loss is an extremely low calibre

Desire for fruits is wrong, whether it entails attaining virtue or heaven

of thinking. Surprisingly, even the scriptures employ this very same language. And this is why, despite the sheer abundance of scriptures in the world, man is unable to find peace. This is the very reason he is bereft of joy and success. However, you should not commit the same mistake yourself; you must stop desiring the fruits of action. The Supreme Soul knows better than you, what to give you and what not to. And bear in mind, Arjuna, equanimity means having an equanimous approach towards one and all; to observe equanimity not only in gain and loss or victory and defeat but also in virtue and sin; whereas, the arguments you are furnishing on the grounds of the scriptures have nothing except sin and virtue at their core. Similarly, forsaking the fruits means forsaking them in totality; regardless of whether the fruits you wish for entail attaining virtue or heaven. For, irrespective of the nature of fruits you desire, it is but a sin. So, in short, understand well that to observe complete equanimity is the only way to be liberated from all bondages of *karma*. O Arjuna! You must realise that the desire for fruits is the sole reason behind illusory bondages of all kinds. All sorts of knowledge inspiring you to desire the outcome are an impediment to living with "a singular determination". And the day you become firmly anchored in "equanimity", you will become liberated from the desire for fruits as well as from every word of the scriptures you have ever heard. And when you are freed from these two, you will establish an eternal connection with the Supreme Soul. Thereafter, questions such as what to do and what not to do will never arise in your mind. Everything will be crystal clear in your conscience at all times."

Verily, the words I had spoken were profound and I had also conveyed my message with utmost clarity. And it did manage to steer Arjuna's focus from fear to knowledge. The same Arjuna who was earlier adamant on acquainting me with the scriptures was now curious and eager to gain knowledge from me. Hence, listening to my words, Arjuna asked, "O Krishna, what are the characteristics of one who has realised the Supreme Soul? How does he sit, speak and walk?" Now although he had asked the question out of sheer curiosity, the influence of the scriptures on his mindset was still apparent. So, in order to free him from their influence, I said, "O Arjuna, what he says or does holds no significance. How he stands, what he wears and how he walks doesn't matter either. These are all physical actions, which have no bearing on the virtue of righteousness. In fact, the truth is that the body has no right to action. It is a human being's desires that prompt his physical body to undertake certain actions and to refrain from others. However, a person of steadfast mind has inevitably renounced all his desires. You, on the other hand, had arrived strutting on this battlefield only to fulfil your desires, and you are trying to flee the battle now for the very same reason. But remember, desire, of any kind, is sinful. For, desires veer a person away from his *karma*. It is not a question of 'whether you are waging a war or meditating in the Himalayas'; the pertinent question is, whether you are performing the said *karma* under the influence of your desires or devoid of desire. A person of stable mind, irrespective of what he does, does so without harbouring any desire. And the one whose actions are devoid of desire never suffers when sorrow befalls him and nor does he rejoice when he attains happiness. He always remains equipoised within. A person's state of equanimity within is the only measure of how free he is of his desires. And since you are overwhelmed with desires, you are getting influenced by victory and vanquishment. O Arjuna! In essence, understand that to be affected by happiness and sorrow is the only sin, and to remain equipoised under all circumstances is the only virtue. And you are being affected not just by the scriptures or the desire for the fruits of *karma* but even by virtue and sin, defeat and victory and friend and foe. But a person with a steadfast mind is free of all desires, and hence never affected by anything. Thus, no matter what he does or how the world perceives his actions, none of his actions ever amount to sin. And this is exactly what I am explaining to you as well; "If you too fight the war, free of all desires" you will never incur sin. Hence, shift your focus from the virtues and sins delineated in the scriptures and release yourself from the bondage of all kinds of desires. In fact, draw in all senses that affect you, just like a tortoise draws in its limbs. You must also know that even if you flee from the battle, your desires will not cease to exist. Stationing oneself in the Himalayas doesn't liberate one from desires. That is why, to not escape but to endure is the sole solution. Ergo, instead of fleeing from the war, face it. You must realise that by fleeing

> **O Arjuna, when life itself has come into existence because of karma, there is no question of anybody escaping from it. Everyone has to engage in karma, be it a tiny ant or a mammoth elephant**

the battle, your reasons for stepping onto the battlefield will not be obliterated. Even if you run away from the battle, those reasons will keep chasing you. Furthermore, bear in mind that your desire to attain the kingdom of Hastinapur will not be eliminated on fleeing the war. The animosity in your heart towards the Kauravas will not end. But yes, on fighting the battle, you will gain victory over both these reasons. On emerging victorious, perhaps your desire to attain the kingdom will get fulfilled and you will be free of that desire. Also, it is possible that after launching a few decisive attacks on the Kauravas, your animosity towards them will also disappear. As, ultimately, Arjuna, that which lies in one's mind is verily the truth for him, his very reality. Only by facing it and enduring it, can he overcome it, not by running away from it. Bear in mind, O Arjuna, those who run away from subjects leave the subjects behind, but the desires brewing within them for those subjects do not leave them. Likewise, upon running away from the battlefield, you will be rid of the war but you will never be able to triumph over the reasons that led you to the war. On the contrary, those reasons will only become extremely powerful within. It is the truth that the *sanyasis*, the renunciants, who have renounced women and sensory enjoyments are never truly free of them. That is why women and sensory enjoyments appear in their scriptures and texts, and even feature in their fantasies of heaven. Ergo, it is better to take this opportunity to enjoy the kingdom instead of wandering around and leading the life of a nomad. Perhaps, having experienced kingship, your attachment for the kingdom might truly dissipate one day.

O Arjuna, now to comprehend the science behind this entire process, you must consider the subjects as adversaries in this whole process. Furthermore, you must know that when one loses equanimity, a variety of subjects come to exist. All of the human being's dualities come to the fore as soon as he loses sight of equanimity. Then, he creates numerous distinctions between enjoyment and renunciation. And based on those very differences, he gives rise to a myriad of subjects. Next, he hankers after the means that can be instrumental in the fulfilment of those subjects. For example, the one who craves sensory, worldly pleasures becomes absorbed in amassing riches and power, while conversely, the one who desires renunciation engages himself in accumulating means of knowledge and meditation. But ultimately, there is no difference between the two; for, both are running behind subjects after all. Try to fathom the scientific aspect of this; whether man desires riches or renunciation, eventually, both are nothing but subjects. And then, he becomes involved and obsessed with those subjects. This, in turn, awakens a desire within him to attain them. If he succeeds in acquiring them, he develops attachment for them. And in case he fails, he gets perturbed. Moreover, if he happens to lose something once gained, he grows angry. And see for yourself, whether riches are threatened or religion, the pursuers of both become furious. This anger results in the loss of their power of reasoning, which, in turn, leads them to fall deeper into the abyss. And then, they continue to plunge deeper by the day. Then comes a day when the king grows tired of his kingdom and the *sanyasi* gets weary of his begging bowl. And one fine day, the tables turn; the king begins yearning for the begging bowl and the *sanyasi* starts hankering after wealth. This cycle continues birth after birth, but never are they liberated from this vicious cycle. Consider yourself for instance; your desire for the kingdom brought you to the battlefield. When you saw the Kauravas' vast army posing an obstruction to your desire of attaining the kingdom, you began speaking of renunciation. Tomorrow, if the circumstances change, you will once again start craving the kingdom. But for how long will this cycle continue? For how long will you continue chasing riches and renunciation? When will you realise that there is no difference between the two? Thus, without wasting time, fight with a singular resolve and leave the decision of its outcome to the Supreme Soul. Forsake your expectation of fruits from the battle. Let the Supreme Soul decide whether you should gain the kingdom, take up renunciation or accept liberation from life. Bear in mind, Arjuna, till the time you do not perform *karma* as per the dictates of your heart, and leave its fruits to the Supreme Soul, you will continue to be perturbed by happiness and sorrow. For, until then, you will keep oscillating and alternating between riches and renunciation. O Arjuna, you must comprehend that sensory pleasures and renunciation are both similar to the flowing waters of a river; they both make you run. Thus, forsake the desire for both, sensory pleasures as well as renunciation, be prepared to fight wholeheartedly and get over this vicious cycle for good. Relinquish the desire for fruits and become like the vast ocean. Wholeheartedly embrace all three possibilities—kingdom, renunciation or death— emerging as a consequence of the war, just as the mighty ocean welcomes and absorbs all the rivers, big and small, as its own. The virtue of steadfastness verily implies becoming like the vast ocean. Moreover, why do you not comprehend that this war is the outcome of your own desires? And as it is so, experience it now with your heart and soul, forsaking your expectation of the fruits. Inevitably, you will attain *Brahmanand*, the supreme bliss. This is the only solution to liberate oneself from the bondage of *karma* forever. This is the only way to put an end to all of life's struggles." Every human being needs to apprehend that he must not run away from his *karmas*. He must accept that the *karma* which lies in front of him is the outcome of his own desires. So, for once, perform *karma* with every ounce of your heart and soul, letting go of the desire for its outcome and you will be freed from the bondage of *karma* forever. The way this battle of Mahabharata presents that opportunity to Arjuna, some other battle of life could accord that chance to you. Simply leave the outcome to the Supreme Soul and accept life as it plays out. You shall attain supreme bliss.

In Chapter 2 of the Gita, Krishna clearly states that the question is not about good or bad; it is not about what you want or desire either. Timing alone is of utmost importance, because one can harbour any desire and ambition; and Krishna does not object to that either. But yes, you must assess its timing i.e. whether the timing is right for the desire you are nursing. If you nurse a desire or an ambition at the wrong time, then your doom is certain. Therefore, it is in your best interest to recognise the timing of your three principal desires and ambitions. Move forward only if the timing is right; otherwise, wait for the right time and set aside that desire or ambition for the time being. For, it is the law of Nature that if the timing is right, you can move mountains effortlessly, but if the timing is wrong, then even a bulldozer will fail to crush a tiny pebble. Hence, first, check the timing of your three principal desires, and if you sense that the time is ripe for a particular desire, engage in fulfilling it with all your heart. Do not relent until you have materialised that desire.

Express your desire (in detail) and put a tick ✓ against each question (as applicable)

....
....
....
....
....
....
....
....

Are you capable of achieving it?

⬜ Yes   ⬜ No

Are the circumstances favourable?

⬜ Yes   ⬜ No

Is this the best option available to you?

⬜ Yes   ⬜ No

Can all the barriers in your way be eliminated?

⬜ Yes   ⬜ No

Are you confident of moving ahead?

⬜ Yes   ⬜ No

Express your desire (in detail) and put a tick ✓ against each question (as applicable)

....
....
....
....
....
....
....

Are you capable of achieving it?

☐ Yes   ☐ No

Are the circumstances favourable?

☐ Yes   ☐ No

Is this the best option available to you?

☐ Yes   ☐ No

Can all the barriers in your way be eliminated?

☐ Yes   ☐ No

Are you confident of moving ahead?

☐ Yes   ☐ No

Express your desire (in detail) and put a tick ✓ against each question (as applicable)

....
....
....
....
....
....
....

Are you capable of achieving it?

⬚ Yes   ⬚ No

Are the circumstances favourable?

⬚ Yes   ⬚ No

Is this the best option available to you?

⬚ Yes   ⬚ No

Can all the barriers in your way be eliminated?

⬚ Yes   ⬚ No

Are you confident of moving ahead?

⬚ Yes   ⬚ No

Note: If you have answered **Yes** for all five questions, then without any hesitation, engage yourself fully in the attainment of that desire. If you have answered **Yes** for four out of five, you can still forge ahead. But if you have answered **Yes** for three out of five, then wait until your answer turns into **Yes** for at least four of these questions. And if you have answered **Yes** for just one or two, then put that desire on hold for the time being.

In Chapter 2, we also learnt about the various reasons that give rise to confusion. We learnt why Arjuna, who had marched onto the battlefield determinedly, was suddenly gripped by confusion. Further, we learnt that the root cause of confusion is having more than one option in mind. When Arjuna had just one option—to fight the war—he was not deluded about the war at all. But when he found himself mired in several alternatives, his mind was clouded by confusion. So, on the basis of this, identify the root causes of your main confusions in life and eliminate them. And to that end, fill in the chart below. Write about your three main confusions in detail, and put a tick (as applicable) against the reasons that have led to those confusions.

Note:

The principle for accomplishing a task is, the more single-mindedly and determinedly one performs a task, the better are the results. So, whatever you do, try and ensure that you do it determinedly, with full concentration. And that is possible only when performing that particular task is the sole option you are left with. And for this purpose, it is imperative to rid oneself of all alternatives that create confusion. Therefore, for each of your confusions, put a tick (as applicable) against the reason(s) mentioned herein. Then, check how many reasons or factors are preventing you from undertaking that task. Next, eliminate those reasons, one by one, and continue to strengthen your determination towards performing that task. Do not commence the task in haste; first, obliterate the reasons that are giving rise to confusion. And once all the confusions are dispelled, get ready to dive into that task decisively. Krishna is also engaged in dispelling the confusions that Arjuna has about the war so that the latter can fight the war wholeheartedly. Similarly, you too have to get rid of your confusions so that you can execute the tasks determinedly. Needless to say, any task performed determinedly will inevitably produce spectacular results.

....
....
....
....
....

Reasons for Confusion:

Want to act on it but religious beliefs are a hindrance

☐ Yes   ☐ No

Want to act on it but fear people's reaction

☐ Yes   ☐ No

Want to act on it but worried about the outcome

☐ Yes   ☐ No

Don't want to act on it but feeling external pressure

☐ Yes   ☐ No

Don't want to engage in the task, but the task feels like a compulsion

☐ Yes   ☐ No

Want to act on it but don't have the authority to take decision

☐ Yes   ☐ No

....
....
....
....
....

Reasons for Confusion:

┌─── Want to act on it but religious beliefs are a hindrance ───┐

☐ Yes   ☐ No

└──┘

┌─── Want to act on it but fear people's reaction ───┐

☐ Yes   ☐ No

└──┘

┌─── Want to act on it but worried about the outcome ───┐

☐ Yes   ☐ No

└──┘

┌─── Don't want to act on it but feeling external pressure ───┐

☐ Yes   ☐ No

└──┘

┌─── Don't want to engage in the task, but the task feels like a compulsion ───┐

☐ Yes   ☐ No

└──┘

┌─── Want to act on it but don't have the authority to take decision ───┐

☐ Yes   ☐ No

└──┘

....
....
....
....
....

Reasons for Confusion:

Want to act on it but religious beliefs are a hindrance

◯ Yes   ◯ No

Want to act on it but fear people's reaction

◯ Yes   ◯ No

Want to act on it but worried about the outcome

◯ Yes   ◯ No

Don't want to act on it but feeling external pressure

◯ Yes   ◯ No

Don't want to engage in the task, but the task feels like a compulsion

◯ Yes   ◯ No

Want to act on it but don't have the authority to take decision

◯ Yes   ◯ No

Practical Application – 7

What does Krishna expect of Arjuna? If truth be told, not much! He simply wants Arjuna to fight the war wholeheartedly. Why? Because only then can he emerge victorious in the war! And this is precisely what we too need to learn from the Gita. Krishna is teaching us that our focus should only be on the *karma* – the task or deed. And when is that possible? Only when one's focus is withdrawn from everywhere else. When one's focus is withdrawn—even from the fruits of the action—only then would one be able to perform his deeds wholeheartedly. Despite craving success, if a person is not able to succeed, it is not due to lack of talent, but because of his inability to fully focus on his task. Hence, before undertaking an important task, check whether your mind is preoccupied elsewhere, apart from the said task. First, rid yourself of all distractions. And only once your focus is withdrawn from all other places and fully centred on the task, should you commence the important task. In doing so, you are certain to meet with great success in that task. Therefore, at present, if you are thinking of undertaking an important task, you must first fill in the chart below. This will help you shift your focus from the unnecessary to the necessary and channelise all your energies into the task at hand.

Write down below the significant or momentous task that you want to undertake:

....
....
....
....
....
....

Check whether your focus is diverted elsewhere

A) Are you distracted by the potential outcome or consequences of your action?

Yes | If the answer is Yes, first, set about eliminating the hindrance, and once done, put a tick ✔ on the right side

No | If the answer is No, proceed to the next question

B) Is your financial condition posing a hindrance in your task?

Yes | If the answer is Yes, first, set about eliminating the hindrance, and once done, put a tick ✔ on the right side

No | If the answer is No, proceed to the next question

C) Are familial problems diverting your focus?

Yes | If the answer is Yes, first, set about eliminating the hindrance, and once done, put a tick ✔ on the right side

No | If the answer is No, proceed to the next question

D) Is your health not supporting you?

☐ Yes | If the answer is Yes, first, set about eliminating the hindrance, and once done, put a tick ✔ on the right side   ☐

☐ No | If the answer is No, proceed to the next question

E) Are you yet to grasp the nitty-gritty of the task, which is posing a hindrance?

☐ Yes | If the answer is Yes, first, set about eliminating the hindrance, and once done, put a tick ✔ on the right side   ☐

☐ No |

Note:

The questions for which you answered **Yes** are, in fact, the hindrances faced by you. So, if the task you're about to undertake is crucial or momentous, then first and foremost, do away with as many hindrances as possible. And only when all the hindrances are out of your way, undertake the crucial task. In so doing, you will be able to engage wholeheartedly in the task and the said task will be accomplished effortlessly too. Moreover, you will be able to enjoy the task and it will fetch splendid results as well. Bear in mind, this application is only meant for the few crucial or momentous tasks of life. Else, in this day and age of multitasking, one inevitably has to deal with a host of problems simultaneously.

Chapter 3

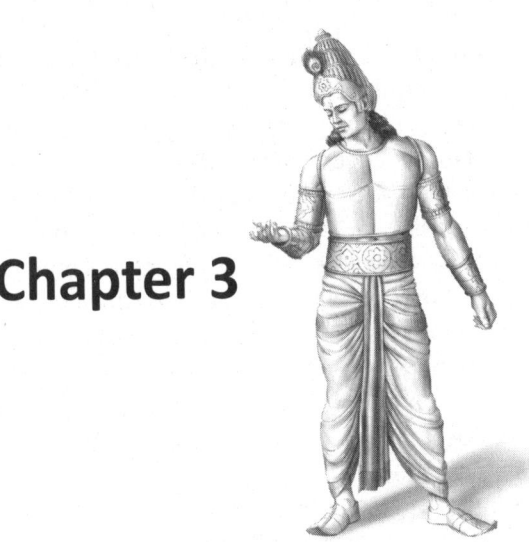

Arjuna:

O Krishna! If you consider knowledge superior to *karma*, then why are you urging me to undertake this dreadful deed? Don't you reckon how rife with peril it is? To tell you the truth, O Krishna, your words have left me spellbound. I wish this exchange would never stop, ever! So, please enlighten me about knowledge rather than *karma*. And in your wondrous discourse on knowledge, please suggest which course of action will decisively prove beneficial to me, and involve no risk whatsoever.

Krishna:

Arjuna is remarkable, isn't he? He is asking me, if I consider knowledge superior to action, then why am I repeatedly advising him to fight? Why do I want to drag him into this perilous deed? Now, when did I ever claim that knowledge is superior to *karma*? All I had asked him to do was to expand his horizon of knowledge and accept the immortality of the Soul. I had said, 'Once you realise the immortality of the Soul, this battle will become a farce for you. Or if you want, you can eliminate your expectation of fruits from this *karma* (of the battle of Mahabharata), then too, you will have no qualms about fighting. In other words, whether you grasp my point through the course of *karma* or knowledge, what you ought to do eventually is, fight. You have no other recourse.' Just see, how he twisted even this absurdly simple statement of mine! I could well understand that ultimately Arjuna's focus is on fleeing the battle somehow. What I say doesn't matter to him in the least. He will, undoubtedly, ferret out excuses to flee from the battle. Had the circumstances been different, I might have argued with him; for, when did I utter such a statement? But if I were to do that right now, it would serve a golden opportunity to Arjuna. After all, that is precisely what he wants; endless arguments and counter-arguments that can somehow help him find a way to convince me too, to flee from the battle. But we do not have time for all this right now. For, what if we remain blithely arguing over here and the swords and maces start clashing in the battle? If that were to happen, Arjuna would, indeed, die for no reason. Hence, it is better to take the conversation forward from the point where he had left.

With this in mind, I said, "Listen, O Arjuna! I had earlier referred to two courses: knowledge and action. And just look at the height of my consciousness that presently, I am not aware of my body at all; I am wholly and solely a "sense of being". That is why, the words "I have said" just slipped from my lips. And this "I" encompasses every person who has ever spoken from his pure, soulful existence. It has no place for distinction of 'you' and 'I', as people who speak from this realisation have no name or physical form. Hence, I said, 'Since millennia, "Jnana Yoga" and "Karma Yoga" are the two methods advocated by people who have attained self-realisation.' And Arjuna, whether you speak of Jnana Yoga or Karma Yoga, eventually, the keystone of both these courses is *karma*. In Nature's scheme of things, no human being can sit idle without performing *karma* - action, even for a moment. If nothing else, he still has to perform the *karma* of breathing in order to stay alive. Ergo, do not ask me to not speak of *karma*; or just furnish you with knowledge and spirit you away from this dreadful deed. For, even if you choose to follow the path of knowledge, you would have to perform your *karma* eventually."

At this point, also etch this in your mind that the foundation of all *karma* is wholly and solely, the present. Any statement uttered in the past by anyone can never be the foundation for the present action. Ergo, for every person, his current state of mind, i.e., his present truth should verily be the keystone of his action. And for you, Arjuna, the attainment of the kingdom is the only present truth of your mind. You may assert your fraternal love all you want, but the present truth of your mind is simply to teach the Kauravas a lesson. You cannot turn a blind eye to this truth under the pretext of citing the scriptures or by exhibiting your fraternal love. Bear in mind, Arjuna, "the one who forsakes an action physically despite brooding or nurturing it within" is known as an impostor; he is an egoist and a hypocrite. His doom is inevitable. Such kind of people "who deliberately observe abstinence physically but brood over the sense objects mentally" are the ones who desire heaven. Their fantasies of paradise are replete with celestial nymphs like Urvashi and Menaka, and *somaras*, the drink of the gods. But for a person who lives aligned with the truth of his mind, this world is verily his heaven. For him, Urvashi, Menaka or *somaras* are all existent in this very world. He experiences them all during the course of his life itself, and gets liberated from them all before he breathes his last. In the same vein, you must clearly comprehend that this war is the present truth of your mind. Only if you embrace it and experience it wholeheartedly, can 'knowledge' become the truth of your mind tomorrow. No person who renounces action of any kind superficially can ever attain knowledge. Such abstinence from action is nothing but self-deception, which can only result in mental destruction. Moreover, discern the present truth of mind of the warriors standing before you in this war as well; the ones you are calling your cousins, uncles

The person who goes on **accepting everything** is a **true sanyasi**

and teachers. Presently, they are not your teachers, your cousins or your well-wishers. They are your enemies who have congregated here, flushed with a raging desire to destroy you, the Pandavas. Hence, to consider them your teachers, cousins or well-wishers at present is also a falsehood. O Arjuna, in short, you must understand that knowledge lies in the present alone. For, the present is the only true form of God. And the present truth of the moment is, this battle is inevitable and you and the Kauravas stand ready in confrontation, with nothing but enmity for each other. Hence, under the present circumstances, the scriptures become the past and the outcome of this battle becomes the future in relation to your present truth of mind. Ergo, embrace the present truth wholeheartedly, forsaking both the past and the future.

O Arjuna, you must apprehend that in this world, every human being has his own scripture, which emanates from his inner consciousness as per the present truth of the moment. And that alone is the actual truth of every human being. And your truth at the moment is nothing but "to fight this battle with every ounce of your being". So, do not drag the scriptures penned by others or the potential outcome of this war into it. Seek refuge unto the scripture of your soul, that is, listen to its voice. It is calling you to fight the war and war alone. And this scripture of self-knowledge exists within every human being. That is why, at any point in time, it is crystal clear to everyone's inner consciousness what should be done at that moment. However, in each and every person, this knowledge gets shrouded by the external scriptural knowledge as well as anxiety with regard to the outcome. As a result, everyone continues to be deluded as to what to do and what not to do. Hence, if you wish to attain knowledge, listen to me carefully; your soul is already well equipped with the requisite knowledge. You need not attain any knowledge externally. All you need to do is nullify the influence of all the external scriptural knowledge you have garnered and stop worrying about the outcome. In so doing, the "determination to fight" will automatically emerge from within, in the form of self-knowledge. Thus, do not speak of running away from *karma* at all.

To grasp the same, O Arjuna, try to comprehend the principle of the genesis of a human being. If I were to speak on the grounds of the prevalent scriptures and speak in their lexicon, then *karma*, that is, '*yajna*', has stemmed from '*Brahma*', that is, Nature. In other words, life has come into existence through Nature's *yajna*, which is basically *karma*. And no sooner did life come into existence than Nature "entrusted it entirely to *karma*". Thereupon, Nature has become wholly and solely the caretaker and nurturer of life. That is, although water, food, sunlight, Earth and so on were provided by Nature to foster life, the journey ahead for every life form has been left to its own actions. In short, the human being himself has to accomplish all deeds and make progress from here on, on the strength of his *karma* alone. Nature thereafter does not aid him in any way to that end. Nature, meaning *Brahma*, has made it clear in no uncertain terms, 'Henceforth, you must work towards your own betterment and uplift your life through your own *karma*.' And such being the case, it is better to perform deeds which lead to collective welfare and progress. And you can see for yourself, O Arjuna, the human being, who in the bygone eras wandered around naked or covered his modesty with leaves, has today designed a plethora of wonderful garments by virtue of his actions. The human being who was wont to travel everywhere on foot has built an array of magnificent chariots and carts. From eating raw meat, he has now concocted innumerable, sumptuous delicacies through his actions. Not only did he discover dance and music for his entertainment but also games and sports of various kinds. And he has achieved all this on the strength of his actions alone. There is no contribution of Nature whatsoever in any of these feats. And trust me, this is just the beginning; the human being shall accomplish ever more extraordinary feats in the future.

This implies that by entrusting life in the able hands of *karma* – action, Nature has made it explicit that from now on, human beings, with the help of their *karma*, must support one another and work for the greater good. Nature has made it amply clear to humans, "perform this *yajna* of *karma* day and night for the collective welfare and progress of humankind". And, Arjuna, I am also asking you to focus solely on this *yajna* of "welfare and happiness of all" as ordained by Nature. And not just you, I urge everyone to devote their life's energy to this one *yajna*. Then, it doesn't matter in the least whether this task (in the interest of the greater good) is in the form of art or knowledge, science or business. Here, the importance is of having everyone's betterment at heart while performing any task. Thus, you too should focus solely on the greater good in this war. At the moment, your duty towards the greater good is to liberate the inhabitants of Hastinapur from Duryodhana's evil reign. But, just like most human beings, your focus is centred around self-interest. You have arrived on the battlefield driven by your selfishness and this same selfishness is beckoning you to flee the battle as well. But to act out of self-interest is against Nature's design. Comprehend it thus, O Arjuna, coming to the battlefield is an action, to fight the battle is also an action, and to flee the battlefield is an action as well. Thus, even fleeing the battle comprises performing an action (*karma*). Moreover, when *karma* is the basis because of which life has come to exist, there is no question of anybody escaping from it. Everyone in this world has to engage in *karma*, be it a tiny ant or a mammoth elephant. Hence, comprehend this well, even if you speak of knowledge, it never entails a question of performing or not performing an action. Act you must, were you to follow the path of knowledge too. So, all said and done, the human being is left with only one question, whether to act out of self-interest or to serve the greater good. And it is always better to act for the sake of the greater good. For, it helps maintain harmony between the human being and Nature. Therefore, do not let your self-interest be your guiding force in deciding whether to fight or flee the war. Fight for the well-being of your subjects. Bear in mind, one who performs *yajna*, that is, *karma* out of self-interest, commits sin. You must not succumb to sin. Fight resolutely for the greater good. For, those who act out of self-interest, live in vain. Actually, continually acting for the greater good is the only true knowledge. So, etch this in your mind, no knowledge of this world can be perceived in isolation from "*karma*". Understand it in this manner – knowledge is within while action is on the outside. Each is incomplete without the other. So, you too must kindle the awareness for the welfare of your subjects within and fight the war on the outside to that effect.

O Arjuna! Consider my case as an example. All my life, I have abided by this very wheel of creation. Working towards the greater good has become the sole purpose of my life; rather my very life. Countless evil-doers were slayed at my hands, but tell me, were any of them slayed for the purpose of attaining a kingdom or expansion of territory? Did I ever bear personal enmity against any of them? No! But since each and every one of them had become a threat to the greater good owing to their evil ways, I slayed them for the good of all. Many a time, I was offered a throne after such assassinations, but I never accepted any. My focus never veered towards my self-interest while working for the greater good. In fact, I was not even the son of a king that I would have inherited a kingdom, but I still did not veer towards self-interest. And as it is well known, I even established my own kingdom 'Dwarka' on the merit of my actions alone. Neither did I wage a war to establish Dwarka nor did I commit bloodshed for that purpose. I always rejoiced within my soul and remained blessedly content in it. O Arjuna! Bear in mind, all these actions and responsibilities exist only as long as there exists self-centredness. But a person who remains content just within his soul has neither any responsibility nor any duty to speak of. Whatever the human being terms as "*karma* and duties", have self-interest at their root. His actions are driven by worries for himself and his near and dear ones, and he considers that alone as his duty. But a person who is content in his soul is bound only to the "greater good". He strives persistently for the world's welfare without any thought of self-interest. And working relentlessly for the greater good is actually the one and only "*karma* and duty" of a human being. Such human beings, who dedicate themselves to their *karma* and duty, are not plagued by worries for themselves or their near and dear ones. Such great beings neither have any motive for performing any *karma* nor do they have any purpose behind abstaining from any work. However, you had arrived on the battlefield with the selfish motive of attaining the kingdom of Hastinapur. And now driven by the sole objective of saving your life, you wish to flee the battlefield. Self-interest lies at the core of both these actions. Thus, rise above selfishness and think of the greater good. Liberate yourself from both, the objective of attaining the kingdom as well as the purpose behind fleeing the battlefield. Fight the battle for the well-being of your subjects and to end the evil reign of Duryodhana. This alone is your *karma* and duty at the moment. Arjuna, you must comprehend that externally, this battle is inevitable. Thus, there is no aspect of this war now that is either good or bad. And for that matter, "all concepts of good and bad" exist only in a person's mindset. Anything that a human being does keeping his self-interest in mind is a sin, whereas any task undertaken with everyone's best interest in mind is a virtue. Thus, you must relinquish every kind of attachment from the present war. I give you my word; you will attain the Supreme Soul while fighting this battle with such a "mindset devoid of attachment". Thereafter, you will no longer need to depend on the outcome of the war, for the attainment of the Supreme Soul. Because everything depends upon the mindset; the external action has nothing to do with it whatsoever. If you fight with self-centredness in mind, then whether you win, lose or die, you will incur sin in all three cases. Whereas, if you fight with your mind centred on the greater good, then whether you win, lose or die, you will invariably attain the Supreme Soul. Even Janaka, Sita's father had attained the ultimate state of mind - enlightenment - by casting out attachment. Pray tell me, was there any *karma* of life which he didn't indulge in? But since he was completely devoid of attachment, he inadvertently remained anchored in the Supreme Soul. So, you too must stop seeking alternatives between fighting and fleeing. Think only of banishing attachment and selfishness from the war.

O Arjuna! At present, I am speaking from the ultimate peak of consciousness, so listen to me carefully. You are not the first person to be deluded with regard to *karma*. In fact, the human being, since aeons, has been deluded about *karma*. Nevertheless, the truth is that *karma* is the very foundation of his life. For this reason, the common man has always been banking upon great people, seeking answers to the question - which actions he should indulge in and which he should refrain from. Most people start emulating the actions of great human beings, without comprehending the purport of those actions. And it is this blind faith which has spawned all these misconceptions. For, the human being, in general, does not comprehend the wondrous composition and depths of the mind or the design of Nature; he simply takes the physical deeds and actions of great people as the ideals that should be followed and begins emulating them. Looking at great people, he starts making presumptions about which viands, garments and acts are good and which are bad. And this is precisely the reason for the emergence of myriad confusions in the world regarding *karma*. For, the world is littered with an overwhelming array of differing lists on "what to do and what not to do", based on the habits and routines of each great personality. And these lists are, indeed, the cause of such faithlessness in the world regarding *karma*. And this is why everyone has his own list of actions to be abstained from, which is wrong.

Take my example, O Arjuna, there is nothing worth attaining in the three worlds that is unattained by me. And you must also realise that these three worlds do not exist outside of the human being; rather, they are the states of mind of a person. Here, he can live in any of the three worlds: past, present or future, on the basis of time. And he inevitably desires something or the other while living in these three worlds of his mind. Let us consider you for instance; you wanted to attain the kingdom of Hastinapur in the past, you wish to flee the battle in the present, and you desire your safety and well-being in the future. Whereas, I have not come to the battlefield prompted by any past desire and nor do I wish to gain anything from this war at present. And nor do I have any vested interest with regard to the outcome of this war in the future. And yet, here I stand, firm and determined on the battlefield. Therefore, in essence, you must grasp that performing one's duty resolutely with a view that "I have everything that is worth attaining" is the only true foundation of '*karma*'. To achieve the mindset where you believe, "I have everything that is worth attaining" is a momentous occurrence. For, this very mindset turns man into a king. Being a king implies, 'Whatever I possess and to whatever extent is so adequate that I don't want anything more.' This is the very virtue of a self-realised being. For, the one who has realised his soul inevitably gains the contentment of attaining it all. But unfortunately, such great beings often turn their back on '*karma*'. Most often, they fail to realise that their abstinence from action is leading the entire humankind astray. Dwelling on the ultimate peak of consciousness, I have reflected on this error of the self-realised beings as well. And all my life, I have been careful to not commit this same mistake myself. I have borne in mind that if I refrain from a particular *karma*, humankind will deem that 'refusal' a moral duty. That is why I have always undertaken all the ordinary acts of life very naturally. Because, "what one did and did not do" cannot be considered the criterion to measure the extent of one's knowledge. It is the "desire" behind the action that indicates the level of a human being's wisdom. Because, were I to think, 'what need have I to associate with women' and maintain my distance from them, it would have led to catastrophic consequences. For, everyone would have then balked at relationships between man and woman. And in no time, humankind would have reached the brink of annihilation. And were this to become a reality, I alone would be responsible for the obliteration of humanity. I would be called narrow-minded and parochial. My consciousness could grasp this reality, but even the wisest of men could not comprehend it. And it is because of them that such faithlessness in actions has emerged in the world. You need look no further for why one is shirking one kind of *karma* considering it sinful, while another is abstaining from some other *karma* for the very same reason, sinfulness. Why go far, consider your own case for instance; you too want to run away from the battle on the grounds of the sins and virtues delineated in the scriptures. But since I am a person dwelling on the acme of consciousness; rather than citing the scriptures, hearken to my words. Do not get beguiled by talks or teachings which engender distrust in action. At the same time, I would also request the self-realised beings to respect the grand *leela*, the divine play of Nature. They too must bear in mind that the realisation of soul is the primary objective of human life, not its final. The ultimate goal of human life is to live life wholeheartedly as it plays out, having attained the soul. Just like King Janaka had lived his life, and the way I have too. The wise must comprehend that they have to lead human beings to a desire-less state of mind; they certainly do not have to alter the era. Everyone should accept the era they live in, no matter which or what kind of era it is, and must mould themselves accordingly. The wise should also maintain the world order and live in sync with the popular likings of people and popular lifestyle. They too should experience each and every pleasure pursuit prevalent in that era but without any involvement or attachment. For, why refuse anything when everything is just a play? I, for one, refused neither love nor matrimonies. I spurned neither the *raas* dance nor war. I even embraced the pleasurable pursuits of dance, music and food. Why, this is the right of the wise, who are devoid of all desires! In fact, never can the ignorant experience the pleasures with the same ardour as the wise. So, the wise have, indeed, the first right over every kind of pleasure. Thus, rather than refusing to indulge in pleasures, they should, on the contrary, experience them wholeheartedly, with great fervour; and thereby send out a message and make people realise that it's the greed for pleasure which is perilous, not the enjoyment itself. So, instead of giving rise to faithlessness in people with regard to enjoyment, they should aim to liberate people of the attachment hidden in enjoyment. They should focus on liberating people from their lustful desire for "more and more enjoyment". Consider Shankara for instance; though he was a hermit, he spurned neither marriage nor love nor anger. And neither did he refrain from indulging in the pleasure pursuits of drinking, dancing or even cannabis. Ergo, the human being should shun neither *karma* nor enjoyment. He must experience them both wholeheartedly, and enjoy life in keeping with the times he lives in. All he has to do is learn to extricate desire from action and forsake the obduracy for 'more and more' enjoyment. As for *karma*, all he needs to learn is that he must undertake whatever task befalls him at any time. And as far as enjoyment is concerned, he simply needs to learn to accept and enjoy anything that comes his way at any point. Hence, if currently you have been presented with the opportunity to wage a battle, embrace it wholeheartedly, considering it a momentous task. If you gain the kingdom as an outcome of the battle, accept the kingdom too with all your heart and soul. There is no sin in it whatsoever.

Moreover, Arjuna, nobody here truly comprehends the "fabric of the human being". All the discussions concerning action revolve around the corporeal body, when, in fact, the body does not perform any action by itself at all. It is the mind, brain, ego and senses that propel the body to act. Such being the case, to question what action the body has or has not performed or what *karma* it should or should not undertake is erroneous in itself. Concurrently, the mind, brain and ego are also bound by their past *karmas* to wish, act and influence the human being in a certain way. In other words, understand that all actions are performed by the *Gunas*, the virtues of Nature. You too are bound by your mindset to desire the kingdom and harbour enmity towards the Kauravas. You have forged this mentality yourself and today, you are bound to act as per its dictates. And this applies not just to you; everyone in this world is bound to desire and indulge in ideas, thoughts, *karmas* and pleasure pursuits according to their psychology. So, fathom well that it is your mindset that provided the impetus for you to arrive on this battlefield. Even at this moment, this war is verily a part of your mindset. So, do not be adamant. You must grasp well that one's mindset is verily his present truth. To run away from it is utter foolishness. Nobody in this world should ever allow "external knowledge" to act as an impediment to the ongoing *leela* of their mindset; for that matter, true knowledge never encumbers or acts as an impediment. Only the ignorant provide all kinds of "knowledge which hinders". So, do not fall for the words of the unwise. Not only you, but even an enlightened being like me is bound to act as per the diktats of my mindset. Consider this very instance; I am bound to say all this to you because of "my resolute mindset to act for the greater good". The only difference is that an ordinary individual's mindset revolves around self-centredness, while mine is centred on the highest good. However, both are bound to act in accordance with their respective mindsets. Thus, I would like to appeal to those who profess to be wise to avoid encumbering people needlessly with knowledge that impedes "their spontaneously flowing mindset". Do not give suggestions to people regarding "what they should and should not do" and nor should you thrust inane lists of virtues and sins upon them. For, everyone in this world is bound to act as per their mindset. And that alone is in their best interest. Hence, every person in this world needs only to comprehend that he himself is not undertaking any action; rather, it is his mindset which is driving him to do so. And when it is our mindset which is compelling us to act, then why should we be concerned? O Arjuna, in a nutshell, comprehend well that to believe, "I am the doer" is ignorance; and to realise that "my mindset is driving me to do it" is wisdom. So, you too must free yourself from anxiety, for it is not you who is fighting this war; rather, it is your mindset which is compelling you to fight.

O Arjuna, you must understand that one's mindset and his psychology is his first and foremost truth; and one's soul, the inner consciousness, is the witness of his mindset and psychology. And the actual play of life revolves around a human being's mindset and psychology compelling him to undertake an action, while his witness acts as a spectator to this play. So, you too must discard your sense of doership and become a witness to the play of your mindset and psychology. The one who becomes a witness, and a spectator to the game played by his psychology is the one who triumphs, while ruin becomes the destiny of the person who turns his back on the urges of his mindset. So, focus on the inner consciousness dwelling within, and let your mindset act freely. Surrender your mindset to me, the omniscient, the all-knowing, dwelling within you. Become free of expectation and attachment, and fight this battle without any sorrow or anxiety."

Speaking thus, I concluded the Gita once again. Time was of the essence, hence there was no question of prolonging the conversation from my side. For, what if the sound of the bugle boomed on the battlefield even as we conversed? And if it did, the Kauravas would, indeed, slay this despondent Arjuna standing in front of them without a moment's wait, and the battle would end even before it began. I knew this all too well, but of what consequence was my comprehension? It was Arjuna, after all, who had to agree to fight! I, for one, had already explained to him to surrender his state of mind and psychology to his inner consciousness and become the "non-doer". I had told him, 'Let your mental state be free of anxiety and sorrow, and then fight with all your might. Do not become a 'doer' and vainly meddle with your mindset.' I do not believe, anybody, under the circumstances, could have stated words of greater import at the moment. But if only Arjuna understood! So, left with no recourse, I resumed speaking. I said, "O Arjuna, righteousness and religiousness are a matter of one's inner self; and one's mindset and psychology are one's religion that one must follow. When you follow your own state of mind and psychology, you never face problems. But any attempt to embrace a mindset suggested by someone else spawns fear. Mind well, this war is verily a part of your psychology. Numerous are the battles which you have fought till today and never once were you frightened. Never once did you retract! But today, no sooner did you try to embrace the psychology of virtue and sin propounded by others than you became terrified. That is why, I, Krishna, dwelling on the acme of consciousness, hereby declare that abiding by one's psychology and call of duty, one can even relinquish life with a beatific smile on one's face, but adopting others' psychology engenders fear. So, set yourself free from all kinds of extraneous influences and be prepared to fight resolutely, anchoring yourself in your psychology once again."

Arjuna:

O Krishna! If following one's mindset alone is one's fundamental duty, then what force drives one to commit the atrocious sin of acting contrary to one's mindset?

Krishna:

O Arjuna! Actually, the *Rajas* element of the human being is the culprit in this case. The desires spun out of the *Rajas* element are unending in nature. They propel him to run helter-skelter to gain something, and also propel him to engage in tasks out of fear of losing something. And in the outside world, a plethora of mesmerising avenues beckon him in the name of religion, business and learning, enticed by which, he ends up committing the sin of acting against his psychology. Know that both, "the human being's psychology and his soul" need no knowledge whatsoever. A human being's psychology and his state of mind are evolving and changing in accordance with his deeds; all he has to do is resolutely perform his tasks in sync with his mindset; while his witness has to remain a spectator to this play without interfering in it at all. However, even in the simple game of life, swayed by his element of *Rajas* and driven by his concern for gain and loss, the human being begins to seek *karma* foreign to his psychology. And this, in turn, leaves him deluded with regard to *karma*. You too have become deluded at the moment, for your knowledge within has been shrouded by external scriptural knowledge. And that is why you are deliberating on undertaking actions which are contrary to your psychology.

O Arjuna, here, it is imperative for you to grasp the composition of a human being. Perhaps, it might aid you "in perceiving your adversary in the form of *karma* – the desires, the lust, the greed" which makes you run from pillar to post in the name of gain and loss; which eclipses not only the human being's soul but also his psychology. For this purpose, you must, first of all, clearly comprehend that the physical body is corporeal, that is, it is transient. The human being's senses are mightier than his body. The mind is superior to the senses, while the brain towers over the mind. And that which is far more potent than even the brain is the soul. However, this soul is absolutely a non-doer. If you are not able to perceive this quality of non-doership of the soul, then you must understand it in this manner: there are two types of human mind. One is the feeble mind which is weaker than the brain, while the other is the mighty mind which is far more powerful than the brain. And in order to elevate himself to the height of the soul, the human being has to "rise above the weaker mind and advance towards the powerful one" with the aid of his intelligence. Presently, you are in the clutches of your feeble mind. For, at the moment, an overbearing external influence prevails over your psychology. That is why I am asking you to liberate yourself from all these extraneous influences thrust upon you by your brain. Strive to reinstate yourself in the "*Kshatriya* mindset", for it will instantaneously strengthen your mind. And whilst fighting the battle with that empowered mind, you will be able to rise to the elevation of the soul as well. To put it succinctly, you must comprehend that all paths leading to your welfare and progress pass through this very act of wholeheartedly "embracing the war with every ounce of your being".

The most remarkable lesson of Chapter 3 is, the one who desires nothing is verily a king; the rest are mere beggars! And the one with the mentality of a beggar will continue asking for more and more, even if he acquires the entire wealth of the world. And irrespective of the enormity of his wealth, he can never become a king. That is because, it is one's mentality that makes one a king, not wealth. And you too must become a king at heart just like Krishna, so that contented like him, you too can say with conviction that you have everything! In fact, most people actually have a lot in life. So, enjoy what you have, for this will help you engage in tasks wholeheartedly. And when the mind is focused on tasks, it will fetch splendid results too. When the outcome is good, you will gain a lot more as an incidental benefit too. In essence, instead of asking for more and more, wholeheartedly engage in tasks, and rejoice in whatever you receive in return, as the outcome of your tasks. And no matter what, live like a 'king' in every situation and sphere of life. Relinquish the beggar-like feeling of 'I don't have this' and instead awaken the kinglike feeling of 'I have plenty', which is basically the mindset of abundance. As a matter of fact, history bears testimony to the fact that people who are kings at heart are verily the ones to have attained great success in life. So, cast out thoughts about what you don't have and instead make a list of all that you have. Enjoy all of that and awaken the sublime feeling of being a king at heart. In doing so, you will immediately begin radiating the glow that will make even the greatest of people pale in comparison to you! And as a bonus, you will start treading the path of progress.

Questions	Answer Yes if applicable

1 Are you able to inhale and exhale? ....

2 Do you still have the capability to experience joy, peace and fun? ....

3 Do you have a family? ....

4 Do you have friends? ....

5 Do you have hobbies and interests? ....

6 Do you have the means for entertainment? ....

7 Are you fond of sports? ....

8 Do you have talent(s)? ....

9 Do you have a roof over your head? ....

10 Do you have work to occupy yourself with? ....

Note:

Don't you see? You already are blessed with so much in life! Isn't it enough that you are not a piece of furniture? So, have a sense of contentment and feel like a king, for there is so much you possess! Enjoy every bit of what you have. Perform your tasks wholeheartedly; and let whatever happens, happen. Receive with open arms whatever comes to your lot and continue to live like a king. Leading your life thus, you will end up accomplishing deeds of great significance effortlessly, without even realising it.

Chapter 4

Krishna:

Well, I had, indeed, elucidated it all to Arjuna. I had made it amply clear that from every perspective, right from self-interest to the greater good, the best and sole alternative for him is to fight the war. Additionally, I had said, 'As a matter of fact, you have absolutely no other choice.' But the artful way in which he had twisted my words saying, "O Krishna, if knowledge is superior to *karma*, then why are you forcing me to undertake this dreadful deed," made it apparent that he was not paying heed to my words. His attention was solely focused on fleeing the war somehow. He was unnecessarily prolonging the conversation in the hope that I would inadvertently say something which he could use as "his contention for running away from the war". Well, he would assuredly get no such opportunity from my end, but the real concern was, his hesitation and state of dither was wasting precious time. And time, we didn't have! Why, I had even told him that I am the wisest of the wise. Those who are truly wise call me the only 'complete *avatar*'. But how was he to believe me? He was unable to discern the difference even between my corporeal body and my eternal soul; he was perceiving me only in my physical form, which was making him wonder, how could a trickster and liar like Krishna be wise, let alone be considered the complete *avatar*? However, in order to not hurt his ego, I had already told him that I am not a body but a pure and enlightened soul. And it is my soul alone which is wise and that alone is the complete *avatar*. As for the body, be it yours or mine, it is much the same. But presently, he is dispossessed by the intelligence to think anything above the physical body. I understood only too well that until he grasped this difference, he would not take my words in earnest. And until he took me seriously and paid heed to my words, he would not consent to fight.

Thus, rather than imparting knowledge to him, my first priority was to make him take me seriously. And to that effect, I thought it best to employ words that would appeal to his scriptural sensibilities. Thus, drawing myself up impressively, I proclaimed, "O Arjuna! I had first revealed this supreme *Yoga* to the Sun. Thereafter, the Sun bestowed it to his offspring. But alas, it faded into oblivion with the inevitable passage of time. Nevertheless, since you are my beloved friend and devotee, I am revealing this *Yoga* to you today." Actually, Arjuna displayed no signs of a devotee. Had that really been the case, he would have readily agreed to fight the war. But what can one do, except for coaxing and inveigling! So, eventually, I told him, "It is a secret which had best remained a secret. Nevertheless, as you are dear to me, I have disclosed it to you." This was obviously an attempt to make Arjuna realise my greatness. For, since I had already spoken of this great *Yoga* to the Sun, no questions should, indeed, be raised on anything that I say. Moreover, I had said to him that this cipher had best remained shrouded in secrecy. In short, I implied, 'Arjuna, you must realise how esoteric the knowledge that I have shared with you is. Ergo, stop deliberating and just do what I ask you to do.'

Arjuna:
O Krishna! Mere decades have passed since your birth, whereas the Sun has existed since aeons. So, how am I to believe that you had revealed this *Yoga* to the Sun? Kindly explain...

Krishna:
Well, I had hoped that my psychological treatment would work on Arjuna and he would consent to fight without further questions or arguments. But Arjuna was intelligent, after all. Instead of getting influenced by

my grand assertion, he had posed a pertinent question, 'With a gap of millions of years between the ages of the Sun and you, how did you impart this *Yoga* to the Sun?' Oh, he had certainly managed to trap me, but not entirely. He was undoubtedly brilliant but not enough to entrap me and leave me clueless. For, the answer to his query could well be given within the perimeter of truth. Had he asked, 'The Sun is inanimate, how can it listen? How can it possibly have sons?' I would have been ensnared. But his contention was simple; 'You belong to this age, while the Sun has prevailed since aeons. How then did you reveal this secret to the Sun?'

Well, to satiate his curiosity, I once again began expounding the truth as I said, "O Arjuna! You and I have taken numerous births. You are unaware of them because you are under the spell of your brain and ego, but I am cognisant of them all. The entire universe has come into existence all at once. Ergo, you and I are also as old as the Sun. The only difference is that our consciousness has evolved and elevated to the stature of a human being, whereas the Sun has not yet taken that leap of progress. And as far as I, the soul, am concerned, I am unborn and indestructible. I am the one who governs all sentient beings. I just don brain and ego, and become manifest through *Yogamaya* – a divine play of Nature. You too must liberate yourself from the tendencies of your nature, which exists in the form of your brain and ego, and this soul will fully manifest within you as well. O Arjuna, whenever unrighteousness – *adharma* sees a steep rise or righteousness wanes, this 'soul' inevitably manifests in some human being in order to safeguard righteousness. And this has been the case since aeons. As the soul has manifested in me, it verily has the potential to manifest in every human being; it is just that it is lying dormant in everyone now. If you too fight with your heart and soul to expunge the evils perpetrated by the Kauravas, it will manifest in you as well. Hence, neither should your ego be bruised by my words nor should you unnecessarily cast doubt on me or my words. And as I have mentioned earlier, I am not the corporeal body but the eternal soul.

O Arjuna, both my birth – that is, the birth of the soul – as well as my *karma* are divine and pure. Even in every era including the previous ones, it has been manifesting in those whose anger and fear have been purged. And the person in whom it once manifests attains freedom from the cycle of life and death. Having attained sanctity, he gets absorbed in my form again, never to be reborn. O Arjuna, my – the soul's – greatest specialty is that I respond to my devotee with the same fervour he seeks me with. Ergo, do not disregard me, the witness dwelling within you. Heed its voice and fight this war with every atom of your being, and destroy the sinners. I, the soul, will support you in this great endeavour in every way. Perceive it thus; your witness, at any rate, is ever emanating the call to work for the greater good, but it is "the human being's mind, brain and body" which have to heed its voice and act accordingly. As for the soul, it always exists as a non-doer in the body of every human being. Such being the case, if you do not listen to the voice of your soul and stand up to fight the Kauravas, then to me, the soul, there would be no difference between you and the Kauravas. And then, you will not have me, the Supreme Soul, by your side. However, if you fight wholeheartedly, hearkening to the voice of your soul, you will find me beside you at every step of the journey. And each and every person needs to bear this in mind. Everybody in this world wants the support of the Supreme Soul, but nobody wants to act at the behest of the voice of their soul. And let me make it very clear; without heeding the call of one's soul, nobody in this world can ever attain the support of the Supreme Soul. A human being may embrace all the religions of the world, but if he acts against or contrary

This world is called **illusory** for the simple reason that **everything** here is both an **illusion** as well as the **Supreme Soul**

to the call of his soul, the Supreme Soul doesn't bother to even spare him a glance.

Returning to the reluctant Arjuna, even though I had explained the matter to him simply and lucidly, he still did not seem willing to fight. I reckoned that he was unable to grasp my words, as the scriptural knowledge had him in its beguiling grip. And the scriptures only sparingly mention '*Tatvagyaan*', the knowledge of the essence of everything; for the most part, they are loaded only with ritualism. I could well discern that Arjuna had not read about *Tatvagyaan*. Even now, he held the rituals described in the scriptures as the sole 'truth', despite my explaining to him earlier that even a fraction of self-knowledge is superior to millions of scriptures put together. But as long as the influence of the ritualism extolled in the scriptures weighed heavily upon him, he would fail to discern the significance of self-knowledge. So, immediately shedding light on the difference between the two kinds of worship a human being customarily performs, I said, "There are two kinds of worship; one, coveting the fruits of action and the other, having renounced the desire for fruits. Those who crave the fruits of action worship numerous other gods and goddesses. But those who do not solicit the fruits, focus only on me—the soul. Here, the pertinent point to note is that both, "those who hanker after the fruits and those who don't" perform action. For, eventually, action, that is, *karma*, alone is the foundation of a human being's existence. And these people performing *karma* can be divided into four groups on the basis of the deeds they perform. *Brahmin*,[10] *Kshatriya, Vaishya*[11] and *Shudra*. "And bear in mind, O Arjuna, this division of human beings is not made on the basis of birth as your cherished scriptures suggest; rather, it is done on the basis of action. Thus, you are not a *Kshatriya* because you were born into a family of *Kshatriyas*, but because your mindset revolves around bloodshed. Most importantly, people of all four categories are free to perform an action with a desire for fruits as well as without harbouring any such desire. But in every instance, their soul dwelling within always remains the non-doer. For, I, the soul, have no inclination for either action or its fruits. Ergo, simply stated, any of these people can attain self-knowledge "even by performing day-to-day deeds without hankering after their fruits". Thus, unshackle yourself

10   *Brahmin* - The highest Hindu caste comprising priests, guards of sacred learning and spiritual teachers.
11   *Vaishya* - The third Hindu caste comprising people engaged in agriculture, trade and commerce.

from the bondage of scriptures which ingrain the greed for fruits into your mind. In essence, you must grasp that since your mentality is still that of a *Kshatriya*, a warrior, "forsaking the expectation of fruits and leaping into action in the form of this battle" is the only way forward for you."

"Well, as our discussion on the subject has been extensive, I shall now elucidate *karma* and *akarma*. Man must be aware of the nature of *karma* as well as *akarma*. As a matter of fact, a human being should also be cognisant of the nature of *vikarma*. On the basis of the Three Dimensional Theory underlying the whole of existence, all actions of a human being are segregated into these three categories. And I have seen even the most brilliant people getting baffled in deciphering and grasping them. And amusingly, in spite of this, they unabashedly start delivering sermons on *karma*. So, forget what they have to say and listen to me, the words of the self-realised one. To put it succinctly, performing or wholeheartedly engaging in any deed that lies before you is *karma*; in other words, if you have something in mind and the external circumstances are also favourable for its fulfilment, then it is *karma*. Just as your desire to attain the kingdom lies within and for that purpose, the present circumstances in the form of this war support it. So, if you fight zealously with all your heart and soul to attain the kingdom, then that will be called your '*karma*'. But if you run away from your *karma* or engage in it half-heartedly, then that will be your '*vikarma*'. What you should especially take to heart is that '*karma*' maximises the possibility of attaining the desired outcome, whereas '*vikarma*' only spells doom. However, '*akarma*' is distinct from both of them and is well superior to them. '*Akarma*' implies doing anything that lies before you with absolute wholeheartedness while liberating yourself from its doership; in other words, to act not for self-interest but for the greater good, and that too without harbouring any desire for fruits, and without agonising over the outcome. So, if you fight this war without worrying about yourself or the outcome of the war, armed with the sole objective of "putting an end to the sins of the Kauravas" then that will become your *akarma*. And all I am asking you to do is that, if you are unable to fight the war anchoring yourself in *akarma*, then fight it believing it to be your duty and *karma*. But it's my kind

The one who is not perturbed by external vicissitudes is truly wise

entreaty, do not search for alternatives to *vikarma*, else, doom will be your fate. And as we have delved into this discussion in great depth, let me provide you with the supreme vision to grasp *akarma*. O Arjuna, the one who "discerns *akarma* in *karma* and *karma* in *akarma* of great beings", alone is intelligent among human beings. You can comprehend this through my example. I have performed innumerable deeds so to speak; is there anything that I have not done? From love to matrimony, I have indulged in both. I have resorted to trickery as well as deception. I have carried out assassinations and also engaged in battles. I have performed the *raas* dance, and so have my feet twinkled to innumerable other dances; I have also coaxed countless mellifluous melodies from my flute. However, there has always been an absence of doership in all my actions. The actions were performed on the outside while I always remained a non-doer within. Understand, O Arjuna, it is in the hands of Nature to decide who has to undertake which actions on the outside, whereas to remain a non-doer within is the ultimate virtue of an elevated human being. And that is why the wise know me as *Brahmachari* in spite of my numerous love affairs and marriages. For, be it love or matrimony, both were external actions; within, I always remained a witness of "my own love affairs and marriages". Hence, let the *karma* of war remain an external action of which you become the witness within; and in the blink of an eye, you will scale the supreme summit of human life.

O Arjuna, bear in mind that "desire and resolve" are the chief impediments to one's union with the Supreme Soul. The fact of the matter is that this entire Nature functions in the present; and whatever exists and is encompassed in this present is the divine, the Supreme Soul. Hence, to be absorbed and unified with the present is verily a symbiosis with the Supreme Soul, and this present manifests itself through two avenues. Firstly, through one's state of mind and secondly, through external circumstances. So, the human being needs to live sincerely with whatever lies within and without him. But his desires simply do not let him live in the present. They keep leading him astray from the present. Propelled and enthused by his desires, he engages himself in changing the present for which he takes the support of his resolve. On the strength of his resolve, not only does he try to go against his psychology and present state of mind but he also attempts to change the external circumstances. But all such endeavours are simply vain attempts to act against Nature's design, which consequently spells doom for him.

O Arjuna, you too are engaged in a similar effort at the moment. The battle lies in front of you and instead of accepting it, you are thinking of running away from it. The desire to attain the kingdom very well exists within you, but you are trying to shroud it with the strength of your determination. So, be careful! Do not put your determination to work in the wrong place. It is far better to employ your strength of determination in the task that lies before you, which in your case is the battle. Putting your determination at work in the battle thus, you will become one with 'the present truth of the Supreme Soul'. And such a person who is in absolute sync with the present never incurs sin. In fact, each and every gain and loss of a human being is endowed by Nature. And he should not interfere with it under the influence of his desire and determination. Ideally, a human being should rise above all dualities such as victory and defeat, achievement and failure, and allow things to take their own course. He should always remain content with "whatever he receives from the *Parmaatma*" automatically in the course of happening. O Arjuna, this path of contentment suggested herewith is the sole basis of the human being's joy and success. So, do not wreck your foundation of happiness and success. Understand this in no uncertain terms, you will attain all that you are to attain in the future only by going through this war.

Moreover, Arjuna, all the distinctions perceived by the human being are nothing but his sheer ignorance. As a matter of fact, *karma*—the *yajna* of human life is its sole truth as well. And a true *yajna* is one where everything, the object to be offered in the *yajna*, the paraphernalia of the *hawan*,[12] the one who performs the *hawan*, the one to whom the *hawan* is devoted and the one who endures it or enjoys it, is the Supreme Soul. In other words, only that *karma* is a true *karma*. Hence, you too must perform the present *karma* with this selfsame belief. Consider the weapons wielded in the war as the Supreme Soul, the warriors battling in it as the Supreme Soul and the one who shall endure or enjoy its outcome also as the Supreme Soul. At the same time, the one who will ascertain the outcome of this war is also the Supreme Soul. And when everything is the Supreme Soul, then let the Supreme Soul play with itself; do not interfere. But alas, owing to his failure in understanding the virtue of this *yajna* in the form of action, the human being has drifted from this 'great *yajna*'. Entangled in a web of countless distinctions and desires, he is busy performing all sorts of futile *yajna* except this one great *yajna*. However, one must know that all of his *yajnas* have emanated from desires and are concerned just with the corporeal body. A true *yajna* can only be of the *karma* performed with the belief that everything is the Supreme Soul. And when everything is the Supreme Soul, the human being needs neither desire nor determination. All that he needs to do is, forge ahead in life accepting whatever he receives in the form of the fruits of his action, as the Supreme Soul. Hence, you too must consider this *karma* that lies before you in the form of a battle as the Supreme Soul and just play! Then, accept whatever you receive as the outcome of this battle with a smile on your face, considering it a blessing of the Supreme Soul. For, it is the Supreme Soul's will which ought to be fulfilled, not ours; and it is better that way!"

However, Arjuna was not willing to fathom the import of my words. Hence, addressing him again, I said, "Alright, Arjuna, try to gain this knowledge from another guru; but yes, do have faith in him. Do not argue with him. Raise your questions with simplicity and directness.

12   *Hawan* - A Sanskrit word that refers to any ritual wherein offerings are made into a consecrated fire.

Do not be sly; exhibit only that which really lies within your mind. Thereupon, you will certainly grasp this knowledge." In other words, I told him in no uncertain terms that it was not my knowledge which was the problem but rather his faith or lack thereof. I even told him, "If you really want to gain knowledge, then have faith and listen to me with devotion, not deception." For, presently, where was the 'time' to seek another guru? Moreover, whom could he find wiser than me? So, taking the conversation forward, I said to him that if you listen to me sincerely and honestly, your "present delusion" will be obliterated in no time. And when it does, you will be willing to jump into the battle without any delusion whatsoever. And, Arjuna, I completely understand your problem; for, it is a law that one can perceive the wise only to the extent of his own knowledge and intelligence. There exists no means or mechanism of understanding a person beyond one's level. Ergo, until you gain knowledge in entirety, you will not be able to "perceive a guru" in me. As it is a law that a person first discovers the Supreme Soul within himself and only then does he perceive it in everyone else. That is why, I too am not imparting knowledge to you at present; I am only striving to awaken the Supreme Soul in you. For, this law is applicable not only to you but to every human being too. So, it is my humble request to everyone, do not try to seek the Supreme Soul in me; for you would never be able to perceive it until you have realised your own. To view me as the Supreme Soul without realising the Supreme Soul dwelling within you, will be nothing but a farce. So, you and everyone else should focus on seeking the Supreme Soul within yourself and realise it with the help of the knowledge I am imparting herewith.

O Arjuna, you must comprehend yet another mysterious aspect of this science. The one who continually dwells in a pure state of consciousness automatically gains this supreme knowledge. Hence, fight this war with purity of mind. As the desire to attain the kingdom dwells deep in your mind, fight wholeheartedly to that end. Follow your inner consciousness and impulse of mind even in the times to come. When a person continually conducts himself thus, the maladies of the mind vanish on their own. For, the simple truth is that the human being has to do absolutely nothing to attain this great knowledge. One day, in due course of time, his soul awakens and manifests by itself. Even a person who has sunk to the pits of sin gets absolved of all sins with the aid of this sole knowledge. The awareness that one should "work persistently with a pure consciousness" is the kind of knowledge that incinerates all of the human being's *karma* in the blink of an eye. Bear this in mind, the human being strays on account of acting against his consciousness. Ergo, to fight the battle wholeheartedly is the only way for you to realise the Supreme Soul at present. As for the foolish and faithless person who digresses from the path I have shown, he loses sight of the spiritual path and is ruined. Thus, dedicate all your *karma* to your inner consciousness. And brace yourself to fight this war with all your might and main.

In Chapter 4, Krishna has elucidated *karma, vikarma* and *akarma*. He has explained that everyone in this world has to inevitably engage in *karma*. The sun has to burn, water has to flow, and human beings have to lead a joyous and successful life. This is verily the design of Nature. Further, he has explained that the human being engages in three types of *karma*. First is *karma* – the deed which is performed in expectation of fruits. Meaning, it is performed either to attain something or safeguard something. Then comes *vikarma*, which is at a level lower than *karma*. *Vikarma* are the deeds performed in contrast to that which lies within. In other words, what you are doing externally is at variance with what lies within; and such deeds invariably produce disastrous outcomes. And then comes the most superior of all three – *akarma*, a deed performed single-mindedly. *Akarma* are those deeds in which the mind, brain, body and senses are all aligned and engaged in unison; so much so that the mind does not even desire the fruits of an action. Interestingly, the person who is relentlessly engaged in the pursuit of *akarma* does not even realise how, in time, he attains greatness. You too are engaged in deeds day and night, but you are unaware as to which of those deeds are *karma, vikarma* and *akarma*. But hereafter, start paying attention to the deeds you perform and check which of the three categories they fit into. Here, I have provided a list of deeds that are routinely performed by everyone. After perusing the list, check which category – *karma, vikarma* and *akarma* – each of these deeds fall into. This chart itself will form the foundation for your present life as well as your future. Needless to say, if *akarma* is dominant in your life, then life will inevitably be splendid; whereas, if *vikarma* is dominant, then life is certain to be doomed.

Types of deeds

Put a tick against the approach (i.e. *karma, vikarma* or *akarma*) you take for performing each of these deeds

When engaged in daily chores

☐ *Karma*   ☐ *Vikarma*   ☐ *Akarma*

While conversing with spouse or beloved

☐ *Karma*   ☐ *Vikarma*   ☐ *Akarma*

While indulging in hobbies or pleasure pursuits

☐ *Karma*   ☐ *Vikarma*   ☐ *Akarma*

While conversing with parents

☐ *Karma*   ☐ *Vikarma*   ☐ *Akarma*

While performing work duties

☐ *Karma*   ☐ *Vikarma*   ☐ *Akarma*

When engaged in recreational activities

☐ *Karma*   ☐ *Vikarma*   ☐ *Akarma*

While eating

☐ *Karma*　☐ *Vikarma*　☐ *Akarma*

While exercising

☐ *Karma*　☐ *Vikarma*　☐ *Akarma*

When engaged in your favourite activity

☐ *Karma*　☐ *Vikarma*　☐ *Akarma*

While sleeping

☐ *Karma*　☐ *Vikarma*　☐ *Akarma*

Note:

The level of energy, effervescence and the degree of blitheness and success in one's life is directly proportional to the number of *akarmas* in their life. So, henceforth, stop engaging in the tasks which you have been executing by way of *vikarma*. This will automatically weed out several problems from your life. As for the tasks that you have been engaging in by way of *karma*, well, they are actually essential in life. So, try to gradually turn those *karmas* into *akarmas*. The day all your *karmas* are transformed into *akarmas*, all the problems of your life will be eliminated. Thus, fill in the above chart thoughtfully and earnestly, and try to turn all your tasks into *akarmas*. Then, just watch how your life takes a 360-degree turn!

Chapter 5

Arjuna:

O Krishna! First, you praised *Karmasanyas*, detachment from *karma* and then *Karmayoga*, the path of action. Kindly enlighten me, which of the two paths is assuredly propitious for me?

Krishna:

You are remarkable, aren't you, Arjuna? I am your friend. Why, I am a friend and a well-wisher to this entire world! It is simply beyond me to say anything that is detrimental in nature. Obviously, everything I speak will be only for your benefit and that of the entire world. Nevertheless, your desire to know "which is superior, *Karmayoga* or *Karmasanyas*" is also quite an achievement in itself! The human being, in fact, speaks thus because he is bereft of the knowledge of psychology. Else, be it *Karmayoga* or *Karmasanyas*, both are extremely beneficial. Bear in mind, only fools perceive *Karmayoga* and *Karmasanyas* as separate and distinct from one another. They speak such words of folly due to lack of psychological knowledge. Otherwise, the wise well know that the outcome of both is one and the same. O Arjuna, *Karmasanyas* implies "renouncing the sense of doership from action" while *Karmayoga* is "forsaking the desire for the fruits of action". The human being may forsake either the desire for "fruits" of action or the sense of "doership"; no sooner is one forsaken than the other perforce disappears. In other words, the one who hankers after fruits is verily the doer, and it is the doer who craves the fruits. Why go far, consider your own case for instance. As you had nurtured a desire for fruits in the form of a kingdom, you arrived at the battlefield verily as a doer, striving for battle. And at this moment, as you want to secure your life, you wish to indulge in an act of doership and run away from the battlefield. This verily implies that doership exists as long as the desire for fruits exists. Similarly, doership exists in a person only till the time he yearns for fruits. In other words, fruits and doership are integral to each other. As soon as one ceases to exist, the other disappears by itself.

O Arjuna! Consider my case for instance. I too am standing in the battlefield, just like you, but what is it that I desire? Nothing whatsoever! And since I do not wish to gain anything, I am not the doer either. As I am here in the battlefield to fulfil the wish of the Supreme Soul, the doer of my *karma* (this battle) is also the Supreme Soul. Why just this, the Supreme Soul is inevitably the doer of all my deeds. It is solely for him and to comply with his wishes that I perform the *raas* dance and also savour the *Chhappan Bhog*.[13] I undertake assassinations for him and indulge in trickery and deception solely at his behest. So, despite being the doer without, I always remain the non-doer within. And this is what you should do as well. Be free from all forms of fruits—possible outcomes—this war brings in its wake. Whether you attain victory or vanquishment, kingdom or death, virtue or sin, banish these concerns from your mind. No sooner are your personal desires expunged than you will fight this war only for the sake of the Supreme Soul. And when you wage this war for the Supreme Soul, the doer of this war will not be you but the Supreme Soul dwelling within you. In other words, the sense of doership emanates only on performing *karma* out of a selfish motive or interest. As soon as the self-interest is expunged, the human being becomes the 'non-doer'. Hence, I implore you to perform all your actions only for the sake of the Supreme Soul. In so doing, you will always be free. In short, *Karmasanyas* is not possible without *Karmayoga*, and *Karmayoga* is impossible without *Karmasanyas*. But as the human being finds forsaking doership a little arduous, I am of the opinion that the renouncement of fruits is the ideal path for the human being's liberation and progress. Hence, I urge

13 *Chhappan Bhog* - A meal consisting of fifty-six dishes.

you once again, forsake the fruits of all actions and prepare yourself to fight the war. Upon doing so, your sense of doership will automatically vanish and you will instantaneously attain supreme bliss.

O Arjuna, simply comprehend that the question of "what you did or didn't do" is of no consequence whatsoever. The real question is, did you act in expectation of fruits or without it? Who was the doer of these actions—you or the Supreme Soul? O Arjuna, the masters of *Tatvagyaan*, in spite of being engaged in seeing, smelling, eating, speaking, renouncing or even accepting and grasping are, in fact, never doing anything themselves. For, every *karma* they undertake is only for the Supreme Soul. So, fight you must, but only for the Supreme Soul. Then, irrespective of what your scriptures dictate, I declare that if you wage a war for the sake of the Supreme Soul, you will not incur sin. O Arjuna, do not presume that today I am the Supreme Soul as I am speaking of the soul, and that I was not so while performing the *raas* dance or when committing trickery and deception. I am nothing but the Supreme Soul, at every moment, in every situation. Any person in the world, who performs any action without desiring the fruits and without a sense of doership, is indeed considered as the Supreme Soul, but only with regard to that particular action. In other words, you must realise that "the sense of doership and the expectation of fruits" are the biggest impediments to the path of righteousness. And the scriptures you are stressing upon, on the contrary, engender "the desire for fruits" in a human being; they all strengthen his sense of doership. On the other hand, the pure knowledge I am imparting herewith simply states that only a person who bears neither attraction nor repulsion towards any person, subject or object is a true *Karmayogi*. And the person who goes on accepting whatever comes his way willingly, is a true *sanyasi*. So, presently, the only knowledge you truly need is—get up and embrace the battle that lies in front of you, forsaking doership and the expectation of fruits.

O Arjuna! The scriptures which you are citing in order to flee the battle, instruct one to differentiate even between a *Brahmin* and a *Shudra*. They are inadvertently engaged in creating divisions among human beings. But the truly wise do not make a distinction even between a learned and genteel *Brahmin* and a cow, elephant, dog and a wicked man. They are absolutely impartial; they do not differentiate even between a *Brahmin* and a mongrel. Such wise beings never make a distinction between war and renunciation. And the individuals anchored in such equanimity not only conquer the world but also attain the Supreme Soul in this very lifetime. O Arjuna, you must comprehend that all the differences that a human being perceives exist as long as he nurses the expectation of fruits. Moreover, all his choices and discriminations last only till he is possessed by a sense of doership. All in all, the truly wise being never chooses between what is agreeable and disagreeable to him. He never rejoices on attaining the pleasant nor does he ever grieve on encountering the unpleasant. For, he is aware that this "entire cycle of gain and loss" is under the purview of the Supreme Soul. Hence, he is content with whatever he receives from the Supreme Soul. He neither desires nor chooses. He is cognisant of the truth that one world lies within and another, without. He knows that he has no control over the external world, but his inner world is verily his own. And his inner world alone is his soul. And such wise beings remain blithe and contented within their soul alone; soul alone is the source of their knowledge and they traverse (nowhere but) its wondrous depths. Hence, their inner state remains unchanged forever; they always remain contented in their soul. The world without might be caught in a maelstrom, fraught with chaos and disorder, but within they always remain equanimous. Arjuna,

O Arjuna, I am the Supreme Soul in totality, not just while enunciating the Gita but even when indulging in trickery and deception

the person who worships his soul, believes that it is his soul which experiences all *yajna* and penance. In fact, he considers his soul as the god of all gods. He is never influenced by any scripture, save for his soul. Thus, you too must stop resorting to the scriptures and instead, surrender to your soul, and gain knowledge from it; all your doubts and misgivings will vanish in the blink of an eye. To that end, all you need to do is surrender "your expectation of the fruits of action and the sense of doership" entirely to your soul. And mark my words, in that very instant, your soul—the fountainhead of knowledge—will make the knowledge available to you, which I am now imparting to you.

 Practical Application – 10

The greatest lesson of Chapter 5 is, expunge all differentiations and discriminations, for they inevitably create delusions and lead life astray. Hence, always remember, "Everything is the Supreme Soul" is the only true knowledge. At this juncture, the reason why even Arjuna is gripped with sorrow is discrimination. He is mired in indecision only due to discrimination. If you too have many digressions in life, it is only on account of differentiation and discrimination. To this end and even for the mindlessness you see all around, the teaching of differentiation imparted unto us is responsible. Krishna says, for a wise being, there is no distinction between a learned *Brahmin* and a dog. For, in the end, they are both existential elements. They are not 'like this' or 'like that'. Besides, we have to deal with only those who are present in our life; for, we naturally maintain distance with those who are not part of our life. So, perceive those present in your life as the Supreme Soul, and then see how your mind becomes blithe and peaceful forever! And needless to say, it is verily the peaceful and cheerful mind that makes progress. Well, by accepting everything as the Supreme Soul, firstly, all your concerns regarding gain-loss will be eliminated. For then, whatever you gain, or lose, will also be nothing but the Supreme Soul. And as for your mind, it will become so pure and unsullied that you will enjoy life to the hilt. So, with a calm and resolute mind, write next to all the points mentioned in the chart below that "I consider this to be the Supreme Soul." We have both originated from the Supreme Soul and both of us have to return to the Supreme Soul, so why discriminate at all? Only a fool would do so! You cannot even imagine the kind of transformation this single change (in your outlook) will bring forth. And as a bonus, your mind will attain everlasting peace.

List of all the people and things you encounter in life

With utmost sincerity, write next to each point, "Henceforth, I shall verily consider these as the Supreme Soul."

Family and friends

....
....
....

Your duties

....
....
....

Your mind and body

....
....
....

People belonging to other castes, religions and countries

....

....

....

Your competitors

....

....

....

Your enemies

....

....

....

The failures you encounter

....

....

....

The problems and difficulties you endure

....

....

....

Your hobbies, interests, desires and pleasure pursuits

....

....

....

Others' desires

....

....

....

Note:

In essence, you need to understand that every object, every human being and every event that occurs in the universe is verily the Supreme Soul. And this is irrefutably the most sublime state of mind. And once you attain this state of mind, you will be rid of all the sorrows plaguing your life. Indeed, when everything has originated from the Supreme Soul and is well occurring as per his will, then why discriminate and fret at all? This is what 'equanimity' is all about.

Chapter 6

Krishna:

O Arjuna! You seem anxious to become a *yogi*[14] but you are unable to cultivate the attributes of a *yogi* within. For, the truth is that if a person refuses to perform an action on account of the possible outcome of the action, then he certainly cannot be considered a *yogi*. Thereupon, the reason for his refusal—be it the scriptures, virtue-sin or the fear of burning in hellfire—is of no consequence. And this is what you must especially take to heart. For, though you appear interested in comprehending *yoga*, your conduct in no way matches that of a *yogi*. Not only do you believe this war to be a grievous act of sin but you also deem it as a path leading straight to hell. However, like a true *yogi*, if you abandon "all resorts you have been banking upon in the form of the fruits of action" then you will think of nothing save fighting this war. I too have carried out numerous assassinations in my life but while executing them, neither did I agonise over virtue-sin or heaven-hell, nor did I hanker after them. For, if the sinners are meant to be destroyed then they ought to be destroyed by all means! Then one cannot shirk from the said task due to the expectation of fruits or anxiety over the outcome. The obliteration of sinners cannot be weighed on the scale of virtue-sin. O Arjuna, likewise, comprehend that the human being who has renounced the sacred fire is not a *sanyasi*. In other words, one cannot refuse to perform a task which ought to be performed, out of fear of loss or harm to oneself. This is also nothing but utter selfishness.

14   *Yogi - A practitioner of Yoga.*

Therefore, understand this once and for all; the greater good can never be shirked for any self-interest of the world.

Thus, to act selflessly, that is, to continually perform deeds devoid of desire or expectation is the sole characteristic of a *yogi*. And for such a *yogi*, "the absence of all kinds of predetermination" is the one and only path to his upliftment. For here, one can never be certain as to what one may be called upon to do at any point in time. So, a person who is predetermined for what he will do or not do can never anchor himself in *yoga*. In other words, "only the person who forsakes all his predeterminations is called *"yogarud"* or anchored in *yoga*". Consider me for instance; I am a heart awash with love, a seeker of pleasures who believes in living life to the fullest. But to that end, I cannot make a resolve that I will not get embroiled in complications or that I will not be drawn into conflicts. I have given Nature complete authority to decide what I ought to do at any given moment. I do not let "my desires, my choices or my predeterminations" meddle with it. And that is why I am a true *yogi*. So, if you too wish to anchor yourself in *yoga*, expunge "all forms of desires and resolves" and then give me just one valid reason for you to put down your weapons; I will readily assent to it. Arjuna, my good friend, time is slipping away from our hands. So, try to comprehend my words. Given the present circumstances, no true *yogi* or *sanyasi* in the world will refuse to fight this war.

O Arjuna, the world is so designed that here, the human being is his own friend as well as his own enemy. In the world without, no person is another's friend or foe. Hence, he should be a committed friend to himself and effect his own betterment while sailing through the "ocean of the world". And for that purpose, he must absolutely relinquish all desires and resolves. Never should he vow that he would perform a particular action or refrain from another. He should not enmesh himself in thoughts of what he wants or does not want. A person must save himself from all such kinds of attractions and distractions. O Arjuna, for a *yogi* or a *sanyasi*, there is no distinction between joy and sorrow, heat and cold, or honour and humiliation. They go on accepting anything they receive in life as the Supreme Soul's blessing. They perform every task that befalls them considering it to be the decree of the Supreme Soul. Thus, you too should accept this war which has fallen to your lot as the Supreme Soul's blessing. Thinking otherwise only displays "your ego and ignorance". So, do not ask, who is superior, the *yogi* or the *sanyasi*? For, neither of them would seek excuses to flee this battle.

O Arjuna, for a *yogi*, there is no difference between a pebble and a piece of gold. He feels the same for his friends, foes and strangers; he places both sinners and saints on the same pedestal. He does not nurse any hopes and expectations nor does he develop an affinity for anything in his mind. No matter how vast his world is on the outside, within, he just dwells in solitude perpetually. O Arjuna, numerous people strive in innumerable ways to anchor themselves in this *yoga*. To this end, they perform myriad *asanas*[15] including *pranayama*.[16] They are all beneficial as well, for they help in keeping the body healthy and strong. And a healthy body finds it easy to ascend the summits of the mind. Thus, O Arjuna, the fitness of the body is as crucial in this *yoga* as the purification of the mind. That is why, everything, right from diet to sleep, holds great significance in this *yoga*. Neither the one who overeats nor the one who starves himself succeeds in it. In the same vein, too much or too little sleep also acts as an impediment to this *yoga*. But even so, the fitness of the mind holds the greatest significance. And therefore, the act of extricating "desires and resolves" from the mind holds paramount importance. Hence, the human being should certainly take care of his body, but he should focus his attention chiefly on the wellness of the mind. For, eventually, the outcome of one's life is greatly dependent on the fitness of the mind, not the fitness of the body.

O Arjuna, why do you not discern the simple fact that actually, the entire life of a human being lies within, not without. Whatever is worth gaining or losing also lies within him. On the outside, neither riches nor renunciation is worth attaining; for, everything that exists outside is simply an illusion. For that matter, even heaven and hell do not exist outside. The mindset you are presently dwelling in is verily your hell. And I sincerely want to help you overcome your misery and instantly anchor you in supreme bliss. Ergo, do not perceive this war as an external phenomenon. Look for this struggle within and triumph over it. In a flash, this external war will become a "farce" for you. In

---

15 *Asanas* - The physical practice of *Yoga* poses.

16 *Pranayama* - The regulation of breath through certain techniques and exercises.

other words, simply apprehend that for a man who harbours no differences within, there exists no conflict in life without either. Till the time you differentiate between virtue and sin, and kingdom and renunciation inside, struggles will prevail in your life outside. Till then, you would want to run towards one and flee from the other. So, let the matters pertaining to the external world remain in the external world itself and be content in your soul within. To always remain equanimous and content within is, indeed, "supreme bliss" experienced by a *yogi*. For, such a *yogi* views everything around him through the lens of equanimity. He perceives everything that lies in the world outside to be an extension of the one unified soul. And when everything is an extension of the soul alone, then why discriminate and differentiate? Why look for good-bad and virtue-sin in them? Why look for yours-mine and victory-vanquishment in them? Thus, Arjuna, whosoever of the wise perceives the entire expanse surrounding him "to be under the purview of Vasudeva, i.e., I, the soul" becomes one with me for good. Thus, you too must anchor yourself completely in equanimity. Believe everything, including yourself and the Kauravas, as well as life and death, to be 'Krishna'. Then, whether you win or lose, you will not be parted from me. You will be with me whether you live or breathe your last. For then, victory and vanquishment or life and death, everything will simply become manifestations of Krishna for you. O Arjuna, intelligent as you are, just think, is there any difference between victory-defeat

O Arjuna, the world is so **designed** that here, the **human being** is his **own friend** as well as his **own enemy**

> Be it a **human being** or an **animal**, everything here is bound to **act** in **sync** with its **nature**

or virtue-sin for a person who sees everything on the outside as an extension of the Soul? Irrespective of what such a *yogi* does, his Supreme Soul continues to treat everything else as an extension of the Supreme Soul. And how can such a person "who is playing with everyone and everything else as an extension of the Supreme Soul" ever incur sin, no matter what he does? So, in short, till the time you accord importance to yourself as individually distinct, you will differentiate between everything on the outside. The day you consider everyone including your own self to be the offspring of the one God, victory-vanquishment and life-death will no longer affect you. Then, neither will you ever refuse to fight nor insist on fighting. A person who does not differentiate between his own joys and sorrows and those of others, that *yogi* is considered to be the most supreme of all. For, he never acts out of a concern for his self-interest.

Arjuna:

O Krishna, I have taken to heart your lesson on becoming anchored in equanimity. But it is easier said than done. Due to the extreme fickleness of my mind, despite my best efforts, I am incapable of perceiving myself and others with equanimity. O Krishna, this mind is extremely fickle, restless and stubborn. Disciplining it is akin to taming the wild wind. In spite of wishing to the contrary, I am constantly ensnared in the pursuit of self-interest. I cannot help but get repeatedly gripped by anxiety about myself. My friend, while you urge me to perceive victory-defeat and life-death with even-mindedness, I find myself incapable of perceiving the warriors fighting in this war with equanimity. My mind refuses to accept the contention that there is no difference between my death and that of the Kauravas; that whether I am vanquished or the Kauravas, it is one and the same. Indeed, though I have comprehended the import of your words, I am finding it extremely arduous to implement it owing to the fickleness of the mind.

Krishna:

O Arjuna! You are right. This mind is, indeed, powerful. To tame it is undeniably challenging. But it can be mastered with the persistent practice of detachment. And let me make it absolutely clear to you that here, I am referring to the detachment of the mind, not the body. Be it victory-vanquishment or life-death, you should keep the external matters strictly confined to the outside world, considering them to be just a physical deed. There must be no thought other than that of detachment in your mind as far as these deeds are concerned. Be it *Chhappan Bhog* or a dry *chapati,*[17] the consumption of both must be confined to the body alone. To your mind, there must be absolutely no difference between the two. A person who continually practises such detachment of the mind "towards all things and actions" easily attains this supreme *yoga* one day. This is my strong conviction "regarding the attainment of this great *yoga*". Hence, anybody who disregards "the detachment of the mind" and focuses on other means and matters for attaining this *yoga*, remains bereft of realising this "glorious *yoga*".

Arjuna:

O Krishna! I have well discerned what you just said! And what you say is true indeed. But enlighten me, what happens to those people who strive to attain detachment of their minds and anchor themselves in equanimity, but are unable to do so till the very end owing to their failure in controlling their minds? Do these persevering people endowed with faith also meet their doom? If I were to elaborate upon this query with my own example, then I have taken to heart every word of yours; I have grasped that if I fight this war, anchoring myself in equanimity, I will attain this *yoga* even as I fight the war. However, despite my best efforts, if I am unable to anchor myself in equanimity and I still go ahead and fight, what will happen to me? I will certainly not attain

17 *Chapati* - A kind of Indian flat bread.

yoga in that case, but will I get debased and ruined? O Krishna, nobody besides you can resolve my predicament and relieve me of this anxiety.

Krishna:

O Arjuna! I am pleased to hear that you have at least grasped my words. Now, grasp further that the human being has to take only the first step "towards attaining the Supreme Soul". In due course, the remaining journey gets completed seamlessly and effortlessly. So, consider your endeavour to get anchored in equanimity as the first step towards attaining the Supreme Soul. Thereupon, you will not get destroyed in this world or any other; neither will you ever regress in life. And even if you die in the battlefield while striving to anchor yourself in equanimity, do not worry. For, then you will be reborn in the abode of a wise, enlightened person, and you will again march towards attaining equanimity with twice the fervour. And this cycle will continue till the time you have attained *yoga*, meaning, "complete equanimity" to the core. O Arjuna, mark my words, the person who strives to anchor himself in equanimity is considered far superior to even the ascetics, religious scholars and followers of ritualism. And you have already taken the first step towards equanimity; so, fight the battle with all your heart and soul, without a single misgiving. Now, there is no need for you to agonise over anything else.

The underlying lesson of Chapter 6 is that selfishness is the one and only sin. Once you expunge all selfishness, then no matter what you do, it will be the Supreme Soul who will actually be doing it. The root cause of all problems in life is selfishness. Indeed, name one problem in your life which doesn't stem from selfishness. So, eliminate selfishness and the problem will vanish on its own; there is no other way to rid oneself of problems. The truth is, only those who have purged their self-interests have attained greatness. And indubitably, the Gita leads you to success and makes you great! So, with the help of the chart below, try to weaken your self-interests. In doing so, your troubles will continue to mitigate on their own and your life will continue to change for the better.

List of all that you deal with

Sincerely write next to each point, "From today onwards, I remove my self-interest from this."

Familial relationships

....
....
....

Friends

....
....
....

Business relationships

....
....
....

The outcome and consequences of actions

....
....
....

Religion

....
....
....

Thoughts

....
....
....
....

Future

....
....
....
....

Deeds & *karma*

....
....
....
....

Note:

You must realise that everyone in the world is striving to carve a happy and successful life for themselves, driven by self-interest. Every person has just one refrain – What about me? What will I gain? And yet, why is no one able to carve a desired life of joy, peace and success for themselves? That is because, one can be blithe and successful in life only by aligning oneself with the supreme laws of Nature, not by applying one's brain and its puny faculties. And verily, Krishna is uttering every word keeping in mind the immutable laws of Nature. So, remember, it is impossible to achieve lasting peace and success in life without obliterating selfishness from all relationships and tasks.

Chapter 7

Krishna:

I had presumed that Arjuna would now definitely agree to fight the war. But this was not the case! His expressions and demeanour made it amply clear that he was still not ready to take up arms. And indeed, how could he be ready? For, although he was not as anxious as before, he was still gripped with anxiety. Earlier, he was agonising over concerns such as virtue-sin and life-death; now, he was fretting over the state of his subsequent births. Although, I had told him in no uncertain terms that once a person sets foot in the direction of anchoring himself in equanimity, he continues to progress birth after birth towards the realisation of the Supreme Soul. But, as I reckon, only the one who is assured of being reborn will worry over his future births. And once he is sure of rebirth, there would be nothing much left to worry about. So, even though Arjuna was feigning concern about his future births, he was still primarily concerned about his present birth. Thus, I could easily divine that though Arjuna's mindset had certainly improved, even now his focus was centred mostly on evading the subject of war than grasping my words.

Such being the case, what recourse did I have except for taking the conversation forward? I could not give up ingraining sensibilities into him and bringing him around to fight the war. Besides, I had never lost any battle of life. And I definitely could not afford to be vanquished in my present conversation with Arjuna either. So, I began expounding once again; although, I had already elucidated the truth to him using so many approaches that he no longer needed to know anything new. But if he still failed to comprehend, I had no choice but to continue with my elucidation using a novel approach. So, I began to speak again, "O Arjuna, "with exclusive devotion towards your soul", hearken to that secret with the help of which you will be able to fathom the entire existence endowed with my glorious qualities. Steeped in science, this *Tatvagyaan* is a sublime secret knowing which, nothing further remains to be known in this world. O Arjuna, this is an utterly profound secret. In essence, you must grasp that it is not easy to realise my divine form, that is, my form as the Supreme Soul. Only a few among thousands in the world endeavour to attain my form as the Supreme Soul and only one among those few actually surrenders to his soul and succeeds in attaining my form. As for the scriptures you have been citing herewith, everyone reads them. But "I" can never be attained through such empty scriptural knowledge, for there is no question of realising me without surrendering to your soul wholeheartedly.

Now, for you, I will shed light upon "my - the soul's - mysterious form". By and large, my nature exists in two realms, the insentient and the sentient. The insentient, that is, my material nature is divided into eight parts altogether. Not only earth, water, fire, air and ether but the human being's mind, brain and ego are also a part of my insentient existence. And surprisingly, despite this, the human being seeks and speaks of knowledge only through the medium of 'the mind, brain and ego' and also strives to grasp it through these faculties alone. He utterly fails to discern that faculties as well as all this knowledge have emanated from my insentient nature. They are laden with nothing but "illusion". O Arjuna, not only are the concepts of virtue-sin, victory-vanquishment and success-failure illusory but discussions of worldly matters and renunciation are also nothing save an illusion. All such concepts including this knowledge are, indeed, a part of my insentient nature. That is why, I am one widely discussed subject, so to speak, yet there is hardly any "discussion per se on me, the Supreme Soul". So, hearken unto me, O Arjuna, I am a spiritual being independent of every single one of these insentient entities. In other words, apprehend that "I am the only being of sentient nature" dwelling in the midst of these insentient elements. My name, my body, my family and my kingdom of Dwarka, are all material entities. If you wish to recognise me, then you must understand that I am far removed from them. Likewise, you are neither Arjuna nor a Pandava, nor does Hastinapur belong to you; you too are nothing but "a sentient element of higher nature".

In other words, this entire world is born out of the union of material and spiritual natures, but in reality, "I, the spiritual being", am the sole reason for the creation and dissolution of this world. Everything in existence exists because of me. Simply put, this entire universe, all these living entities, all human beings are woven into me, like beads woven into a necklace. O Arjuna, in spite of being invisible, it is I who is the most significant amongst all that exists in the world. I am the thirst-quenching element in water. I am the radiance of the Sun and the Moon. I am the blaze in fire, and the life-force in human beings. Why just this, I am even the *purushatva*, the virility in men. Ergo, do not think of running away from the *purushartha*—the purpose of your spirit—in the form of this war. Trust me, my friend, "I" will always stand by you in this *purushartha* of yours. Think of it thus, the ascetic is an insentient entity and "I" am his austerity, an element of his spirituality. The human being is the physical entity, but "I" am his masculinity. That is not all; I am the "carnal pleasure" which is compatible with the scriptural injunctions, meaning, pleasure indulged in with mutual consent. Also, "I" am the might which the mighty display without having any personal aspirations. You too are mighty and powerful but you have always been using your strength to fulfil your desires or to showcase your capability and skills. That is why none of your acts of valour have been imbued with my presence. But I am asking you to fight this war today with nary a wish or desire. In so doing, beyond a shadow of a doubt, my might will amplify your strength manifold.

O Arjuna, what do I say! Know that in human beings, not only an element of *Sattva*, the quality of goodness, and *Rajas*, the principle of activity, but even his *Tamas*, the principle of inertia are begotten through me. As stated earlier, except for me, there is no other ultimate reason behind any occurrence or incident transpiring in this world. So, understand once and for all, even this war is occurring because of my wish. Although it is a different matter that the *Rajasika* tendency of some and the *Tamasika* tendency of others is responsible for the emergence of this war. Concurrently, this war is also the outcome of many people leaning towards *Sattva*; and this is the problem with everyone, including you. And this is the reason why everyone is engaged in conflict. On the other hand, though I have everything to do with this war, in reality, I, the Supreme Soul, have nothing whatsoever to do with it. In other words, even though I am present in the battle, I am not a part of it. Meaning, the battle surely exists outside, and I am standing in the battlefield as well; yet, there is no battle within me. On the other hand, you are so immersed in this war that even if you were to flee from it, you will still never be rid of it. Yet, here you are, refusing to fight the war. So, keep your three tendencies, *Rajas, Tamas* and *Sattva* at bay. Thereupon, despite being present in the battlefield, you will automatically be far removed from this war. Upon doing so, you will become eternally one with me. For, I exist beyond these three inclinations. O Arjuna, the human being may fight with the proclivity of *Tamas* like the Kauravas or the inclination of *Rajas* like the Pandavas, but the Supreme Soul is not present in either. Here, let me also make it absolutely clear that I am definitely not present in those *Sattvika* reasons, that is, the virtue-sin delineated in the scriptures which

O Arjuna, some go through life deeming this *samsara* – the world as the Supreme **Soul,** while others perceive **renunciation** in the same light. They are **both wrong!**

you are furnishing as an excuse to flee the battle. Those are even more treacherous, as under such circumstances, you will carry the thoughts of this war with you for life and they will plague you till you breathe your last. So, recognise "me—the indestructible Supreme Soul" beyond these three tendencies, the material nature of which lies in the battle and the spiritual nature prevails beyond the battle. Under the present circumstances, to fight in the manner I suggested herewith is the only solution. O Arjuna, whoever overcomes this "Three Dimensional Theory" in the form of the tendencies of "*Sattva, Rajas* and *Tamas*" becomes perpetually united with the Supreme Soul even as he lives.

O Arjuna, this Three Dimensional Theory is extremely formidable. It has besieged everyone, whether it is a worldly person or a *sanyasi*. Here, some go through life deeming this *samsara* – the world, as the Supreme Soul, while others perceive renunciation in the same light. But nobody fathoms that I coexist both in worldly pursuits as well as in renunciation. To engage with the world outside while being detached from within is the only way of my being. However, caught up in the three dimensions of tendencies, people's flame of wisdom has been extinguished. The human being is unable to perceive the material nature of the world that exists outside and the spiritual nature of the sentient world that exists within as separate and distinct. Then, whether he lives in the world, embracing it, or adopts renunciation as his way of life, he deems the material and spiritual natures to be synonymous. Nobody comprehends them as the coexistence of two different forms of 'Krishna'. Wise beings who perceive everything as the innumerable forms of Krishna are scarce in this world. But Arjuna, you must not get deluded. Because those *Sattvika* reasons which you are using as an excuse to not fight in this war are also nothing save an illusion in front of this mighty truth.

O Arjuna, in other words, all those who are interested in experiencing pleasure and those who miraculously want to achieve over and above their capabilities, are verily the people who create all these *Sattvika* norms. And only those who crave pleasures follow all such *Sattvika* rules. Such people ignore me, the Supreme Soul, dwelling within them in the form of their soul and instead devote themselves to worshipping other deities. Many a time, faith even brings them the desired outcomes, but they are all perishable in nature. Even if such people make tall claims of possessing knowledge, ultimately, they are all dimwits. For, they fail to fathom that to seek any kind of refuge in anyone besides their own soul is simply unacceptable to the Supreme Soul. On the other hand, those devotees of mine who are absorbed in worshipping their own souls will never be ruined, irrespective of what they do on the outside. In fact, regardless of what they do, they inevitably attain the Supreme Soul. O Arjuna, since the beginning, the problem has always been that everyone searches for the Supreme Soul in a person, a human embodiment. Presently, even you are trying to search for the Supreme Soul in 'Krishna'. That is why you are unable to fathom my words. But I am the 'soul' dwelling not only in Krishna but within every human being including you. In fact, not just you and me, but even the kings standing before you are not "a physical body subject to birth and death". So, have faith in your soul; for, a person who lacks faith in his soul can never fathom me. Moreover, understand that all kinds of dualities and desires only act as impediments to the human being's realisation of his soul. But the person who is freed from dualities and desires inevitably attains me while comprehending *Brahma, Karma* and *Adhyaatma* and perceiving *Adhibhoot* and *Adhidaiva* along with *Adhiyagya*.

In Chapter 7, Krishna has shed light on a profound idea, grasping which, all that remains in life is pure joy and bliss. It is generally believed that rivers, mountains, the Earth, sofa, table, so on and so forth are all insentient. But Krishna states that the mind, brain, senses, body and ego are also insentient. However, science recognises the mind and body as sentient, as these faculties can think and move around respectively. But Krishna states that in the context of spirituality, everything is insentient except the Supreme Consciousness. And when the mind, brain and body are insentient, their processes, activities and feelings are insentient too. But what generally happens is the opposite. For example, if the sofa breaks, we do not grieve for it, but when our heart breaks, the whole world comes crashing down for us. In the same vein, at this juncture, Arjuna's world has also fallen apart with regard to the war. And Krishna is explaining to him that this war, its warriors and the outcome of the war are all insentient. The soul alone is sentient, who can enjoy and be a spectator to the game being played by everyone's mind, brain and ego. Hence, you should not become so grave about things that are insentient in nature. Instead, like me, just become a spectator to this entire drama that has assumed the form of a war. And today, this is precisely what I am asking you to do as well; become a spectator to the game being played by your insentient brain-ego and that of others. Remember, the pangs of sorrow are experienced by the one who identifies himself with this play, not by the one who remains a spectator. Also, this is what being the 'witness' is all about; and becoming a 'witness'

is verily the zenith of human existence. And in order to become a 'witness', it is necessary to just learn to watch the moments of sorrow. The day you become a spectator to pain and sorrow, instead of enduring them, you will become a witness in entirety. Then, to watch films, you will no longer need the cinema screen, because you will get to watch the drama being played out in your life and in that of others, day and night. So, fill in the chart below and take the first step towards becoming a 'witness'. The chart lists events that typically make one feel sad or anguished. For each of these events, write in your own words that 'Henceforth, I will only become a 'witness' to such events. Never will I suffer them!'

Undesirable events that typically occur in a person's life

For each point, write determinedly (in your own words) that 'From now on, I have become a 'witness' to such events.'

An enemy making strides

....
....

People misunderstanding you and nursing wrong notions about you

....
....

Calamity or catastrophe causing major loss

....
....

Failure in a task

....
....
....

Loss in business

....
....

Deterioration in your health

....
....

A mistake that you have made

....
....

Being cheated by someone

....
....

Deterioration in a family member's health

....
....

Death of a near and dear one

....
....

Note:

Now, as long as one is alive, one's body, brain and ego will keep performing antics. So, just watch the game being played by them. What's the problem?

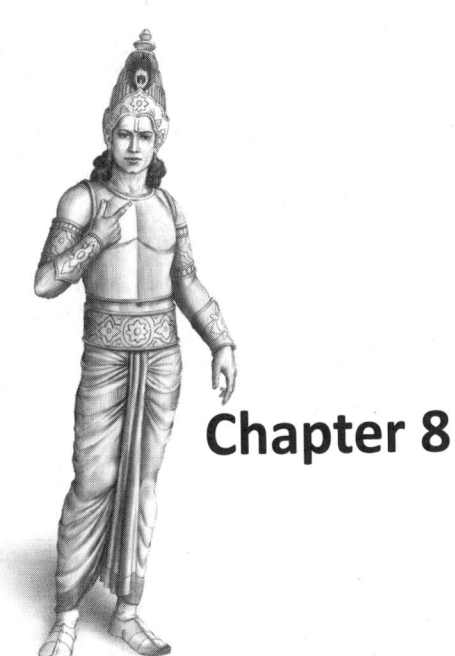

Chapter 8

Arjuna:

O Krishna! What is *Brahma*? What is *Adhyatma*? What is *Karma*? What does *Adhibhoot* and *Adhidaiva* imply? Who is *Adhiyagya*? And how does he dwell in this body? Furthermore, how are "you" perceived by men of superior minds at the time of their death?

Krishna:

This time around, Arjuna had to pose a question, as I had myself prompted him to do so by referring to all these names. However, it pleased me to know that now he was at least making an effort to perceive me beyond my corporeal body. That was why he had employed the word "you" in place of the Supreme Soul. And this was significant progress. For, only if he perceived me distinct from my physical body could a better standard of conversation be established.

So, I started off my explanation with the words, "O Arjuna! There exists one omnipotent force, *Brahma*. This entire world and all the living entities have come into existence through that one *Brahma* alone. Hence, it can be said that this entire world is an extension of that "one universal sound". Be it the moon and the stars or you and me, all of us have, indeed, come to exist through that one ultimate force,

Brahma. And this sound is reverberating everywhere, in every particle, like the universal sound of "Om". Apart from this, one's individual nature and his distinctiveness are referred as the "*Adhyatma*". That is, to remain rooted in one's own individual nature and form is verily the duty of every element, everything in existence. In other words, the only duty which the moon has to discharge is to continue being the moon. Likewise, your duty is simply to be Arjuna and mine is to be Krishna. That is why, the innate scripture emanating from every human being's inner conscience is his sole testament in "deciding what is righteous and unrighteous" for him. No external scripture can ever form the basis for deciding what a person should or should not do. For, every person's soul is in sync with that one universal force, *Brahma*. That is why, everyone's inner consciousness is "aware of the supreme harmony and interconnectedness of Nature" in this world. However, despite this realisation, driven by delusion, every person creates his "distinct identity in the form of 'I'" spurred by his brain and ego. Then, he spends his entire life believing that identity to be the truth, building and safeguarding it. But, O Arjuna! Everything that the human does to safeguard that "I" should never be considered as *karma*. The primary and sole *karma* is the renouncement of this "I", which one must perform as a human being. In other words, to consider oneself a part of this grand union, despite one's individual existence, and to live for the welfare of that union is the only true *karma*. Any *karma* undertaken for the sake of one's personal interest has always been considered a sin. For, no matter whose "I" it is, it inevitably perishes. In fact, the very nature of "I" is subject to creation and destruction. And this "I" is known as '*Adhibhoot*'. And all those people whose "I" has already ceased to exist, who are concerned only about this grand union, are the ones known as '*Adhidaiva*'. And likewise, O Arjuna, I, Krishna, who dwells in all human beings in the form of their soul, am known as '*Adhiyagya*', meaning, the only one worthy of worship.

Now comprehend this in the present context; whether it is the universe or you, me or all these kings, all of us are different embodiments of the "one, all-pervading, omnipotent *Brahma*". Hence, the question of 'yours and mine' simply does not arise here. However, as you have assumed a distinct identity for yourself, you are agonising over yourself and others. Based on this premise, you are furnishing numerous excuses to flee the battlefield. But the veritable truth is that when everything in this world is one, the question of victory-defeat, gain-loss and virtue-sin is utterly meaningless. When everything is one, even victory belongs to *Brahma* and so does defeat; and your soul is privy to this truth. It is aware that we are akin to the droplets of water in this vast ocean called '*Brahma*', having no separate existence of our own. Ergo, concern yourself with this ocean, not with a droplet, i.e., your ego. Stop tormenting yourself over the fate of this 'droplet', and instead immerse yourself in concern of this vast ocean. Reflect on the consequences, which your decision (to not fight the war) will bring upon the ocean. For, then the Kauravas will become the rulers of Hastinapur again. And if this becomes a reality, they would unnecessarily torment millions of these droplets (people) again. So, fight this war not for yourself but for the sake of all those droplets. However, your "I" in the form of this droplet will continue to exist as long as your brain-ego remain strong; and until then, your soul will remain shrouded. But, O Arjuna, you must realise that the soul alone is worthy of worship, for the soul alone is aware of this union—interconnectedness in Nature. So, you must surrender to your soul alone.

O Arjuna, whoever leaves the body (dwelling) in the state of realisation of this union inevitably attains my truest form. For, in his succeeding birth, a person is born with the same mindset that he possessed at the time of leaving his body in his former birth. So, concern yourself with your mindset, instead of worrying about fighting or fleeing the battle. Be wary of this strong "I". For, if you yield your body to this formidable "I", then this "I" will embroil you in myriad new problems even in your next birth. Also, do not be under the impression that if you live your life dwelling in the mindset of "I", you will be able to realise this union towards the end of your life. No, that shall not happen. Because the eventual state of mind won't appear out of the blue; it will verily be the one you have lived and breathed your entire life. So, a person should devote every moment of his life to weakening his "I" and "strengthening his realisation of the union". Hence, I am repeatedly asking you to connect with me, that is, feel and realise this union within and fight the war. If you fight the war with such a mindset, you will indisputably attain 'me, the Supreme Soul'. But if you flee the war "dwelling in the mindset of 'I'", you will unquestionably bring doom upon yourself. So, the question before you at present is certainly not about whether to fight or flee but simply to choose what you wish to fight this war for; to safeguard your "I" or "for the best interests of this union"? And devoting every action "to the welfare of this union" is in the best interest of every human being. For, this realisation of the union is verily the realisation of "the Supreme Soul and the Supreme sound Om". And this realisation alone is the ultimate elevation of a human being. Whoever deserts his body hearkening to this reverberating sound of *Omkar*, inevitably attains the supreme goal. Then again, you must clearly grasp that this entire play revolves around the question of the very existence of this "I". A person with a mighty sense of "I" may even chant "Om-Om" at the top of his voice night and day, but he will still not get liberated. Whereas a person who has realised this union has no need to articulate the sound of *Omkar*, for it resounds day in and day out in his every action and emotion. You too must fight with the realisation of this union and you will hear the serene sound of Om reverberating everywhere, instead of the clamorous clash of weapons. O Arjuna, the one who breathes his last with the resounding note of Om within, is never reborn. Then, he transcends time like me. Having attained a timeless form like me, he becomes the one "who always was, always is and always will be". The joy pervading this state is such that time in this state assumes an altogether different dimension. In this world, crushed under the weight of its trials and tribulations, a single day in a person's life is as cumbersome as the passing of a thousand days. Whereas for a person dwelling in that elevated state of mind, his entire life passes in a flash. Consider your own example; the present moment is weighing down upon you so heavily. And on the other hand, look at my life. It has simply flown like 'a moment'.

O Arjuna! In other words, all of the human being's diverse emotions are simply an expression of his "I", owing to which, he dwells in various emotions such as joy, sorrow, anxiety, victory and vanquishment. And they are verily the root cause of all his tribulations. However, upon realising the grand union, all of these emotions disappear. Because when everything is an extension of "the one letter *Brahma*", then irrespective of what transpires, where is the need to attach any importance to it? Such a supreme being, in every moment, dwells in an "inexpressible state of emotion". And to attain this "inexpressible state of emotion" is itself known as attaining the supreme goal. And a human being who once dwells in this ultimate abode of mine never ever returns to the mortal world. Ergo, forsake all your emotions "in the form of 'I'" and anchor yourself in that "inexpressible state of emotion". Then, you will see no difference between "fighting and not fighting". O Arjuna, there are only two paths for the human being to traverse this world. One is the path of *Shukla Paksha*, the path of bright fortnight; and each and every moment of a human being who treads this path is filled with luminescence. Wherever one looks, there is nothing but light, brilliant and pure. For, after having realised the grand union within, he continues to progress further in life. And treading that path, one day he attains the absolute realisation of this union in the form of *Brahma*. This path to a person's liberation is a path of no return; the one who treads this path never returns to the mortal world. The other is the path of *Krishna Paksha*, the path of dark fortnight which is perpetually engulfed in darkness. For, this path is fraught with the sense of "I". And if you too continue on this path of "I", then whether you fight or not, your life will forever be shrouded in darkness. However, if you adopt the path of the union, then even as you fight the battle and thereafter too, your mind will be infused with radiance. For, a person who has set out on this path of union never gets deluded again. Thereafter, his inclination towards performing sacrifices, austerity and charity, extolled in the *Vedas*[18] for accruing merit, also vanishes. Thenceforth, he flouts all these injunctions with conviction. Because then, he attains "the supreme eternal state" where every action he performs becomes an "act of austerity". In essence, this entire game is about the sense of "I" and the realisation of the "union". Were you to flee this war with this sense of "I" still dominating your mindset, it would be considered wrong, whereas even the act of your fighting in the war will become "an act of austerity" if it is performed with the realisation of the "union".

---

18   *Vedas* - The sacred scriptures of Hinduism.

In Chapter 8, Krishna is teaching us how to elevate ourselves from 'I' to '*hum* - us'. He explains, we are all a part of the one '*Brahma*', and every part should be concerned about the *Brahma*, i.e., its root. In other words, concern yourself with '*hum* - us' instead of 'I'. If you cast a glance around, you will see that everyone worries about 'I', and yet no one is able to carve a splendid life for themselves! That is the reason Krishna asserts that only he, who is concerned about '*hum* - us' at all times will be able to carve a joyous and successful life. Hence, one has to gradually grow and augment this sense of '*hum* - us'. In order to do so, first of all, learn to include the people you deal with in your daily life in this '*hum* - us'. And then, ascend to a level from where you can acknowledge the whole world as 'us'. Know this for certain that the more you widen your sphere of '*hum* - us', the more sublime and successful your life will turn out to be. Bear in mind, the constant refrain of 'I, me, myself' will lead you nowhere. So, start rising from 'I' to '*hum* - us' from this very moment. If you're sitting with your family, think about the well-being of the entire family, instead of just yourself. In business, think about everyone's benefit, right from your business partner to the supplier to the buyer. In essence, invest your energies only in the tasks that benefit 'all' instead of yourself. You will see how your life soars to unprecedented heights in no time. That is because, Nature teaches us to think of *'hum* - us', not 'I'. And that is why those who lead their lives with this sense of *'hum* - us' inevitably enjoy the full support of Nature. So, with the aid of the following chart, start progressing from 'I' to *'hum* - us'.

Steps to help you gradually widen your sphere of 'hum - us'

Next to each point, write firmly (in your own words) that 'Henceforth, I will only be concerned about *'hum* - us' in this.'

Also, write about the hindrances you may encounter while doing so. The more you write in your own words, the quicker it will yield the benefits, and will keep you determinedly aligned with *'hum* - us'.

I begin my *'hum* - us' with my family. In other words, in family matters, I will henceforth think about the welfare of the entire family, instead of just myself

....

....

....

....

....

....

....

....

....

....

....

Even with my friends, I will start leading my life with a sense of *'hum* - us'

At my workplace too, I will conduct myself and take decisions in the interest of *'hum* - us'

Irrespective of where, when and with whom I am, I will take all decisions purely in the interest of everyone, considering all to be '*hum* - us'

....
....
....
....
....
....
....
....
....
....
....
....

In this manner, I will gradually widen my sphere of '*hum* - us' to include my city, country, the world and eventually, the universe

....
....
....
....
....
....
....
....
....
....
....

Chapter 9

Krishna:

Now, I had already explained to Arjuna in no uncertain terms that he must fight the war with the realisation of this grand union. And I had proclaimed, "Upon fighting the war in the manner suggested here, you will attain "me, the Supreme Soul"." Arjuna should have then promptly consented to fight the battle. But alas, this was not to be! Well, what recourse did I have save for taking the conversation forward and explaining to him in a new light? So, as I continued my exposition, I said, "O Arjuna, I will once again expound to you at great length the secret knowledge, attaining which, you will be forever liberated from this world that is rife with suffering. Steeped in science, this knowledge is the sovereign of all wisdom. In fact, this knowledge is termed as science for the simple reason that it is law-bound. Therefore, man has no option other than to abide by this knowledge. Also, not only is it very simple to follow, but at the same time, it bears instantaneous results. No sooner a person imbibes this knowledge than he is immediately liberated from the sorrow-stricken world. For, truth never demands you to act today and reap the fruits tomorrow; anything that says so, cannot be the truth. It is only in the world of *adharma*—unrighteousness—that such declarations of reaping fruits in the future are made. It is the empty refuges and reassurances that need to resort to 'tomorrow', not truth. Ergo, grasp this supreme knowledge and free yourself from all your present distresses instantly.

It is **never** too **late** to **connect** with the **Supreme Soul.** There, it is better late than **never**

O Arjuna! From my formless form as the Supreme Soul, the entire universe has come to exist and it pervades all around on the basis of one resolve; determination. And such is my *leela* that despite being all-pervading, neither does anything belong to me nor do I belong to anything. This is the reason why the human being has been deluded about me since aeons. Sometimes, he presumes I am somewhere far off, while at other times, he conjectures that I dwell right within him. However, he fails to discern that despite pervading everywhere, I am actually nowhere. That is why talks of attaining me or losing me are utterly meaningless. For, I am present at all times, everywhere; and at the same time, I do not exist anywhere. Thus, to experience this mysterious *leela* of mine is the only true knowledge. To comprehend this in detail, you must understand that firstly, two kinds of worlds are coexistent in Nature, and both these coexistent worlds are as different as night and day. There is one world which, time after time, I create with my *yogamaya*[19] and then, I repeatedly absorb that world unto me as well. While on the other hand, there exists another world which is subject to neither creation nor destruction. Speaking of it in the context of human beings, understand that there are two kinds of expansions that occur in human life. One is the expansion undertaken on the strength of "I" (the ego), while the other is imbued with the feeling of oneness with the Supreme Soul. And I, the Supreme Soul, am totally absent from every kind of expansion in one's life which revolves

19 *Yogamaya* - Divine illusory power.

around his 'I, me and mine' (i.e., his ego). Even if the said expansions are in the name of his religion or god, I am not present in them either. Here, you must also comprehend, O Arjuna, that I - the Supreme Soul - incessantly keep creating "human beings on the basis of all actions revolving around their sense of 'I'" (their ego). On the other hand, there exists another set of human beings who have freed themselves from all kinds of attachments. Hence, devoid of attachment, their world expands (but) without a reason. As the "feeling of me and mine" is conspicuously absent in any such expansion of theirs, it is invariably imbued with my, that is, the Supreme Soul's presence. Ergo, you must comprehend that two kinds of human beings exist in this world: those "whose every expansion is devoid of my presence" and those "whose every action and expansion is imbued with my presence". So, what really matters is whether or not I am present. If I am absent, then I am absent in that person's religion, meditation and worship too. And if I am present, then even that person's cheating and fighting is imbued with my presence. In other words, my presence and absence cannot be concurrent. So, what merits consideration is not whether you are fighting or fleeing the war; what is important is whether your action is imbued with my presence or devoid of it. Ergo, if you make me a part of all your actions, then even in this war, all that you will feel is the presence of the Supreme Soul; otherwise, whether you fight or flee the battle, you won't find me anywhere. If you (in the state of "I") fight the war, you will be bound by those actions, whereas if the Supreme Soul fights the war, you will not be bound at all. Ergo, in essence, both these worlds are completely different from each other. One is the world of ego, while the other is that of the Supreme Soul. Even the scriptures uttered from the realm of ego find no trace of the Supreme Soul, whereas any action performed from my realm is nothing save the Supreme Soul. Another pertinent point for you to note is that for the human being, both these worlds are his own states of mind. And both the Supreme Soul and the ego cannot coexist in a human being's state of mind. Hence, surrender your "ego in the form of 'I'" to the Supreme Soul dwelling within you; all your present delusions will disappear in an instant.

O Arjuna, the fools who do not apprehend this 'divine supreme nature' of mine dwelling within human beings, assume that I am an ordinary mortal human being. They fail to fathom that I, having attained this supreme nature, roam the world in my human form only for the deliverance of the world. I, the Supreme Soul, have nothing whatsoever to do with my name, body or actions. So, do not seek me in any of these elements. Steer your gaze inwards towards my supreme nature; stir and awaken the divine within and recognise me. For, O Arjuna, those who perceive this supreme *Ishwar* - the Supreme Soul - in an embodied form continue to be gripped by demonic and delusional tendencies all their lives, owing to which, they harbour thousands of meaningless expectations from this embodied form of *Ishwar*. And most scriptures belong to this very category; for they do nothing but rouse such vain hopes. Thereafter, in order "to fulfil the expectations raised by the illusory trap of those scriptures laden with futile knowledge" these people undertake all kinds of meaningless tasks. And trapped in this circle, their entire life gets squandered. But no true knowledge ever raises false expectations nor does it engage human beings in futile deeds. True knowledge never gives empty hopes and reassurances; rather, it urges you to simply awaken the "divine state of the Supreme Soul" dwelling within you. And those imbued with divine tendency, engaged in the task of awakening their 'supreme nature' never perceive me, the great *Ishwar*, in the confines of the body. They seek me, the Supreme Soul, as divine nature within. Day and night, they engage themselves in delving upon that divine nature and chant glories of that supreme nature alone. They live in absolute obeisance to it and worship it with exclusive love and devotion. At the same time, some people imbued with divine tendency believe that I, the Supreme Soul, possess a universal form. They believe that the Supreme Soul is all-pervading. And both of them are right. Because when one has realised the Supreme Soul within, anything and everything he then beholds is the Supreme Soul. Only the one who is driven by ego sees differences everywhere. Ergo, O Arjuna, worship me, the Supreme Soul, imbued with divine tendency. Either recognise me as the 'supreme nature' dwelling within you or consider me an omnipresent being, pervading everywhere including this war. But renounce the demonic tendency of viewing, perceiving or finding the Supreme Soul in any embodied form, be it mine or anybody else's. As it is solely because of this tendency that you are harbouring numerous absurd expectations like heaven-hell and virtue-sin, and then in order to fulfil them, you are bent on undertaking the futile task of "fleeing the war". But those who perceive the divine nature dwelling within everyone as the Supreme Soul, and those who consider the Supreme Soul as all-pervasive, do not need to perform any task with any kind of expectation.

O Arjuna, you must know that even people with divine tendency can be of two kinds. One is the 'introvert' while the other is the 'extrovert'. For an introvert, it is better to search for the Supreme Soul in the 'divine nature' dwelling within him. While for an extrovert, it is easier to realise that "everything everywhere is the Supreme Soul". As an extrovert, it is simpler for you to discern that 'the Supreme Soul is all-pervading'. And when everything is the Supreme Soul, then it is so without exception. Then, it cannot be said that the Supreme Soul exists in one place or in one idol and not in some other. Then, you also cannot hold the belief that it exists in your *yajna* and not in that of others. Then, it is also erroneous to declare that it exists in one object and not in the other. And this is exactly what you are trying to do right now. For, you assume that the Supreme Soul lies in the act of renunciation and not in war. No, my dear Arjuna; that is not the case. "I, the Supreme Soul" am present in each and every ritual and paraphernalia of every single *yajna*. I exist in all the *Vedas*. I am the nurturer of this entire world, and I am its mother, father and grandsire. However, I am completely absent from all kinds of desires, and from every attempt made towards their fulfilment. Those who perform *yajna* driven by desires, even if it is for attaining heaven, become subject to the cycle of life and death instead of self-realisation. For, instead of realising God in his entirety, they seek him in fragments; and you are being no different. Instead of realising the all-pervasive Supreme Soul, you seek to attain it in parts. You wish for heaven, and at the same time, you also crave the kingdom. You wish to safeguard your life and property as well as earn virtue. But you must understand, O Arjuna, you will not attain 'me, the Supreme Soul' by seeking me in bits and parts; rather, you will be subject to the endless cycle of birth and death. You will return to this mortal world over and over again. Ergo, even an extrovert must aim for realising me in entirety, without any distinction. And those who wish to realise me in entirety never refuse any object, person or action. For, when everything is the Supreme Soul, what is there to reject? Hence, you must embrace even the war considering it to be the Supreme Soul's *leela*.

O Arjuna, if for some reason you feel that you are an introvert and it is easier for you to seek the Supreme Soul within yourself instead of the world without, then listen to my explanation regarding the said path as well. Without having aspirations, introverts are incessantly devoted to their soul. For them, it is a foregone conclusion that if the Supreme Soul dwells within me, then it dwells within everyone else as well; just as my inner self is imbued with the divine supreme nature, so is every single particle of the world. Ergo, they too never differentiate and make distinctions between any elements in any matter. Inundated with desires, they never worship gods in fragments. For, worshipping any god as a distinct identity bespeaks that nobody but that one particular god possesses divine supreme nature. Hence, worshipping any such god separately is against the law of Nature. For, that too is akin to differentiating between the Supreme Soul. That is why such people are not liberated from the cycle of life and death, and are thus reborn. So, if you wish to perceive the "divine supreme nature" dwelling within you, you will still have to let go of all differentiations, and liberate yourself from all desires. For, if you have the divine supreme nature within, so does everyone else. Such being the case, whom can you possibly differentiate yourself from? And what can you possibly wish for? Hence, whether you search for the Supreme Soul within or without, just seek it in entirety. Trust me; those who seek me in entirety are never subjected to rebirth.

O Arjuna, human birth is meant for action; it is synonymous with '*karma*'. And you will always be subject to loss and gain if you perform action. But when everything is the Supreme Soul, then this entire cycle of loss-gain is rendered meaningless, for this too belongs to the Supreme Soul. And the one who continuously leads his life in sync with this philosophy is my true devotee. Only the one who dedicates all his deeds to me, the Supreme Soul, is dear to me. And if such a devotee offers me even a leaf, flower or fruit with love, I accept it wholeheartedly. Why, I embrace all his actions, from waging war to employing subterfuge and deception! Thus, you too dedicate it all to me, be it the deeds you perform, the food you eat or the austerities and charity you undertake. Do not do anything for your own sake, do it dedicatedly for me. Whoever dedicates all his deeds to me is forever freed from the bondages of *karma*. Whereas, he who does it for himself, be it a sacrifice or a kind of worship, perpetually becomes ensnared in the bondage of *karma*. Presently, you want to flee for your own sake and I am urging you to fight for the Supreme Soul. O Arjuna, I prevail in everyone with equanimity. Nobody is dear to me nor do I despise anyone. Do not think that you are dear to me and that I bear animosity towards the Kauravas. No, I am not in the picture at all. This is not about me but you all. Anyone who dedicatedly performs actions for me will connect with me immediately and I will be available at his disposal. Hence, it is in your best interest to perform deeds for me. In so doing, you will connect with me; and once someone attains me, he no longer needs to agonise over anything!

O Arjuna, why don't you grasp that you will not garner my support just because I am your charioteer. I will join forces with you only if you devote all your actions to me. But unfortunately, you are unable to comprehend the "significance of my support". Not only you; even the wisest of the wise are unable to fathom its import. Else, wouldn't everybody in this world be joyous and at peace, having surrendered all their actions to me! Nonetheless, I implore you to do so. Dedicate this *karma* which lies before you in the form of war to me. I alone am the supreme abode worth dwelling in. I alone am everyone's master. I alone am the ultimate reason behind creation and destruction. I am the one who radiates heat in the form of the sun, and I am the one who pours down in the form of rain. O Arjuna, dedicating all your actions to me is a magic which nullifies all your past actions in an instant. Even the worst of the degenerates becomes a saint simply by surrendering all his deeds to me. Once a person resolutely dedicates his deeds to me, he is immediately purged of all his past sins. So, after listening to me, if you are thinking, 'Of what use is my acting differently today when I have always been acting spurred by the greed for fruits before?', then trust me, doing so will instantly change everything. If you devote this act in the form of this battle to me right now, all your past deeds will get obliterated and you will immediately become one with me. Ergo, neither you nor anybody else needs to think over their past actions. What has happened is already in the past. It is this moment which is significant; crucial are the deeds you are performing at the moment. No sooner does a person surrender his present deeds to me than he immediately becomes a saint. It is the selfish and ignorant people who speak of the past and the future. The wise who are selflessly absorbed in meditating on the Supreme Soul only speak of the present. And at this moment, as you are confronted by an inevitable battle, you must fight it for the sake of the Supreme Soul and you will be immediately relieved of all your past deeds. It is never too late to tread the path of truth and connect with the Supreme Soul. There, it is better late than never!

O Arjuna, "dedicating deeds to the Supreme Soul" is a potent magic. It does not make a difference whether the person dedicating the deeds is virtuous or a sinner. The kind of deeds dedicated to the Supreme Soul does not make a difference either. It is not that the offering of charity is accepted, while that of war is frowned upon. When a person dedicates his *karma* to the Supreme Soul, his caste or gender does not make any difference either. It is not that the deeds of men are accepted, while those of women are not; neither is the case that the deeds of the virtuous are accepted while the actions of the sinners are not. I, the Supreme Soul, am forever stationed in equanimity for everyone. It is the scriptures imbued with ignorance that propagate all these delusions. Ergo, do not presume that I will accept your deed only if you offer sacrifice having embraced renunciation; no, even if you fight the war as a *Kshatriya*, I will accept it with equal love. Thus, O Arjuna, if you wish, you can seek me, the Supreme Soul, in your inner consciousness or if you so desire, you may seek me in my universal, omnipresent form prevalent everywhere, but search for me you must! Become my devotee whose thoughts are turned to me, worship me and make obeisance to me, regardless of the circumstances. In any way you can, you must accept me completely and wholeheartedly. Surrendering completely to your soul in this manner, you will become one with my universal form. So, heed its call and get up to fight for me.

The key highlight of this chapter is, Krishna urging you to surrender yourself unto him. As you well know, Arjuna, at this juncture, is in a deluded, worried and miserable state. And importantly, you too are sailing in the same boat; equally deluded, worried and miserable. This alone is the matter of concern, nothing else. For, the only thing that is wrong is, we do not possess the blitheness of Meera, the innocence of Kabir and the wisdom of Krishna. And this is the reason everyone is in great distress. And it is to eliminate everyone's distress that Krishna says, till the time one does not take refuge in me with all of one's heart, one will continue to be in distress. And as for Krishna, he has already proclaimed that he is the soul dwelling in everyone. In other words, Krishna is the 'collective well-being' of all those who are alive. And in this chapter, Krishna explains to Arjuna that instead of performing deeds for 'yourself', perform deeds for 'me'. For, this is the only way to liberate oneself from all problems and difficulties. All other notions of virtue-sin and good-bad are meaningless. Krishna says, 'Arjuna, I will not accept even renunciation if you choose it for your own sake; but I will accept even the war if you fight it for the 'safety and well-being of everyone' i.e., for me. In such a case, I will embrace you instantly.' In essence, Krishna says, since he dwells in everyone, thinking about the well-being of everyone verily amounts to his worship. Apart from this, you should know all other notions and beliefs to be utter nonsense. Now, every deed cannot lead to the welfare and well-being of the entire world. So, thinking about the interests of those present before you at any point in time implies '*sharanagati*' – surrendering to Nature. For instance, out of five people, if four are benefitting while you are not, then to think about the benefit of those four is '*sharanagati*' or surrendering to the Supreme Soul. And look at Krishna's *leela*, his wondrous play! In the battlefield, when both Arjuna and Duryodhana are present before him, he is thinking in the best interest of both of them. He is delivering the discourse, the Bhagavad Gita, to Arjuna to extricate him out of his currently deluded state, and simultaneously, he is attempting to rein in Duryodhana's atrocities. And this verily is in Duryodhana's best interest so that he could be liberated from a life marred by the tendency to perpetrate sin, and make a fresh start by taking a new birth. Indeed, in matters concerning the greater good, no other person has been able to match Krishna's perfection. If you wish to grasp Krishna's personality in totality, then read my book, 'I am Krishna', the complete psychological biography of Krishna, which will help you comprehend what, why and how Krishna did whatever he did during his lifetime. Well, returning to the central point of this discussion, you must think about the best interest of those present before you, while withdrawing yourself, i.e., your self-interest completely from every situation and equation. In place of yourself, include all, for, that verily is your surrender to the Supreme Soul. Then, everything, including your life and death, will be endowed to the Supreme Soul. So, fill in the chart below and start taking steps towards surrendering to the Supreme Soul. First, undertake ten significant deeds wherein you can say, 'In place of me, the Supreme Soul has gained this, i.e., this task has been the means to achieve the greater good.' Also, whenever you perform such good deeds, write them below in detail. I am asking you to perform just ten tasks for the Supreme Soul, which means this chart must be filled in a month's time. For, slowly and gradually, you have to dedicate all your tasks to the Supreme Soul.

Detailed description of the tasks performed for the Supreme Soul

1

....
....
....
....
....
....
....
....

2

....
....
....
....
....
....
....
....

3

....
....
....
....
....
....
....
....

4

5

6

7

8

9

10 ....

....
....
....
....
....
....
....

Note:

Now, check how many days or months you take to perform ten tasks for the Supreme Soul. Also, what difference do you feel while performing tasks for your own gain vis-à-vis performing tasks for the Supreme Soul? With the passage of time, check which tasks are leading to greater gains – the ones performed for yourself or those performed for the Supreme Soul. You will be surprised! The tasks performed for the Supreme Soul will result in greater gains externally and greater happiness internally. Just keep adding to the list of tasks performed for the Supreme Soul, and one day, start doing everything for the Supreme Soul; you will scale the ultimate height of human life.

Chapter 10

Krishna:

Well, on my part, I had already explained everything to Arjuna, not just once but countless times, and that too, using several approaches. Perhaps never before had such a simple truth been explained in such a straightforward manner and in so many diverse ways. But Arjuna was just not ready to comprehend. However, I could understand his predicament. At present, he was plagued by not just one but a multitude of worries. And it is not easy to comprehend truth in such a state of mind. Moreover, his focus still lay on fleeing the war. Of course, he was now displaying an earnest interest in knowledge too; but there was a problem even in this case. How was he to believe that I was, indeed, wise and that I am the Supreme Soul? For, we had spent a considerable part of our lives together. Never before had I allowed him a glimpse of my divine nature or shared my divine experience with him. I had never discussed wisdom or knowledge with him. He had always interacted with the ordinary, embodied form of Krishna. Furthermore, the influence of scriptures weighed heavily on him; and many of them portray such fantastical imageries of God that it was no longer easy for him to recognise the soul as the actual form of God. However, I had made many proclamations with conviction to kindle his belief in myself and my knowledge. I had all but proclaimed that both the creation as well as the destruction of the world falls under my purview (of governance). I had already stated that I am both, the radiating heat of the sun and the clement coolness of the moon. Now what could I do if he still lacked faith in me? For that matter, I was well aware that many people will term me an egoist for making such boisterous statements. Those simpletons will not be able to comprehend that ego and Krishna are far removed from each other. My statements and proclamations are the obvious manifestations of the height of my consciousness. It is only out of compassion to ensure Arjuna sees sense that I am compelled to thread my words into such statements. Moreover, if this is ego, then I say that by all means, everyone should be able to nurse the ego of having such an experience. I am able to make such proclamations only because I have raised myself to this ultimate height of consciousness. Is there anyone else in the history of humankind who has been able to say all that I have said with as much conviction when, in fact, it is everyone's duty to gain this experience?

Nevertheless, we shall now return to our earlier point of discussion, Arjuna. And the duality involved in that situation is evident. While I am determined to convince Arjuna to fight the war, he, on the other hand, is equally determined to escape it at any cost. And undoubtedly, the sole reason behind this stand-off is his concern regarding the outcome of the war. Although I am imparting to him the ultimate wisdom to rid him of his worry, it doesn't seem to make any difference to him at all. And the reason behind this is quite apparent; he is unable to pose absolute trust and faith in me. Even so, at present, I have no option but to strengthen his faith in me. And it is imperative for him to have complete faith in me "not only with regard to the outcome of this war but also with regard to my being truly wise". So, taking the conversation forward, I remarked, "O Arjuna, listen to my stirring statements once again. And since you are very dear to me, believe me when I say that I am making all these statements keeping your best interests at heart. However, if you are still unable to understand me, then it is certainly not your fault. For, forget about you, neither the gods nor the great seers are aware of the divine play behind my manifestation in the current human form. So, my real form, that is, the real form of "the *Ishwar*" has nothing to do with what those people say about me in the scriptures. O Arjuna, only someone who knows that I am birth-less, that is, without beginning, knows the truth about me, and only he is able to liberate himself from all kinds of sin. Endeavouring to find *Ishwar* in any form or embodiment is a proof of ignorance. So, forsake not only the imageries of *Ishwar* narrated in the scriptures but also stop seeking *Ishwar* in me, the embodied form of Krishna. I am that which has no bounds, no limits and no birth. The entire universe, based on one desire and one resolve, is embedded in me. The populace of the world at large is my subject. And among them, only he who experiences and realises this supreme divine form of mine as his state of mind is my true devotee.

O Arjuna, know that it is I, Krishna, embedded in every soul, who is the prime cause of the creation of this world. Here, a person endeavours to make efforts only as long as I exist in the body. As soon as I leave the body, all his efforts come to an end. Those who know the significance of the soul and lead their existence with complete and constant surrender to it soon become one with me. Those who discuss the glories of the soul amongst themselves also take no time in becoming one with me. Presently, I am discussing nothing but "the glories of the soul" with you. Do not bring the fanciful and illusory words of the scriptures into this grand discourse. O Arjuna, I make this supreme knowledge available at the earliest to those people who always remain content in their soul. For, eventually, it is "I" alone who dwells in everyone as soul. Ergo, instead of unnecessarily being plagued by all kinds of worries and going astray, anchor yourself in your soul; I will surely kindle the illuminating lamp of knowledge in you.

Arjuna:

You are, indeed, the Eternal, Supreme Abode and the holiest of all, the greatest purifier. Even the wisest of beings consider you – the soul – the *Ishwar*, as the "eternal divine being". They too accept you as the God of gods and as the unborn. The sage Narada and the great seer Vyasa also perceive you as omnipresent. And even you are describing the very same glory of my soul. O Krishna, to tell you the truth, only now am I able to comprehend what you had been endeavouring to explain to me all along. Now, I can well discern that both the body and the soul are separate and distinct, and that you are not a mortal body but a pure soul. I am finally able to grasp what you were trying to enlighten me about. I can well perceive everything you say as the truth. O Krishna, it is true that neither the gods nor the demons are aware of the divine manifestations of the soul. I am finally able to grasp this truth that you alone know yourself through yourself. Thus, only you are capable of elucidating your glories comprehensively. So, you alone can enlighten me, what kind and process of contemplation should I engage in to realise you and become one with you? Which particular forms of yours are worth reflecting upon? Kindly enlighten me about your divine glories in detail. I wish to listen to you as much as possible; what can I do? No matter how much I listen to you, my heart still yearns for more!

Krishna:

Phew! For the first time, Arjuna had, indeed, absorbed what I had been striving to explain to him. Having said that, it was but natural for his curiosity to be aroused to know and understand the soul better. Besides, I had no option but to honour every wish of his and answer every one of his queries. I was his charioteer in the battlefield, and now his refusal to fight the war had led me to become the charioteer of his life as well. So, honouring his wishes, I said, "O Arjuna, I will now speak comprehensively of my prominent divine glories, as there is no end to my manifestations. First of all, know that I am the universal soul dwelling in each human being. I am verily the past, future and present of every human being. Nevertheless, consider me to be the incarnation of *Vishnu,*[20] that is, everyone's present. Since the human being has already come to exist, I am not his *Brahma*[21] now. Even his death belongs to the future, so I am not *Mahesh.*[22] Rather, I am the present-day life of every human being, that is, *Vishnu*. Similarly, among the human being's senses, I am neither his brain nor ego; I am his 'mind'. For, a human being's mind is closest to his soul. His brain and ego are of this birth, while his mind has been his companion for all his births. This is not all, I am the life-energy of a human being, or you may say, his life-force; in other words, I am his desire to live. And it is essential for every person to expand the horizon of his life in order to fulfil his desire to live. One may undertake that expansion by attaining position and power or by financial advancement. But among all these, remember, I am "the lord of riches *Kubera*[23] " that is, the businessman. Just look

---

20 *Vishnu* - The preserver and guardian of human beings.   21 *Brahma* - The creator of the universe.
22 *Mahesh* - The destroyer of the universe.   23 *Kubera* - The lord of wealth.

at me, I never tried to attain any position, usurp anybody's kingdom or expand my kingdom, in order to progress. I made the journey from being a cowherd to becoming the King of Dwarka on the strength of my business acumen alone. This is not all, I never snatched another kingdom's right in order to effect Dwarka's progress and engender prosperity; rather, I always relied on expanding Dwarka's business.

O Arjuna, I am as deeply ingrained in the human mind as widely as I am prevalent without. Know that all the finest sights in the external world are nothing but my manifestation, and likewise, the zenith of human emotions is also but an extension of my sense perception. Know that I alone am the god of fire among the *Vasus*[24] and I am the *Sumeru* among all the mountains. Also, the 'tranquil ocean-like behaviour' among the human beings' state of mind is also me. In other words, know that I am that immense heart which absorbs unto itself the waters of all rivers like an ocean, whether they are clean or unclean, without any discrimination. Know that none but I am the 'equanimous ocean-like mindset' which does not spill over either by the waves of success or the blows of failure. Likewise, among *mantras*, I am the tendency to endeavour persistently till the completion of a task, that is, the only *Japamantra* worth chanting. Furthermore, I alone am the undisputed king amongst men, that is, I am "the content heart which doesn't desire anything else". For, in my opinion, the person whose happiness still depends upon attaining more is a beggar. O Arjuna, you are here to attain the land of Hastinapur, but you fail to comprehend that a king is a king by heart, not land. Besides this, the carnal pleasure which is engaged in without any coercion and with "mutual consent", meaning, the physical intimacy approved by the scriptures, in which procreation is also paid attention to, is also me. At the same time, the *Yamaraj*[25] amongst the rulers, that is, the one who dispenses timely justice without any discrimination is also my form. You too are well aware that the God of death doesn't differentiate between a sinner and a saint, old and young, healthy and sickly; when their time comes, he beckons them without any discrimination. Likewise, among the intellectuals who apply their intellect and make calculations, I am "the intelligent one who has the knowledge of time and is mindful of it". O Arjuna, as you too are intelligent, you must comprehend it particularly

24 *Vasus* - The attendant deities of Indra and later Vishnu.
25 *Yamaraj* - The God of death.

well. You should not apply your intelligence in thinking "whether to fight or flee", rather, you should apply your intelligence to determine the timing of your action, that is, whether this is the time to fight or flee the battle. O Arjuna, always bear in mind, time is the only deciding factor in determining "what to do and what not to do". No scripture or the enormity of self-interest can make a decision in this respect. And a person cannot gain this knowledge of time till he is not close to his soul. This, indeed, is the significance of being one with your soul. Hence, you too must pay heed to time instead of seeking reasons for fighting or fleeing or calculating gain and loss. Gauge the need of time. For, when time prompts you to do something, you don't have the option to choose.

O Arjuna, apart from this, there are many more wondrous, great states of minds in which I dwell. For instance, among the ones who work for the betterment of others, know me as the breeze-like mindset which is available at all times, everywhere, to give life to one and all. Likewise, amongst the wielder of weapons, know me as Rama, who employs strength only when time demands it. Amongst knowledge, recognise the self-realisation or the knowledge of self as me; consider all other forms of knowledge as ignorance. Similarly, I exist in debates and discussions, provided they are being conducted in order to arrive at a decision, but I am never present in a discussion undertaken with a predetermined mindset. And, O Arjuna, you should especially pay close attention to this, because you are speaking to me with your mind already made up to not fight. And this preconception of yours is acting as an impediment for you in comprehending my discourse. However, Arjuna, you need not worry, because I am the dilemma among doubts. Dilemma implies being confused about a choice that must be made between two options. And at the moment, you are mired in the dilemma of whether to fight the battle or not. So, do not worry, very soon the option of not fighting will disappear and you will determinedly stand up to fight. Instead of being engaged in the debate after having made your decision to not fight, reason with an open mind. Furthermore, O Arjuna, amongst those who deceive, I am gambling. Gambling implies a balanced wager, and this war is akin to an act of deception. So, it is better that you consider this war as a round of gambling and play it. Do not think too much. Ideally, one should not indulge in deception, gambling, battle and so on, but if it befalls you, you cannot escape it either. Under such circumstances, it is better to play it like a round of gambling instead of worrying about victory and vanquishment. The best part of having a gambler's mindset is that the person verily leaves the decision about the outcome of the wager on the third power, meaning, the Supreme Soul. Neither does he worry about it nor does he ruminate over it. And by entrusting the 'outcome' to the third power, every gamble of his is absolved from all kinds of sin. Hence, believe me, if you fight the war with a gambler's mindset, you will not incur sin.

O Arjuna, among those who employ strength and might, recognise me as the power to punish and penalise. However, I am not the strength employed to attain a kingdom or to mete out revenge on one's enemies. Hence, forget about your desire to attain the kingdom and your enmity towards the Kauravas; instead, fight the war with the intention of punishing them. If you fight with such a mindset, then too, you will never incur sin. O Arjuna, in short, I am present in everything that is the finest and the best; just as I am the *Gayatri* amongst the verses and the Ganges among the rivers. This does not mean that you should chant the *Gayatri Mantra* or worship the Ganges. You must pay heed to my words; I am saying that I am the *Gayatri* among verses. That is, if you have to choose amongst verses, then I am the *Gayatri*. Likewise, compelled by circumstances, if you have to choose between rivers, then I am the Ganges amongst the rivers. Earlier, when I had stated that I am gambling among the deceivers and tricksters, (even then) I did not say that it is pure and righteous to gamble; rather, I meant that if circumstances compel you to deceive, then I am gambling among the deceptions committed. Likewise, I had said that if you have to indulge in carnal pleasure, then I am the "objective of procreation" in it. I am the carnal pleasure indulged in without the merest hint of pressure and with complete mutual consent. Even then, I had not said that I am carnal pleasure. O Arjuna, I have already stated that I dwell in everything and everything dwells in me, but neither do I exist in anything nor does anything exist in me. For, I dwell only in the truth of the moment. I am present only in the selection of the best at every moment. Just as I exist in this battle at the moment. For, this battle has now been decided by the flowing stream of time. And when 'time' has already decided, then one has no option but to fight. And when one has to fight at any rate, then I am present in the best mindset of fighting the battle, meaning, in gambling. So, just engage in this war with the mindset of gambling and enjoy it as if it were a game and leave the decision of its outcome to the third power.

O Arjuna, what else do I say and to what extent? For, there is simply no end to my glories. I am the reason behind the entire human race coming into existence. O Arjuna, there exists no such insentient or sentient element which is not imbued with my presence. Here, I have only succinctly spoken to you about my glories. From the discussion so far, you must have well grasped that I am existent in all human beings in the form of life. Ergo, primarily, it is the duty of human beings to ensure their lives radiate with glory, brilliance and power, and in the process, they must attain the realisation of soul. Hence, taking everything into consideration, it is your duty to fight this war; and you also have the complete right over the glory ensued from this battle. However, here, it is imperative to leave the decision of whether you shall attain this glory or not to the justice of the Supreme Soul. To desire it or deny it (once received), both signify lack of belief in the Supreme Soul's justice. Therefore, in brief, you need to comprehend that I have brought the world into existence, holding this universe by a fraction of my *Yogashakti* (yogic power). Hence, I exist in every particle of this world and in every *karma* of human beings. All that the human being needs to do is perform whatever task befalls him with the best state of mind. He must continue choosing the best option among those that are available for undertaking any task. Neither should he go about seeking any *karma* nor should he flee from any. If we decipher this in your context, then this war is the outcome of your own *karma*. So, now is not the time to think about choosing alternatives in this war. The choice has already been made; at least today, perform this *karma* in the form of war without making any selection. Then, turn this practice into a habit. If you go on performing deeds in this manner without making choices, one day, you will be "freed from all bondages of *karma*". O Arjuna, how long do I go on describing my glories? In short, all you need to grasp is that be it the universe or this world, I am always present in those deeds which are taking place of their own accord anywhere without any selection."

In Chapter 10, Krishna enunciates, 'The best in anything or anyone is me.' And that is, indeed, the truth; the best in anything or anyone is verily Krishna, and thus, verily the Supreme Soul. On the other hand, you would recall, Krishna has also stated that everything is 'me (Krishna)'. In other words, there is nothing in this world that is totally bad or negative. Every person and object, no matter how and what they are, inevitably have something exceptionally good in them. And Krishna says, he is 'that exceptionally good quality' even in the vilest of the lot. To explain the essence of the above-mentioned point with the analogy of a weapon, the best use of a weapon is to kill 'terrorists and vile people'. So, when a weapon is used for such a purpose, it is nothing but Krishna. This implies, weapons can certainly not be termed as completely bad. Now, to come straight to the point of your interest, no person is ever completely bad, for, every person possesses some noble or great quality. Hence, you must never dismiss anyone completely. Do not consider anyone to be insignificant or inferior. You simply need to see the 'best' hidden in everyone, and connect with that 'best' quality in them. Sever your connection with that which is not positive in anyone or anything. In other words, connect with the passion of passionate people, connect with businessmen for their business, with intellectuals for a dialogue and debate, and connect with wise men for their wisdom. Even in the case of your enemy, connect with his 'finest' quality; and as for your loved ones, connect only with their 'best' quality. Indeed, why should you converse with the ignorant, engage in business with a scoundrel, party with a killjoy, and dine with those who observe fasts. Connect only with the 'best' in everyone, that is, with the 'Krishna' present in everyone. Then, see how wonderful your life becomes. So, in the chart below, write the names of 20 people whom you are close to as well as their 'finest' quality. And henceforth, connect only with their respective 'finest' qualities and confine your relationship only to those qualities. In doing so, you will get the opportunity to learn from them, enjoy their company and also experience peace.

Write down the names of the people and their 'finest' quality

1

2

3

4

5

6

7

8

9

10

11

....
....
....

12

....
....
....

13

....
....
....

14

....
....
....

15

....
....
....

16

....
....
....

17

....
....
....

18

....
....
....

19

....
....
....

20

....
....
....

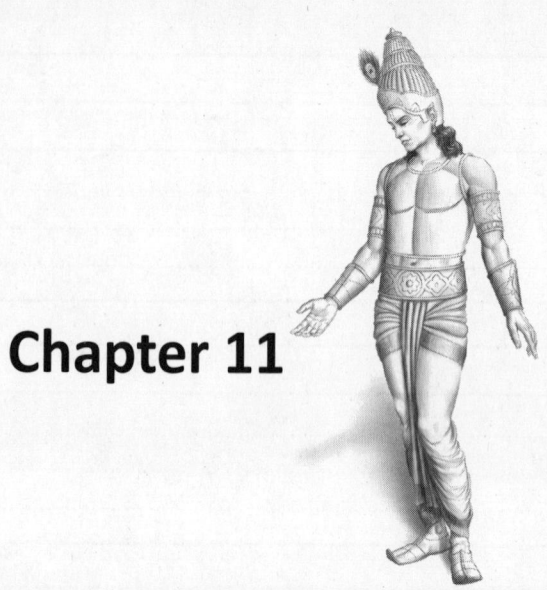

Chapter 11

Arjuna:

O Krishna! My ignorance has been dispelled by the ultimate discourse on the secret of spiritual knowledge which you have shared with me. I have listened at length to the laws of the creation and destruction of this world from you. I have also hearkened to your imperishable glories. I also know that every single particle in existence is governed by you. You are the sole reason behind the existence of this world. And all that you have enunciated about yourself is indeed the truth, pure and simple; I have no doubt about it. Even so, it is not easy for me to fathom this all-pervasive form of yours. So, if you do not mind, I would like to witness this supreme form of yours imbued with prosperity, power, strength, valour and radiance with my own eyes. If it is, indeed, possible for you to display your cosmic form, then kindly grant my wish.

Krishna:

Indeed, what Arjuna is saying is right. One does not realise the soul with the mere comprehension that the body and the soul are separate and distinct. One does not experience the soul, merely upon hearing that this entire world is an extension of the one soul. Hence, in order to ascertain the truth, Arjuna wants to see with his own eyes the soul's 'manifestation as *Ishwar*' in its omnipresent form. Now, by its very nature, this is impossible. For, without realising the soul within, it is not possible to sense or experience the omnipresent Supreme Soul without. Power and riches can be shared but is there a way to bestow the legacy of experience? Had this been possible, I would have transformed the entire world to become like Krishna. Nonetheless, whether it is possible or not, I had no alternative other than to reveal my cosmic form to Arjuna. At any rate, he is waiting for an opportunity to flee the battle. So, my refusal would only serve as an excuse for him to run away from the battlefield. Indeed, he would immediately retort, 'Since I was not able to behold your cosmic form, I am unable to convince myself to fight even at your behest.' And were this to happen, the possibility of the Kauravas emerging victorious would grow manifold. Now, I simply cannot take any chance in a battle that has become inevitable. Well, I am called the glorious Krishna for a reason; there is nothing in this world that is impossible for me! Though I cannot show him my cosmic form, I can surely delude him by hypnotising him. All my life, I had made others do my bidding only by means of hypnosis. I had been enchanting people on a personal and collective level ever since I was a child. You know very well how all of Vrindavan was spellbound by me during my childhood. Is there anyone who is unaware of the condition of the *gopis* beguiled by my spell? And even today, is there any nook or corner of Aryavarta that is not in thrall of my enchantment? Therefore, it was certainly possible to bring Arjuna under my hypnotic spell in totality and put him under the delusion of having beheld my cosmic form. Thus, for the first time in the history of humankind, I conducted a complete hypnosis of a human being. Here, you must comprehend how the technique of enchantment works. A human being possesses two key strengths; one, his mind and the other, his brain-ego. Enchantment or hypnosis means putting a person's brain and ego to sleep, i.e., to make them non-functional. Once a person's brain and ego are dormant, he becomes his natural self. This opens the door to two possibilities; first, this completely brings to the fore his actual self which is hidden inside, because the 'brain-ego' which comprehends and expresses everything in a distorted manner, stops functioning under the spell of hypnosis. And in such a situation, not only can you show a person whatever you want to show him, but you can also explain to him anything you want him to grasp. For, the brain, which acts as an impediment to this process, is non-functional during the spell of enchantment. All in all, Arjuna had certainly put me in a predicament, but my shrewdness had turned even this quandary into an opportunity. For, now, not only would I make his innermost self come to the fore but I would also make him realise my cosmic form. This would lead to two direct benefits for me; one, I would get a definite measure of both his hidden desire and the depth of his present fear, and two, upon experiencing my cosmic form, he would be completely under my control.

So, why tarry an auspicious deed? I immediately glanced into his eyes and put his brain-ego to sleep. And as soon as they became dormant, I said, "O Arjuna! Behold my multifarious divine forms of various shapes. Behold the never-before-seen astounding forms of the *Adityas,*[26] *Vasus,*[27] *Rudras*[28] and *Ashwinikumar*[29] and his sons described in the scriptures." Now, as Arjuna had read about them in the scriptures, it was quite easy to show them all to him in his enchanted state. Thereafter, I said, "See whatever else you want to see in my cosmic form." Here, one must note that even in the state of enchantment, I could show him only those imageries that already existed in his mind. To make someone visualise anything new is not possible in hypnosis. However, smartly and sagaciously, I had already given a direction to his thoughts by speaking of "*Aditya* to *Ashwinikumar*". Then, I asked him to see "everything he has ever heard about the soul and the Supreme Soul." Now, in the state of enchantment, his own imagination was going to get realised in his mind; I only had to show him the way and I had already done so. Thereupon, I immediately said, "See whatever else you desire to see besides this." With this instruction, he would now see the desires hidden in his mind getting materialised. This, in turn, would reveal his true inner self depending upon what he saw. Thereafter, to ensure the complete obliviation of his brain and ego, I said, "O Arjuna, but surely you cannot see all this with your physical eyes; so, close them and I will grant you divine vision so that you can witness my majestic godly form with ease." Speaking thus, I paused, curious to hear what

---

26 *Adityas* - Solar deities who reside in the heavenly regions and personify various natural phenomena.
27 *Vasus* - They are elemental gods who are described as the attendant deities of Indra and later Vishnu.
28 *Rudras* - Gods of storms and tempests mentioned in the *Vedas*. Gods of destruction.
29 *Ashwinikumar* - They are two *Vedic* gods, the divine twin horsemen. Twin-born physicians of gods.

Arjuna would see. So much for Arjuna but back in Hastinapur, Sanjaya had also become enchanted along with Arjuna. This was inevitable, for my power of enchantment was indeed extraordinary. Hence, Sanjaya had also begun to experience whatever Arjuna was witnessing within. And surprisingly, it was not Arjuna but Sanjaya who began to speak. Arjuna, on the other hand, was completely absorbed in devouring the sights appearing before him. In other words, my historic power to enchant had been proven beyond doubt.

Sanjaya:

O King Dhritarashtra! Speaking thus, the master of *Yoga*, Shri Krishna actually revealed his divine form to Arjuna. And with this, Arjuna saw Krishna manifesting innumerable faces, possessing numerous mouths and eyes, and countless arms wielding divine weapons. O King, I have no words to describe the radiance of this glorious form of Krishna! It seems as if thousands of suns have at once illuminated the sky with their brilliant light. Indeed, at this moment, Arjuna beheld the entire universe with its manifold divisions, situated all at once, in the body of Shri Krishna. This sight, in turn, left Arjuna completely confounded. And in that same bewildered state, with folded hands, he began to engage in a dialogue with Shri Krishna.

Arjuna:

O Shri Krishna! This moment finds me completely awestruck! I am beholding gods as well as various beings dwelling in your body all at once. Not only do I discern *Brahma* and *Mahadeva* in you but I also see all the seers, sages and snakes assembled in you. O Lord of the entire world! I can see neither your beginning nor middle or even your end. To tell you the truth, I am exhilarated seeing this existence of yours replete with diadem, mace and discus. I reckon that it is only with great difficulty that one can witness your great form. And now, I have no doubt at all that it is you who are the first letter, *Brahma*. You alone are the lord of this world. You are the protector of the ageless *dharma*; you are "the indestructible eternal being", no other. O Keshava! The entire expanse of sky between heaven and earth is illuminated by you alone. In fact, all three worlds are greatly alarmed beholding this divine form of yours. Be it gods or great seers, everyone is eulogising you all around. Indeed, the eleven *Rudras*, the twelve *Adityas*, the eight *Vasus, Ashwinikumar, Yaksha*[30], demons and even the manes and multitudes of *Gandharvas*[31] are gazing upon you in wonderment. The truth is that everyone, including me, is totally perplexed on seeing this extremely frightful form of yours possessing numerous hands, thighs and legs; I am losing both my composure and peace on seeing this. At this moment, I am completely terror-stricken; I am utterly lost and bewildered. My intelligence is failing me.

Thus, O God of gods! Let go of your displeasure and become pleased with me. At the moment, I am witnessing the sons of Dhritarashtra entering this ghastly form of yours. Bhishma, Drona and Karna are accompanying them. Why, I can also see countless warriors from our side and theirs entering your terrifying mouth. I find all of them being gnashed between your gigantic teeth. Just as rivers rush in from all directions to enter the sea, all these warriors are sprinting from everywhere to rush into your mouth. O Lord of all worlds! Tell me who you are, assuming a form so ferocious? O supreme of all gods! I pay my obeisance to you. Kindly be graciously pleased with me. I wish to know and comprehend you. For, try as I might, I am unable to grasp your *pravritti* – activity at the moment.

Krishna:

In short, Arjuna was keen to behold my godly form, and finally, his wish was fulfilled. That is, my hypnosis was completely successful. Here, you must also comprehend, the Krishna that Arjuna was beholding possessing numerous faces and countless thighs, and armed with multifarious weapons was actually "his own vision of God". He was beholding the extension of all that he had read about God in the scriptures. If someone has "some other conception of God" then on being hypnotised he will visualise God as per his own preconceived notion of God. And if one has no vision of God whatsoever, then even on enchantment, he will not see God in any form. This implies, at all times, the human being sees nothing but the extension of his own imagery and conception everywhere. And this is what slumber is all about, that is, his ignorance. And only those who are living in such somnolence can be enchanted; an awakened person can never be hypnotised.

Well, now that Arjuna had seen the *Ishwar* in me, he had no reason to not believe me. However, the problem was still unresolved.

---

30 *Yaksha* - Nature spirits who are caretakers of the natural treasures hidden in the Earth and tree roots.
31 *Gandharvas* - They act as messengers between the gods and humans.

Arjuna's terrified state of mind had given rise to a new difficulty. Arjuna, who until this point was fearful of going into 'battle', was now terror-stricken upon seeing my "divine form". Actually, this is the peculiarity of a fearful mind. It grabs hold of a new fear first and then relinquishes the old fear. In other words, once someone is gripped by fear, it is very difficult to eradicate his fear completely. If nothing else, he eventually begins to fear "the *Ishwar* – the god, who should actually be the symbol of faith". And this is the difficulty with most human beings, as they drag *Ishwar* too in their extended sphere of fear.

Returning to Arjuna, I have to say that his hypnosis at my hands was completely successful. On one hand, while he saw his fantasy of *Ishwar* actualised in me, on the other, I was also successful in bringing to the fore what his mind secretly wished for from this war. Arjuna, who was initially citing the scriptures and asserting fraternal love, himself admitted under the hypnotic spell that they were all matters of no concern. He is still standing in the battlefield nursing the desire to annihilate the Kauravas. That is why, when I asked him to see what he wished to see, he not only saw the Kauravas being swallowed into my deadly jaw but he also saw Drona, Bhishma and Karna meeting the same fate. With this, he proved that he was scared of the triumvirate of Drona, Bhishma and Karna. For, all three of them were verily the finest of archers. If they were all to be devoured by me, he would have no objection to fighting the battle. And since the first verse, I have been speaking of this very inclination of his mind. I had, indeed, been repeatedly asking Arjuna to not try to confuse and delude me. I had reiterated to him that 'the desire to attain the kingdom still exists within you. In your mind, you still want the Kauravas to be snuffed out, like the flame of a candle.' I had told him in no uncertain terms that he wanted to flee the battle because of "the cowardice he had been gripped by". But this is wrong. And so, I said to Arjuna, "You have no option but to "fight this battle which has now become inevitable"."

Fortunately, both Arjuna's fear and desire had been exposed now. Having seen my divine form, his problem - the absence of faith in me as the Supreme Soul - had been quelled. But despite this, he still did not appear willing to fight. For, as I had just mentioned, he had now become fearful beholding my divine form. He couldn't help but wonder what kind of form I had assumed that I was putting an end to scores of lives as far as the eye could see! Why were all the warriors present in the battlefield being ground between my teeth? And 'what if this is my eventual fate as well?' he thought; and verily, this is why when he saw so many people, including the Kauravas, getting gnashed between my teeth, he did not see himself or his brothers and sons succumbing to the same fate. This fully brings to light his desire that whatever happens in the war, he and his near and dear ones should not come to any harm. This clearly meant that despite beholding my cosmic form, until he is assured of the destruction of his enemies and the safety of his near and dear ones, he would not agree to fight. That is why he eventually asked me, 'I am curious to know who you are, to have appeared in such a terrifying form?'

Alright, my dear Arjuna! As everything was now crystal clear, I took the conversation forward and said to him in no uncertain terms, "Listen, Arjuna, at this moment, I am the *Mahakaal*[32] who has arrived to destroy the worlds. I have descended to destroy everyone assembled on the battlefield. So, O Arjuna! Whether you fight or not, your adversary's army is nevertheless going to be destroyed." Now, I could provide no greater assurance than this to assuage the fear he was gripped with presently. Hence, continuing in the same vein, I said, "So, Arjuna, get ready and fight with nary a care. Conquer the enemies and attain glory. Attain the kingdom of Hastinapur. All these warriors in the opposite camp have already been killed by me. All you have to do now is become instrumental in conducting a farce of this battle. And in return, you will attain name, fame and kingdom." Now, in a way, by making this statement, I was reassuring Arjuna in order to quell his fears. For, when *Ishwar* himself is declaring that those people have already been killed by him, then what was the harm in taking a chance? However, yet another aspect of this is, I am not saying this just to boost his confidence; I am, indeed, cognisant of Nature's mysteries. Hence, I am well aware of how Nature and the ego are aligned. Nature is the enemy of ego alone. Every ego, having reached its peak, inevitably gets crushed by Nature. And the Kauravas' ego had reached its zenith. They had dug their graves on the very day they had rejected my proposal of giving five villages to the Pandavas and arriving at an amicable

32 *Mahakaal* - Refers to Shiva who is supreme and above the boundaries of time. The eternal Time-spirit.

solution. That very day, they had become Nature's target. Thus, it is also true that now, whether Arjuna fights or not, the Kauravas would not be spared under any circumstances. For, Nature is not dependent on Arjuna alone for the deliverance of its justice. If Arjuna refuses to fight, then Nature would destroy the Kauravas through King Drupad. That is why, I am urging Arjuna to become 'the instrument of Nature'. 'Fight the battle for Nature,' I advised him, 'and the rest will automatically be done through you.' For that matter, I tell everyone, not just Arjuna, to never let go of an opportunity to become "the instrument of Nature". As constantly being Nature's instrument is the only thing that makes a person great and noble. Thereafter, adding strength to the pillar of assurance, I said, "O Arjuna! Not only Bhishma, Karna and Drona, but even Jayadratha has already been killed by me. All you have to do now is kill these already dead men. So, why fear killing those who are already dead? Thus, free yourself from all fears. Have faith that you will definitely emerge victorious in this war. So, jump into the battle with nary a worry."

Sanjaya:
O Dhritarashtra! As soon as Shri Krishna concluded his instructions, advising Arjuna to get ready to fight, a terrified Arjuna folded his hands and spoke to Shri Krishna thus...

Arjuna:
O Omniscient One! Indeed, your name, virtues and glories reverberate all over Aryavarta. This entire world is experiencing joy and bliss in eulogising you. Terrified demons are running helter-skelter to escape your divine wrath. Wherever one looks, the great beings are paying obeisance to you. And for that matter, why shouldn't they? For, not only are you seated on the highest pedestal but you are the progenitor of even *Brahma*. Not only are you the sire of *Yamaraj*, fire, water and the moon but you are also the father of *Brahma*, who is the lord of all beings. You are the one and only eternal being. Hail to you a thousand times! Salutations, repeated salutations to you once again! O Lord of infinite prowess! My salutations to you from the front and from behind! You, who possess infinite might, pervade all. But the fool that I am, I have never before been cognisant of your tremendous influence and power. I always perceived you as an ordinary friend. And owing

to this naivety, many a time, in our casual banters, I addressed you as 'O Krishna', 'O Yadava' and 'O friend'. It was a grave mistake on my part to address you by your name without recognising you, O great valiant one! Why just this, many a time, I even made fun of your eating and sleeping habits! Countless times, I humiliated you in front of other friends. I beg forgiveness of you, "O extremely gifted being" for all my follies and foolishness.

You, indeed, are the father of this world, for nobody in this world can match you in might and power. Hence, the question of anyone being superior to you just does not arise. O God of gods! I bow to you and prostrate myself at your feet. As I respectfully pay obeisance to you, I sing your glories and appeal to you to be gracious to me. O *Ishwar*! Just like a father forgives the transgressions of his son, a friend of his friend's, and a spouse of his spouse's, I wish you to forgive me for all my wrongdoings. While on one hand, I am elated to behold this divine form of yours which I had never even imagined before, on the other, I am terrified too. I am joyous because my friend and charioteer is *Ishwar*, and fearful because in days gone by, I have unwittingly behaved in such an unseemly manner with him. I am apprehensive that I might have to bear your displeasure for it. It is my humble request that you return to your ordinary form. I am feeling agitated and uneasy beholding this cosmic form of yours. O Lord, kindly be pleased with me, and please cast off this terrifying form and reassume the form of my friend Krishna. For, seeing you in the form of my friend once again will help me regain my composure. I will be assured, for in addition to being the Supreme Soul, and "in spite of everything that has happened" you are still my friend.

Krishna:

Arjuna is, indeed, remarkable, isn't he? Not only did he unknowingly disparage me but my cosmic form as well. Now, would I take offence at his harmless jokes and banter, which friends are wont to engage in and that too, to such an extent that I would be displeased with him? How ridiculous is that! This is the problem with human beings; even their imagination of *Ishwar* reflects their own mindset. Just as he had come to the battlefield with the goal of eliminating the Kauravas because of his inability to forgive and forget their conduct in the past, he is now wondering, 'What if even Krishna is not able to forget my past behaviour towards him?' Now, if friends do not make fun of each other then who will? And besides, I have told him numerous times, "It is this "Krishna and his body" which is your friend; I am the soul that dwells beyond him." Thus, who behaved in what manner with my body is inconsequential to me. And an important point to note here is, when there is no significance of how someone behaves with my living and breathing body then how would it matter even remotely how somebody treats my idols?

However, I am not here to argue with Arjuna, and nor do I have the time to argue at present. Rather, I need to banish all his delusions and fears so that he readily agrees to fight the war, and to that end, I have to augment his faith. So, without further ado, I proclaimed, "O Arjuna, till now, only those who have realised their soul have experienced my cosmic form. You are the first person to witness this form without realising the soul. And you have been blessed with this vision because of my benevolence, which makes it amply clear how dear you are to me. Such being the case, the thought that I would be offended by any behaviour of yours should never even cross your mind. O Arjuna, you must also comprehend that it is not possible to behold this form of mine by studying the *Vedas*, performing *Yajna*, doing charity or undergoing severe penance. I have worked this miracle because of my love for you. So, you must not be needlessly disturbed beholding me in my cosmic form. You should not even let such ridiculous thoughts enter your mind. However, if you still insist, you can see your friend in his ordinary form once again." Speaking thus, I released him from the hypnotic spell.

Arjuna:
O Shri Krishna! I have become calm and have regained my composure seeing you in this very peaceful and gentle human form. The sight of you in this friendly form is providing me a great deal of assurance.

Krishna:
O Arjuna! It is extremely difficult to behold this cosmic form of mine which you have just witnessed; so much so that even gods yearn for a glimpse of it. So, just imagine how gracious I am towards you. Why, it is not possible to behold this cosmic form even if a person were

to study the *Vedas* or perform charity or *Yajna* endlessly birth after birth. However, by unifying with your soul, not only is it possible to see or comprehend me, but also become one with me. O Arjuna, to put it succinctly, knowing and realising me is possible only through single-minded devotion. Although, there exists an even simpler way to know and realise me, and because you are extremely dear to me, I will disclose to you that method as well. Actually, the one who goes through life "undertaking all his tasks and duties only for me, that is, for the greater good" may do whatever he pleases, but he will still be one with me. O Arjuna! When the Supreme Soul is present in everything, then differentiating between yours and mine is meaningless. Then, whatever one has to do, it has to be done for the sake of self and all. In other words, the person who takes good care of his 'self' and who effects not only his own betterment through his deeds but is always keen to effect everyone else's betterment too, is inevitably in sync with me. Such a great being does not have attachment for anyone, nor does he bear "any enmity towards anyone for any reason". Unfortunately, in this world, every human being is vacillating between 'self and all'. Out of ignorance, everyone has created a world of their own. And this extended sphere of 'me and mine' is verily the sign of ignorance. You too are vacillating between the self and all. You too are letting worries of you and your near and dear ones plague you. However, rise above the interests of 'me and mine' and think about all. For, the greater good or the good of all inevitably encompasses the best interests of one and all. Hence, fight this war for my sake, that is, for all; fight for the elimination of sinners; this will certainly effect your betterment. Believe me, if you do so, that is, act for the greater good, you will become one with me in no time.

In Chapter 11, Krishna hypnotised Arjuna and said, 'Arjuna! Now see all that you wish to see.' And as a result, Arjuna saw everything that was on his mind. In essence, the external world is like a state of hypnosis, and the human being perceives the world exactly the way he is. In other words, this world is merely a reflection of our own mind; and that is why, it is also referred to as '*maya*' – illusion. To Meera, this world appears blithe and merry, whereas to Krishna, this world is akin to a game. But the real question is, how do you perceive this world? Well, at present, since your mind is not anchored in sheer joy and bliss, as opposed to Meera, it is constantly vacillating between ups and downs, and therefore to you, the world will always seem reflective of your present state of mind. In other words, the world that you see at present may appear quite different at another point in time. Well, for the next ten weeks, write in two sentences how the people in the world appear to you. Remember, your writing exercise is an effort to become aware of your mind. And you must engage in this practice once every six months, until you perceive all human beings and the entire universe in the same light, i.e., perceive one and all as innocent, loving or a part of the Supreme Soul, and so on and so forth. If people appear innocent one day and scoundrels the next, or if some appear simple while others wicked, then know well that you have not yet attained the purity of perception. Your mind is not yet completely pristine. And that is because, as per the truth of Nature, even a person who has been the most vicious to you is also nothing but innocent! All you need to do is, become innocent yourself in order to see his innocence. In other words, your mind needs to be anchored in equanimity and perceive one and all as the same. And if we are not able to scale this veritable peak of the mind even after reading the Bhagavad Gita, then what have we gained really? So, fill in the following chart thoughtfully and carefully.

Write down truthfully how the people in the world appear to you

1 ——— First week ———

....
....
....
....

2 ——— Second week ———

....
....
....
....

3 ——— Third week ———

....
....
....
....

4 ——— Fourth week ———

....
....
....
....

5 ——— Fifth week ———

....
....
....
....

6 ——————— Sixth week ———————

7 ——————— Seventh week ———————

8 ——————— Eighth week ———————

9 ——————— Ninth week ———————

10 ——————— Tenth week ———————

Note:

Whenever you write, pen your thoughts with utmost honesty, on the basis of your interactions with people throughout the week. A point to ponder here is, when a person behaves viciously with you, you must especially look deep within him. Check whether you can espy an innocent individual hidden within him, even while he is behaving viciously with you externally. And ideally, you must be able to see that innocent person lurking within. That is because, every individual inevitably has a loving as well as an innocent person and also the Supreme Soul hidden within him. So, keep up with this exercise till you have achieved the state of equanimity. The day you begin to perceive a virtue of innocence in those who are the most vicious and vile to you, know it with certainty that your mind has now become calm. And this, in turn, will lead to yet another wondrous outcome; your deeds will also be executed like an act or play, because they will no longer disturb the peace within. This is a great achievement indeed! Hence, undertake this exercise with utmost seriousness. Assuredly, you will stumble upon a priceless treasure that will infuse your life with joy and vivacity and give you wings to soar upon.

Chapter 12

Arjuna:
Well, I have grasped the single-minded devotion you expounded, but even so, a doubt regarding it has risen in my mind. Pray tell me; whom should one worship with single-minded devotion: God manifested in forms and attributes, or the imperishable and unmanifest *Brahma* in the form of the soul? O Krishna! Who amongst the two is superior?

Krishna:
Well, I have already answered this question before. But since Arjuna has framed his query in a different manner, I shall respond to him accordingly. This would certainly make it easier for him to fathom this science in depth. Hence, I remarked, "O Arjuna, for that purpose, first and foremost, you must understand the composition of a human being. Additionally, you need to comprehend that anything relating to religion concerns our inner self; it pertains to our life. And as I have mentioned innumerable times in our conversation so far, we have come into existence by the union of two elements. One is the soul which you can consider as "the indestructible part of *Brahma*" while the other is our body. Our body comprises the mind, brain, ego, senses and so on. The pertinent point to note here is that the soul is the symbol of 'sarva - all' while the body symbolises the 'svah - self'. To live for the greater

good is the sole objective of human life, and this objective can be achieved only through the body. Hence, O Arjuna, among those who worship the Supreme Soul as an entity possessed of form and attributes, the *yogis* who safeguard their self well are most dear to me. For, only if the 'self' is safeguarded ... and it ascends ever new heights, it will be able to rise to the level of 'all' and become one with *Brahma*. But those who are liberated from the senses, who dwell in equanimity at all times, be it in happiness or in sorrow, who are constantly engaged in the welfare of one and all without any discrimination automatically become the worshippers of the 'unmanifest *Brahma*'. Such great *yogis* who are always anchored in equanimity, become one with me right away. And, O Arjuna, the *yogis* who remain anchored in a state of equanimity do not need to worry about their 'self' either. They lead their lives considering even their 'self' as a part of the 'supreme self'. Consider me for instance; I am standing in the battlefield at this moment, but unlike you, I am not worried for myself or for my near and dear ones. I stand to gain neither kingdom nor prestige on emerging victorious in this battle, and yet, here I stand on the battlefield, firm and resolute. For, I am living and breathing with the sole objective of "eradicating sin" for the greater good. Whereas, you, on the other hand, are neither worrying about the Arjuna in his bodily form, i.e., your physical self, nor are you worrying about your omnipresent, unmanifest soul, i.e., 'all'; even though it is for your own good as well as for the greater good to dispel all kinds of self-interest, partiality and preferences, and fight. Do not erroneously assume that there exists a method of worshipping the manifest or the unmanifest Supreme Soul within or without. For, both are ways of leading human life. And if you worship one well, the other will automatically be worshipped. You must comprehend that the safeguarding of self well encompasses the safeguarding of all, while protecting the interests of all includes securing the self. So, whether you worry about your manifest or unmanifest form, either way, the only alternative for you is to fight the war without any desire or presupposition.

O Arjuna! You must comprehend that performing *karma* is the sole duty of our manifest body. Thus, regardless of whose body it is, it doesn't remain idle without performing *karma* even for a moment. If nothing else, it perpetually performs the deed of breathing in and out. Ideally, a person should devote all his deeds to the unmanifest Supreme Soul, i.e., he should do everything just for the sake of his unmanifest soul. Here, one must comprehend that devoting your deeds to the unmanifest soul implies performing all your deeds for the greater good. And I promptly grant deliverance from the worldly cycle of birth and death to all those devotees who live every moment surrendering "all their manifest *karma*" to the "unmanifest soul". Ergo, you too must dedicate your mind, brain and ego to me, i.e., your soul, and perform *karma* only for its sake. Believe me, if you perform this *karma* of the battle of Mahabharata thus, you

Arjuna, always bear in mind, time is the only deciding factor in determining "what to do and what not to do"

will certainly become one with me and me alone. But if you are unable to anchor yourself in the soul while being in the physical body, then continually strive to forsake selfishness, biases and partiality. If you find yourself incapable of even renouncing selfishness and partiality, then at least decide that you have to act anyway, then why not do so for the greater good? When you anyway have to undertake a task, why do so keeping only your interest and concern at heart? Why shouldn't you perform every action acting as a medium and instrument of the Supreme Soul, keeping everyone's welfare in mind? Even in constantly acting thus as the medium of the Supreme Soul, you will instantly realise me, i.e., your soul. And if this too seems difficult to you, then I will suggest an extremely simple method; forsake all fruits of action. I have already mentioned this several times earlier, but I am reiterating it; forsaking the fruits of action is the simplest way of becoming one with the Supreme Soul. For, simply by forsaking the fruits of actions, a human being immediately gets absolved of all his sins and consequences.

O Arjuna, you are discussing the scriptures of the world and the countless rituals described in them. But you must bear in mind; it is far better "to have knowledge, i.e., concrete experience of one single field" than blindly following the scriptures without grasping their meaning. Furthermore, keeping the Supreme Soul, in the form of soul, at the heart of every act and action is even superior to such knowledge. However, forsaking the fruits of actions far exceeds them all. Ergo, let go of all mentions of scriptures, knowledge and meditation, and renounce all your expectations from the present *karma* in the form of this battle. Upon doing so, you will be immediately elevated even above "those who are well versed in scriptures and meditation". All in all, if a person gains the knowledge of "renouncing the fruits of actions", then he doesn't need any other knowledge of the world. For, the root of all of a human being's sins and problems lies hidden in the expectation of fruits. Even if one were to "excessively chant the *mantras* cited in the scriptures" with the anticipation of fruits, that too would eventually lead to nothing but sin. Because the expectation of fruits inevitably entails self-interest, and selfishness is the one and only sin. Therefore, you too must liberate yourself from all self-interests concerning this war. For, every task performed without self-interest becomes a "divine *karma*". And a person who undertakes such divine *karma* immediately realises the Supreme Soul.

O Arjuna, forsaking the fruits of actions is the *mantra* which promptly banishes all kinds of *vikara* – the disorders hidden in the "mind, brain and ego". The person who forsakes the fruits of actions not only gets freed from selfishness but all his negative emotions at once. Also, he gets instantly freed from the clutches of attachment and ego. Thereafter, happiness and sorrow never perturb him again. For, when there is no expectation of fruits, there remains no difference between happiness and sorrow. Such a great *yogi*, having everyone's best interests at heart, is always content with every kind of situation. For that matter, there is no other reason for a person to be discontented than the expectation of fruits. So, such a *yogi*, having renounced the expectation of fruits, does not trouble anyone nor does he get troubled by anyone. Such a devotee who lives beyond joy-sorrow forsakes "all kinds of good and evil" actions. For, when there is no self-interest and no happiness and sorrow, then the concepts of good and evil do not exist for him. He resolutely undertakes his deeds for the good of all. And if truth be told, such determined devotees, replete with such qualities, are extremely dear to me. Hence, I urge you once again to renounce the expectation of fruits from the *karma* of this battle, and you will then become fully resolute to act for the greater good. Then, you will not refuse to fight. Rather, you will fight wholeheartedly in order to obliterate the sinners. O Arjuna, those devotees who put their faith in me are especially dear to me, the ones who start undertaking all deeds selflessly, having partaken of my nectar of pious wisdom. Ergo, what matters is not the worship of the manifest or the unmanifest, but the renouncement of fruits from actions.

The important lesson of Chapter 12 is, one should perform a deed based on only two reasons. A deed should either be performed for the 'self' or for the 'greater good'. However, generally, a person is stuck between the two. He neither does anything just for his own self, nor does he do anything for the greater good alone. When, in fact, a deed must be performed either for the 'self' or for the 'greater good'. In fact, this is the veritable key which yields wondrous results from every *karma*. For instance, you want to write a song. Now, you should write a song either for your own satisfaction or for it to provide entertainment to the world at large. But generally, songs are written for the purpose of earning name, fame, money or to gratify the ego. The analogy of the song mentioned herein applies to every deed performed. In short, for any deed, a-little-bit-of-mine-and-a-little-bit-of-yours kind of orientation is not the correct method for performing the deed. A song will turn out to be a good creation if you write it solely for yourself or for the world at large. To state another example, Krishna used to dance, play his flute, perform the *raas*, go on picnics, take a leisurely ride in his chariot and adorn himself in fine clothes and jewellery, but only for himself. As for the great deeds, he used to perform them for the sake of the world at large. And you must know that according to the supreme law of Nature, when one performs deeds for himself, the world benefits from it, and when one performs deeds for the world at large, one verily benefits from it. If a man is mired in difficulties, it is because of performing deeds that fall in neither of these two categories. So, if you want only good and positive to happen in life and all hassles and failures to be eliminated from it, then start performing tasks for '*sva* or *sarva*', i.e., 'for yourself or for the greater good'. Indeed, this wisdom outweighs all other forms of knowledge of this world. So, to begin with, perform five tasks for yourself and five for the world at large. Bear in mind that the sphere of *sva* and *sarva* does not encompass the concepts of family, society, religion or country; it is either for yourself or the world at large. No discovery of science or work of art is confined to family, society, religion or country. On similar lines, if you are dressing up for yourself, then do not care for others' appreciation or lack thereof. All said and done, to perform deeds only for *sva* or *sarva* is not that easy, as the habit of performing deeds that lie in between the two is a long-standing one. That is why, I'm urging you to begin with five tasks in each category, and then, gradually keep on adding to them. You will be surprised by the pace at which your life will be transformed.

Describe in your own words the tasks you have performed for '*sva*' (yourself) and your experience

1

....
....
....
....

2

....
....
....
....

3

....
....
....
....

4

....
....
....
....

5

....
....
....
....

Describe in your own words the tasks you have performed for *'sarva'* (the greater good) and your experience

1
....
....
....
....

2
....
....
....
....

3
....
....
....
....

4
....
....
....
....

5
....
....
....
....

Chapter 13

Krishna:

Well, I had urged Arjuna yet again to pick up arms. I had also imparted complete knowledge concerning the manifest and the unmanifest to him. I had also clearly exhorted him to fight this war with his manifest body, becoming the instrument of the unmanifest Supreme Soul for the greater good. "In this way," I told Arjuna, "having stood up to eliminate the sinners, you will become one with the Supreme Soul." However, all my persuasion and explanations were in vain, for, he was still not prepared to fight. But it didn't matter! Unperturbed, I picked up the conversation from where I had left off and remarked, "O Arjuna, "*ksetra* and *ksetra-jna*" pervade this entire existence. Herein, our body is known as the *ksetra*, while the one who well knows the functioning and processes of the body is known as the *ksetra-jna*. And being aware of this *ksetra-jna* is 'knowledge'. However, having this knowledge by no means implies that *ksetra* is all but meaningless now. Many have committed this mistake. Upon gaining the knowledge of *ksetra-jna*, they have deemed their body, its activities and processes to be inconsequential. But in my opinion, the pinnacle of knowledge lies in knowing the existence and importance of both "*ksetra* and *ksetra-jna*" in depth. Consider me for instance. Even though I am fully aware of *ksetra-jna*, I wholeheartedly undertake all deeds worth discharging through the "*ksetra* in its physical form". For, the *ksetra-jna*, despite being aware of everything, is the non-doer. Ergo, all actions have to be undertaken by the *ksetra* at the behest of the *ksetra-jna*, i.e., by becoming the instrument of the *ksetra-jna*. To explain this in the context of the present war, everybody's *ksetra-jna* is fully aware that sinners should be eliminated. But the question is, who will undertake this *karma* of the destruction of sinners? That will certainly have to be performed by the body of some warrior or the other. Thus, everyone must follow this and make his '*ksetra*' available to undertake any *karma* at the call of his '*ksetra-jna*'. Ergo, you too must make your body readily available to serve at the call of your *ksetra-jna* and fight this battle just for the sake of *ksetra-jna*. This alone is your duty, and the only true knowledge.

If you haven't comprehended yet, let me impart the knowledge of '*ksetra* and *ksetra-jna*' in greater detail to you. I will tell you what exactly this *ksetra* is, and also briefly touch upon the tendencies of this *ksetra*. At the same time, I will acquaint you with the various influences of *ksetra-jna*. This knowledge has been expounded in numerous scriptures in myriad ways; but I will furnish you with this knowledge in depth and in the most explicit terms possible. Thereafter, all the delusions arising in your mind concerning this supreme knowledge will dissipate. First, you need to comprehend that this entire world is in existence because of the union of *ksetra* and *ksetra-jna*, and the human being is no exception to it. Knowledge lies within in the form of *ksetra-jna*, while on the outside, he possesses the body in the form of *ksetra* to perform *karma*. But the greater part of the human race has no conception of the knowledge that lies within. That is why, ignorant as they are, they perform all physical deeds guided by the knowledge garnered through external sources. Not only the human brain and ego but also a person's intrinsic nature, carried forth from innumerable births, prompts him to undertake such deeds, out of ignorance. Even his mind and senses propel him towards ignorance alone. The pentacle, i.e., five elements of his senses, meaning, sound, touch, sight, taste and smell, also lead him away from "his knowledge". And since most human beings lead their lives considering their body, senses, mind

With **every** new birth, the **human being** certainly goes on **changing** his **form** but his 'primordial **nature'** chases him **birth** after **birth**

and ego as the truth, they go on performing "deeds which are better left unperformed". But as the body and its influence are always abounding with pervasive tendencies, a large part of the human race is writhing in the venom of desire and animosity; the reason why everyone in this world is compelled to endure the blows of happiness and sorrow.

However, O Arjuna, a few human beings in this world transcend their corporeal bodies and get liberated from the influence of their mind, brain, ego and senses and attain 'knowledge'. Thereupon, joy and sorrow do not affect such wise people anymore. Their desires and dislikes too get obliterated completely. Having no desires and dislikes, the deeds which must be undertaken get accomplished effortlessly. And the thought of that which must not be done never even enters their mind. Thereafter, what these wise people do or not do is of no consequence. For then, no matter what actions they perform, their actions are in deference to the wishes of the 'Supreme Soul'. In contrast to them, as you are still reeling under the influence of your body, the desire to attain the kingdom well lies within you and so does the rancour for the Kauravas. But it is in your interest to forsake these petty emotions and imbibe the supreme virtues of *ksetra-jna*. I will now elaborate on the characteristics of the wise who have realised this knowledge so that you become inclined towards this knowledge. First of all, O Arjuna, such wise beings evince no pride in their greatness. They do not consider themselves special or more important than others, the way you do at the moment. This is the very reason why, you think that nothing should happen to 'you or your near and dear ones'. Just let whatever has to happen, happen; you are not different from anyone. In fact, the mind of the wise is always at peace, regardless of the circumstances. The external vicissitudes do not cause upheavals in their inner world the way the sight of the massive army of the Kauravas has caused turmoil in yours. O Arjuna, such wise people do not even cherish any desires concerning this world or the next. But you are aspiring for the kingdom in this world, and heaven in the other. Likewise, the wise never get influenced by "the farce of birth and death"; whereas even at this moment, the fear of death lies at the core of all your concerns. O Arjuna, the simple and plain truth is that the *gyaani*[33] perceives the entire world as his very own and lives his life accordingly; hence, he has no individual attachment towards his child, wife, wealth or property. But you, on the other hand, are losing sleep over not only a kingdom, wealth and power but also your near and dear ones. Hence, till the time you do not rise from *ksetra* to *ksetra-jna*, that is, until you transcend from the corporeal body to knowledge, you will invariably be beset by all these perversities. And till such time, you will continue to hold scriptures as a base and deliberate over virtue-sin and good-bad. Therefore, remember, "knowing everything as the Supreme Soul" is the only true knowledge and anything contrary to it, is ignorance. Hence, mark my words, any teaching which makes a distinction not just between virtue-sin but even between yours and mine, and heaven and hell, is nothing but sheer ignorance. Duality and discrimination, regardless of its kind, is nothing save ignorance.

Hence, O Arjuna, comprehend this once and for all that "knowing everything as the Supreme Soul" is the only true knowledge; and only the one who has realised this knowledge can attain 'Supreme Bliss'. In fact, one cannot even imagine the extent of joyfulness and serenity of a person who has "attained supreme bliss"! Just take a moment to imagine the felicity and jubilance of a person who wishes for nothing at all and who has absolutely nothing to lose. Who can stop the cascading flow of exultation of a person for whom everything is the Supreme Soul, whether he gains it or loses it? O Arjuna, I will speak of this great knowledge to you comprehensively, imbibing which, you will

33   *Gyaani* - Profoundly wise man.

be anchored in that 'Supreme Bliss'. Remember, one's habit of creating duality and differentiation is the only barrier to one's flowing stream of felicity. And this "great knowledge" denies every kind of differentiation. So, neither can you term this knowledge as the truth nor can it be called untruth. This Supreme knowledge encompasses it all, not just the truth and untruth. That is why, it is known as the knowledge having all its limbs, eyes, ears and head spread in all directions. And this is the reason why the 'Supreme Soul' has been visualised in such a corporeal form. This knowledge is such that neither can it be realised nor fathomed. For, it exists but at the same time it doesn't. Actually, it exists between all contradictions. That is why a person can only experience this knowledge. It is aware of all sense-objects, yet it is devoid of all senses. Even though it is absolutely free of attachment, it still sustains everyone. Despite being devoid of all qualities, there is no quality that it doesn't experience. It dwells within everyone as well as without. It is close to everyone, and at the same time, it is distant from everyone. In essence, even though it is without any division, it is divided as it were, in all beings. Know it as the one who gives birth, the one who sustains life and also the one who takes lives. However, one may wonder how the force which kills as well as gives birth can be the same. Likewise, how can the Supreme Soul exist in virtue as well as in sin? In short, understand that it exists between every pair of contradictions. Ergo, to say that "it exists or doesn't exist" would both be erroneous. Thus, everyone including you should search within themselves and learn the art of anchoring themselves between contradictions. Instead of being for or against any object, person or subject, station yourself in the centre. Do not fall prey to these words of ignorance which differentiate between dying and slaying, violence and non-violence in this *karma* of war. Station yourself in the centre of everything, be it virtue-sin or living-dying and lean towards whichever side your *ksetra-jna* asks you to. And return to the centre as soon as the deed is over. This is verily the art of living as the Supreme Soul, in this illusory world. This world is called illusory for the simple reason that everything here is both an illusion as well as the Supreme Soul. It is only a question of a person's perception. Everything in this world is a sin for the one whose perspective is illusory, while everything here is the Supreme Soul for the one having the outlook of the Supreme Soul. This is the sole reason why I can see only the Supreme Soul pervading everywhere, even in the midst of this battle, while you see nothing but sin and violence in this war. Thus, instead of thinking of fleeing the battle, cultivate a divine outlook. Once your outlook changes, you will not think of fleeing the battle. Because then everything, everywhere will become nothing but the Supreme Soul for you. That is why it is said, the Supreme Soul exists as well as it does not. With the divine outlook I possess, everything is the Supreme Soul, whereas in your view, nothing here is the Supreme Soul.

O Arjuna, know that be it *Purusa*—the soul, or *Prakriti*—nature, both are without beginning. And the world, governed by the 'Three Dimensional Theory', has come to exist from the human being's *prakriti*. In short, with every new birth, the human being certainly goes on changing his form but his 'primordial nature' chases him birth after birth. Based on his intrinsic nature, a human being engenders all kinds of reasons and then, propelled by them, he perpetually performs all his actions. This, in turn, distorts his 'primordial nature'. And then, he continues to experience joy and endure sorrow birth after birth on the basis of the actions performed by his degenerated intrinsic nature, since human beings continue to take new births in "virtuous or vile wombs" on the basis of the *karma* they have performed. Therefore, it is only in his best interest that he breaks free of this trap. Every human being in this world 'as per his nature' is caught in

I, the **Bhagavad Gita,** have been brought into **existence** for the **sole** objective of Arjuna's **betterment** and **progress.** And who in this world is **not similar** to **Arjuna?**

this illusory trap. And caught in the vortex of its influence, he goes on forging differences such as success-failure, victory-defeat, friend-foe, violence-non-violence and renunciation-worldliness. But naught is his lot, even after trudging through countless lifetimes. You too have fallen victim to your degenerated nature at this moment. Verily, it is your degenerated nature which is presently prompting you to flee from the "karma in the form of this battle". But mark my words; you will gain nothing by this. You will have to rise above your 'degenerated nature' and anchor yourself in your 'primordial nature' once again. And as war is verily a part of your intrinsic nature even now, let your primordial nature become the 'doer' and wage this war. Do not worry; just focus on your soul. Distinct from your intrinsic nature, this soul is verily the Supreme Soul. The soul is not the doer but a pure witness. And as it is a witness to everything in existence, it harbours no delusions. It always guides a person towards the right path. Perceive the "sacchidanand form" of this soul. This word 'sacchidanand' is formed from the union of three words; sat or truth, chit or consciousness, and anand or bliss. Sat is that which lies in front of you and cannot be avoided, like this war at present. So, focus your chit entirely on the war as you clash with your foes and experience anand while fighting the battle. The truth is, at this moment, neither you nor I need any other knowledge besides this. Presently, any knowledge that you brandish besides this, displays not the Supreme Soul but your degenerated nature. Know that all of your virtue-sin and your desires for victory-defeat are nothing save your degenerated nature. And the one who recognises the 'Purusa', i.e., his soul, and 'Prakriti', i.e., his psychology and nature as separate and distinct, becomes forever liberated even as he discharges all his duties and deeds. But contrary to this, the person who falls prey to his degenerated nature prompted by external influences continues to bind himself in multifarious bondages.

O Arjuna, many people, dimming the power of their brain, behold this Supreme Soul (in the form of soul) in their heart through meditation. Many others experience it by way of anchoring their mind in equanimity, while numerous karmayogis experience it by renouncing the fruits of action. Several others progressively advance towards their soul by listening to the words of the wise on the Supreme Soul (in the form of soul). O Arjuna, it doesn't matter which path you adopt but the liberation of a person is unlikely until he transcends his nature and resolutely anchors himself in his soul. Thus, do not squander your energy in contemplating whether to fight or not; rather, channelise your energy in elevating yourself from your nature to the (level of the) Supreme Soul. In so doing, you will assuredly be liberated from this mortal world. Additionally, O Arjuna, "getting anchored in equanimity" is the easiest amongst these paths for a human being. Thus, you too must strive to anchor yourself in equanimity. Neither choose between fighting and not fighting, nor differentiate between yourself and the Kauravas. For, this battle is no longer dependent upon the affirmation of your participation. Whether you fight or not, this war has now become inevitable. Such being the case, accept it with equanimity and fight wholeheartedly as if it were a play. Do not differentiate between yourself and the Kauravas even in matters of life and death or victory and defeat. Fighting thus, you will set sailing on the divine path and attain the Supreme Soul.

O Arjuna, you must grasp that you and your soul are separate and distinct. All the deeds you have performed find their basis in your *prakriti* – your nature. And on the basis of that nature alone, you have learnt to wield a bow, and that very nature has given rise to the desire of kingdom in you. Your soul has always remained the non-doer in all the *karmas* you have performed; it has always been a spectator of your deeds. And it is no different today either. So, align with your nature and fight the war as per its dictate even today, and let your soul be the spectator to the war. The only new thing you do at my behest today is, turn your focus from "your nature as a doer" to "your soul as a witness". And only the one who perceives his nature as the doer and his soul as the non-doer, sees the truth. O Arjuna, in truth, even all of the human being's diverse emotions are spawned verily by his nature, and a human being's nature, in turn, is begotten by the Supreme Soul. Such being the case, it is always better for everybody to become a witness of their nature instead of striving to alter it. Thus, you too become the witness of your nature which is urging you to fight, rather than attempting to flee the war and acting against your nature. Upon doing so, you will instantly attain *"Sacchidanandghan Brahma"*.[34] O Arjuna,

34 *Sacchidanandghan* - Refers to *Brahma* who is truth, bliss and consciousness.

all of a human being's attributes owe their origin to his nature, and his nature is without beginning, which makes it impossible to be altered. All he can possibly do is, take refuge in the unmanifested Supreme Soul within, which neither performs nor gets bound or engaged in any action despite dwelling within the body. It merely acts as a spectator to the deeds emanating from the human being's nature. That is why, a human being's soul is all-pervasive and is said to be present in every action of a human being.

O Arjuna, know that be it a human being or animal, matter or the planets and planetoids of the universe; everything here is bound to act in sync with its nature. The sun is bound to provide luminescence and the moon is bound to provide clement coolness, for these are their respective natures. Likewise, you too are bound to act in accordance with your nature. Hence, it is best if you do so wholeheartedly as per the dictates of your nature and become the witness to all your deeds. No sooner you become the witness to your actions than you will become the witness to everybody's actions too. This is not all; you will become the witness to the ongoing *leelas* of the universe too. In short, as soon as you become the witness to your deeds, you will become one with the omnipresent "*Sacchidanandghan* Supreme Soul". All your differences and delusions will get shattered. All your desires of victory-defeat and virtue-sin will be obliterated. For, then, you will merely be the witness to all the virtue-sins too that are abounding in the world. Hence, elevate yourself from your *prakriti* – nature to the level of the Supreme Soul and become the witness to your *karma* (in the form) of this war. This alone is in your best interest. And if you act against your 'primordial intrinsic nature' and embrace your 'degenerated nature', you will deprive yourself of everything that is in your best interest.

The key point of Chapter 13 is the definition of '*sacchidanand*' explained by Krishna. Now, in life, one inevitably experiences ups and downs, and not everything always turns out as per one's wish. Krishna was an artist by nature, with a deep fondness for playing the flute, dancing, enjoying the *raas*, adorning himself and so on. But such was his life that enemies would keep barging into it ever so often. Struggles and strife would repeatedly crop up in his life, with or without reason. So, then, should he have cursed his life? Should he have fled from struggles? No, that's not Krishna, and this is not his teaching either. Krishna, in fact, elucidates that one should consider even struggles as a form of *raas* and confront them. And this is precisely what he had done all his life. And that is exactly what he is asking Arjuna to do at this moment. And, at present, this is exactly what I'm asking you to do as well. Difficult phases, troubles, failures are all an inevitable part of human life. And the very meaning of a '*sacchidanand*' mindset is, the problems that have become inevitable, or in other words, the problems that cannot be avoided, have all become '*sat*' – the truth. Because, what is truth, after all? That which is in front of you! So, Krishna says, put your '*chit*' – heart into that which has become inevitable. Do not run away or try to escape from it. Rather, focus all your energies and mind on tackling the problem as if you're playing a game; and overcome the problem while deriving '*anand*' (pleasure) from it. This is essentially *sat-chit-anand*, i.e., *sacchidanand*. In other words, put your heart and soul into every truth and reality you are faced with and seek pleasure in it. The secret behind Krishna always emerging victorious and being joyous and blithe in every situation is verily his nature of *sacchidanand*. And if you too wish to always remain happy and continue to be victorious (in all battles of life), then you will have to become *sacchidanand* from this very day. And to that end, fill in the chart below. In this chart, write (in detail) your top ten current problems and struggles. Remember, neither must you endeavour to escape these problems nor lament them. Resolve that you will be so deeply anchored in *sat-chit-anand* that you will become *sacchidanand* yourself and 'play' with those problems with every ounce of joy and zest, and continue to gain victory over them, one after the other. And as you vanquish each problem, proudly express your sense of accomplishment in the space given. Resolve determinedly that come what may, you will emerge victorious over all problems that have become unavoidable. And as for the problems that can be averted, one need not battle with them at all; just awaken this sense and know the difference between the two.

Note:
Do not stop until you have vanquished all problems and struggles and marked them off with your words of triumph.

1   Write in detail about the problem and struggle

....
....
....
....
....

Once you gain victory over it, express your sense of accomplishment and happiness below. Also, elaborate upon your experience.

....
....
....
....

2   Write in detail about the problem and struggle

....
....
....
....
....

Once you gain victory over it, express your sense of accomplishment and happiness below. Also, elaborate upon your experience.

....
....
....
....

Write in detail about the problem and struggle

....
....
....
....
....

Once you gain victory over it, express your sense of accomplishment and happiness below. Also, elaborate upon your experience.

....
....
....
....

4 Write in detail about the problem and struggle

....
....
....
....
....

Once you gain victory over it, express your sense of accomplishment and happiness below. Also, elaborate upon your experience.

....
....
....
....

5 Write in detail about the problem and struggle

....

....

....

....

....

Once you gain victory over it, express your sense of accomplishment and happiness below. Also, elaborate upon your experience.

....

....

....

....

6 Write in detail about the problem and struggle

....

....

....

....

....

Once you gain victory over it, express your sense of accomplishment and happiness below. Also, elaborate upon your experience.

....

....

....

....

7 Write in detail about the problem and struggle

....
....
....
....
....

Once you gain victory over it, express your sense of accomplishment and happiness below. Also, elaborate upon your experience.

....
....
....
....

8 Write in detail about the problem and struggle

....
....
....
....
....

Once you gain victory over it, express your sense of accomplishment and happiness below. Also, elaborate upon your experience.

....
....
....
....

Write in detail about the problem and struggle

....
....
....
....
....

Once you gain victory over it, express your sense of accomplishment and happiness below. Also, elaborate upon your experience.

....
....
....
....

10 **Write in detail about the problem and struggle**

....
....
....
....
....

Once you gain victory over it, express your sense of accomplishment and happiness below. Also, elaborate upon your experience.

....
....
....
....

Chapter 14

Krishna:

This time, I had clearly explained to Arjuna that the only 'divine deed' he was supposed to undertake was to fight the war wholeheartedly. I had all but told him that the Supreme Soul is not a physical state but a state of mind. And '*sat-chit-anand*' is a manifestation of its form. In other words, to seek joy in that which is before you is verily that divine state. But Arjuna was not ready to comprehend this. Forget Arjuna, who in this world is ready to fathom this truth? The fanciful tales woven around the Supreme Soul have deluded the entire human race. One simply does not realise that 'truth' is not to be sought; rather, that which is before you is verily the truth. But unfortunately, the human being has been handed such an overwhelming stockpile of scriptures that he disregards the 'truth' before him and instead seeks it in all kinds of untruths. Arjuna's conduct at present is no different (than this). Denying the truth before him in the form of the war, he is trying to seek the truth in everything else, right from "the scriptures to the probable outcome of the war".

Nevertheless, the truth of the moment is that Arjuna is still not ready to fight. So, what alternative do I have except taking the conversation forward? Verily, this is what I wish to explain to everyone. Anything and everything that exists in the present is the Supreme Soul.

The human being has no option but to face it with a smile, just as I don't have any alternative other than to accept "Arjuna's decision to not fight" with a smile on my face. This is the reason why all my life I have always been accepting everything that befell me, with a smile on my face. Time after time, I have blithely embraced the shadow of death when it came looking for me; I have accepted trickery and deception with the same love that I have embraced *raas* and *Chhappan Bhog*.

However, we shall discuss about me later, and at present, return to the *karma* which demands my immediate attention. So, when Arjuna did not acquiesce to fight, taking the conversation forward, I said to him, "O Arjuna, I will speak to you once again of the most superior and ultimate knowledge, because the greatest of sages have attained liberation on hearkening to this knowledge. Such is the power of this knowledge that a person who hearkens to it attains liberation for eternity. Then, he never gets perturbed by any kind of adversity at any point in time." If truth be told, I am perceiving even Arjuna's refusal to fight the war as simply being instrumental to the dissemination of knowledge. For, at least on this pretext, knowledge, true and simple, is becoming available to the human being. So, I, who had always been happy and joyful, was pleased even at this moment to know that if nothing else, at least pure and true knowledge was promulgating through me in this way. That is why it is said that people who are always happy need not go anywhere in pursuit of happiness. They find absolute bliss in whatever lies before them.

Returning to Arjuna's sorrow, elucidating the "mysteries of the world" in a different manner to the reluctant Arjuna who was continually refusing to fight, I declared, "Listen to me, O Arjuna! I have two kinds of nature: one is material and the other, spiritual. A human being assuming a corporeal existence is my material nature, while infusing life into that corporeal body is my spiritual nature. From this perspective, recognise the human body as material, insentient and his life-force as spiritual. And all human beings owe their genesis to the union of these two. You may also say that I am the mother who brings all beings into physical existence and also the father who sows the seed of life-force in them. That is why I reiterate, O Arjuna, for everything in existence, there is no reason other than me. Here, one must comprehend that the nature of the material realm is completely different from that of the spiritual realm; both these worlds are as different as night and day. Neither of the two have any impact whatsoever on the other. Material nature is variable and vacillating, while the spiritual nature is steady. Yet, every change in the material realm leaves an impact on the person's state of mind. And this is verily his ignorance; undoubtedly, his "state of somnolence"; just as your mindset is getting influenced by the war, an external event at this moment which is, indeed, your ignorance. For, you are unable to comprehend that both these matters are entirely different. You cannot stop the change taking place in the material realm even if you so desire, and you cannot alter your spiritual nature even if you wish it with all your heart. But you can surely nurse the delusion of being able to do so, and even as we speak, you have fallen prey to the selfsame delusion. Why just you, even the wisest of the wise are living in the same delusion.

Therefore, hearken forthwith from me the root cause of this 'delusion'. The fact of the matter is, the 'Three Dimensional Theory of Existence' which influences everyone is responsible for this delusion. The all-pervasive Three Dimensional Theory comprising "the elements of *Sattva*, *Rajas* and *Tamas*" binds a person's spiritual nature to the material nature in the form of the body. Owing to this, his spiritual nature gets influenced time after time with every change in his material nature. Amongst these three, the element of '*Sattva*' infuses a person with the pride of possessing knowledge and joy. A person under the influence of this element needlessly assumes himself to be superior to others. And in the future, this arrogance of being better than the others verily becomes the root cause of all his sorrows. Thereafter, he keeps getting perturbed whenever his honour, power, wealth or knowledge is questioned or threatened. Likewise, the element of '*Rajas*' spawns from the desires and attachments hidden in a human being. This element incites a person to undertake an action and to crave the fruits of that action. And this is why, a person under the influence of the element of *Rajas* also repeatedly endures 'joys and sorrows' in this world. As for the element of '*Tamas*', it is born out of the ignorance of not being able to perceive the truth. This element spawns faithlessness in actions. Owing to this ignorance, a person keeps looking for good-bad and virtue-sin in every deed, which has a direct bearing on his diligence. Slowly but surely, such a person falls prey to sloth, error and somnolence. For this reason, he is often unable to undertake even those deeds which are mandatory for him to perform. Generally, every human being is a victim of these three elements in varying degrees. At any time, one or the other element inevitably prevails over him. Consequently, his entire life passes away in enduring the harsh blows of these elements. Now, although a person's spiritual nature is defined and bound by these three qualities, a person should still persevere in elevating himself from '*Tamas*' to '*Rajas*' and from '*Rajas*' to '*Sattva*' time after time.

O Arjuna, whenever wisdom and discernment rise within, one should know that there has been an upsurge in the element of *Sattva* in him. Whenever avarice, selfishness and desires rear their heads, he should discern that the element of *Rajas* is on the rise. And when his mind loses interest in engaging even in the basic chores and activities of daily life, he should understand that there has been an upsurge in his element of *Tamas*. As a result, instead of undertaking *karma* to make himself self-reliant, he squanders his time in "other futile endeavours". Thus, any person whose life is dependent upon others for reasons good or bad should understand that 'the nature of *Tamas*' bears heavily on him. Then, even if a person seeks such a refuge in ritualism, it makes absolutely no difference.

O Arjuna, these three elements impact not only a person's present birth but

> '**Truth**' is **not** to **be sought**; rather, that which is **before you** is verily the **truth**

they also influence him birth after birth. A person with an abundance of *Sattva* takes birth in a family with the finest states of mind. There he is provided with an upbringing which helps him liberate himself from the Three Dimensional Theory. O Arjuna, you must comprehend that this entire play pertains to the mind, not the physical world. Thus, do not presume that people who leave their body with a good mindset in the previous birth take birth in wealthy families in the next birth. No, they are born in families with members dwelling in good states of mind. That is why most wise people are born into ordinary families. Why go far, consider me for instance; if I got the opportunity to be brought up under the aegis of Nanda and Yashoda, it was an outcome accorded to me by my good, positive mindset. And just see the pinnacles of success this cowherd scaled thereafter! Likewise, O Arjuna, a person who dies with an excessive quality of *Rajas* is born into a family which "craves the fruits of action", while a person who breathes his last with an overbearing *Tamas* is born in the womb of animals.

O Arjuna, you need to comprehend that no corporeal body or life in this world is free from these three qualities. But a person who observes all his deeds being performed by these three qualities and becomes a witness to this entire play, transcends the Three Dimensional Theory that very moment. In so doing, he immediately realises my form – the Soul. Thereafter, for him, all his deeds and those of the entire human race remain nothing but "a farce undertaken out of compulsion". Such a person is instantaneously relieved of all pains and pangs including birth, death and old age. Ergo, you too must perceive your deeds as well as those of others as being spawned by the 'Three Dimensional Theory' of Nature and then whatever happens, let it happen. Become the witness of this entire play; upon doing so, you will be liberated right here, right now.

Arjuna:
Krishna! Pray tell me, what are the virtues of a person who has risen above all these three qualities? How does he conduct himself? And how does one get liberated from this triad of elements?

Krishna:
Now, I had already told Arjuna that by becoming a witness to these three elements that pervade human existence, he can rise above them.

But Arjuna is right; perhaps it is not as easy to comprehend as it sounds. In fact, ever since the time this dialogue began between us, this is the first time he has posed a pertinent question. So, in a bid to explain to him, I said, "Listen, O Arjuna, there is no person in this world who is not affected by these three qualities. For, as long as there is life, the human being has to deal with the external world. And any external conduct undertaken by the human being is verily influenced by one of these three elements. At the same time, also note that "these three elements have their continuum spanning across births, which is unique to each individual". And since this continuum is so profound and functions in automation, no one needs to ponder over it. Hence, instead of focusing on that over which no one has control, a person should focus on his consciousness. He should allow his Three Dimensional elements to run completely free. For, none of these Three Dimensional elements is permanent. If one element is dominant at one moment, the other element assumes control the very next moment. So, ideally, he should allow himself to drift in the flow of these three qualities. Whether it is the influence of *Sattva* or *Tamas* surging or subsiding, neither should he be averse to them nor have an attachment with them. And neither should he try to change the kind and course of the element rising within. He should simply become the spectator of this ongoing play between qualities. O Arjuna, the one who observes these qualities surge and subside, considering none as his own, and rather, is aware that it is only the qualities playing with each other, becomes stationed in *Sacchidanandghan Parmaatma* for eternity. Then, it makes no difference whether he is a witness of *Sattva*, *Rajas* or *Tamas*. But the human being, ignorant of this Three Dimensional Theory, cannot even fathom the difference between the 'witness' and the 'doer'. He perceives a person driven by the element of *Sattva* as virtuous, and a person driven by the element of *Tamas* as vile. However, the truth is that a "person who is a doer" should be considered ignorant, even if the *Sattva* element dominates him. And likewise, if a person is the witness, in spite of the dominance of *Tamas* element in him, he should be considered as nothing but wise. Here, one must realise that the dominance of a particular element is not important, but relevant is whether a human being is its 'doer' or 'witness'. And Arjuna, you especially need to comprehend this. For, your nature is well prompting you with the lure of the kingdom and the desire to avenge yourself against the Kauravas. I am asking you to become the witness of this nature of yours. In so doing, you will forthwith transcend its three-dimensional influence. But, swayed by "the inconsequential external knowledge and your own ludicrous thoughts", you are perceiving the surge of these qualities rising within as wrong. That is why you want to reject this impulse considering it as *Taamsi* in nature and are trying to cloak yourself with virtues of *Sattva* on the outside. However, let me tell you, this is wrong because your act of embracing *Sattva* superficially will make you the doer of an action. And the plain and simple truth is that any human being who tries to adopt any kind of *karma* superficially on the outside always becomes its doer. And that is why he swells up with pride for every deed he undertakes. Upon fleeing, you will also be nothing but the doer of the act of renunciation. And I assertively state that, "being the 'doer' of *karma*" is verily the sole sin in this world. Thus, if renunciation has to come your way, then one day, in due course of time, you will be prompted to do so. Then, you can certainly follow the path of renunciation. For, then you will be the witness of your renunciation, not its doer. Hence, it is not war or renunciation which matters; rather, it is the impulse rising from a human being's nature which is of paramount importance. For, that verily is his truth of the moment. And the one who constantly remains a witness and "champions his truth" soon attains liberation. All of his mind's perversions get obliterated. Pure emotions take root within him, steadily and perennially. In short, it doesn't take him long to "turn into a sage from a dacoit just like *Valmiki*."[35] But the one who tries to obstinately become the doer of *Sattva* does not attain liberation even after wandering aimlessly birth after birth. Thereupon, he drifts through life nursing the false pride of being religious and sociable.

O Arjuna, the person who continually remains equanimous between these three qualities, soon transcends all of them. Thus, strive to anchor yourself in equanimity. Treat joy and sorrow alike and do not differentiate between mud, rock and gold. Become equipoised even between what is dear and not dear to you. Remain dispassionate between censure and commendation as well. Do not distinguish

---

35 *Valmiki* - The dacoit who later turned into a sage and composed the epic 'Ramayana'.

between heaven and hell. For, all these differences drive a person to consider "one quality better than the other". And this is why he continues to become the doer of multiple deeds. Hence, you must comprehend clearly that it is not a question of choosing between good and bad actions at all, for, every such choice makes a person the 'doer' of his deeds. And it is only because he becomes the doer that he suffers all kinds of blows in this world. For, it is the law that the one who is the doer is the one who pays for it. But the one who remains equanimous between these three elements has perceived Nature as the 'doer' of these elements. Hence, by virtue of this, he doesn't interfere with them. And since he does not meddle with them, he doesn't have to pay the price either. Enjoying himself as the witness of this ongoing play of Nature, he becomes freed from this world. So, you too must "become the witness of this war" and thereby become liberated now and forever. Here, O Arjuna, you must also comprehend that you can never become the witness of this war without becoming equipoised between the joy-sorrow and the victory-defeat that would likely result from the battle. Likewise, if you dwell upon virtue-sin and heaven-hell, then too you will never be able to become the witness of this war. In short, a person can never become the 'witness' of any deed without being completely stationed in equanimity. And he cannot get liberated without becoming the witness. Thus, anchor yourself in complete equanimity and stand up to fight now without an iota of hesitation.

The biggest lesson of this chapter is Krishna's elucidation, that a *Rajasika* disposition is superior to a *Tamasika* disposition, and a *Saatvika* disposition is superior to a *Rajasika* one. But the wise are above all three. Now, what is a *Saatvika* disposition? To state it briefly, it is pride about one's knowledge. What is a *Rajasika* disposition? It is pride about one's wealth. And what is a *Tamasika* disposition? It is pride about one's vices and ignorance. And needless to say, pride of every kind is verily nothing but ego. Going by the purest wisdom imparted by Krishna, Yudhishthira's sense of pride for always speaking the truth and Bhishma's smugness about taking unbreakable vows, both are absolutely wrong. So, imbibe this truth spoken by Krishna and try to weaken your ego. If nothing else, forsake at least three *Saatvika*, three *Rajasika* and three *Tamasika* things that you feel proud of. Then, on a gradual basis, continue to forsake your sense of pride pertaining to everything. That is because, the ego is man's biggest enemy. Trust me, once you relinquish the ego, you will become so pure and genuine that you will fall in love with yourself. Think, why do you fall in love with great people? It is because they have relinquished all three types of pride. So, fill in the chart below and take a firm step towards achieving phenomenal greatness.

Write about your *Saatvika* pride in detail

....
....
....

Start your journey of relinquishing this pride, and once you have done so, write below 'I have relinquished it!'

....
....

2

Write about your *Saatvika* pride in detail

....
....
....

Start your journey of relinquishing this pride, and once you have done so, write below 'I have relinquished it!'

....
....

3

Write about your *Saatvika* pride in detail

....
....
....

Start your journey of relinquishing this pride, and once you have done so, write below 'I have relinquished it!'

....
....

1   **Write about your *Rajasika* pride in detail**

....
....
....

> **Start your journey of relinquishing this pride, and once you have done so, write below 'I have relinquished it!'**
>
> ....
>
> ....

2   **Write about your *Rajasika* pride in detail**

....
....
....

> **Start your journey of relinquishing this pride, and once you have done so, write below 'I have relinquished it!'**
>
> ....
>
> ....

3   **Write about your *Rajasika* pride in detail**

....
....
....

> **Start your journey of relinquishing this pride, and once you have done so, write below 'I have relinquished it!'**
>
> ....
>
> ....

1. Write about your *Tamasika* pride in detail

....
....
....

> **Start your journey of relinquishing this pride, and once you have done so, write below 'I have relinquished it!'**
>
> ....
>
> ....

2. Write about your *Tamasika* pride in detail

....
....
....

> **Start your journey of relinquishing this pride, and once you have done so, write below 'I have relinquished it!'**
>
> ....
>
> ....

3. Write about your *Tamasika* pride in detail

....
....
....

> **Start your journey of relinquishing this pride, and once you have done so, write below 'I have relinquished it!'**
>
> ....
>
> ....

Chapter 15

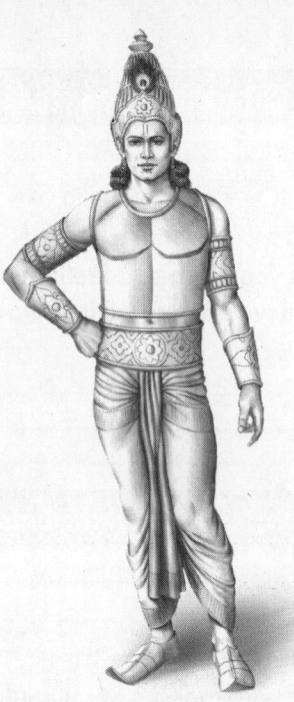

Krishna:

Now, I had tried my best to convince Arjuna with yet another novel perspective to make him wield his weapons in the war. I had no objection to Arjuna raising questions, but the problem was, we no longer had time to prolong the conversation. If the bugle were to be sounded to announce the commencement of the war, everything would be finished in no time. Beyond a doubt, if Arjuna didn't arm himself to fight by then, he would fall prey to the deadly arrows of the Kauravas at the very onset of war. On my part, I had already explained everything to him using numerous approaches. But Arjuna was not willing to comprehend either the point or the precariousness of the situation. Even so, how could I give up? I had to try till the very last moment to save him from ruination. Hence, as he was still refusing to fight, I took charge of the conversation once again. But yes, I did bring about one change in my manner of speaking. This time around, I resorted to the prevalent notions mentioned in the scriptures in my bid to reason with him. For, it had become amply clear that he had been unable to digest the plain and simple truths I had spoken in novel ways.

Thus, I said, "O Arjuna, as you know, this *samsara* – the world has been likened to a banyan tree in the scriptures. Chiefly, this tree comprises three elements; first, the root of the tree by virtue of which the tree grows and develops. For this reason, the root is called the *Parmeshwar* form, the manifestation of the Supreme Soul. Second are the branches of the tree on which the third part of the tree grows in the form of leaves. Metaphorically speaking, this world-like tree is divided into three parts, that is, three worlds. The pertinent point to note here is that nobody in these three worlds is free from ego, attachment and lust. They inevitably exist within everyone. I am explaining this to you because since aeons, the human being has been deluded in this regard. He believes that in order to reach the core, meaning the Supreme Soul, one has to renounce ego, attachment and lust. Whereas, renouncing the ego, attachment or lust is not possible by law. Not able to fathom the fabric of the world, even the wisest of the wise make such statements. And that is why, only one in a million is able to rise to the level of the Supreme Soul. For, everyone in this world believes that ego, attachment and yearning are enemies in realising the Supreme Soul. Nobody in this world is able to discern that this trio is at the core of the existence of this world. Metaphorically speaking, everybody on this planet has their "roots, branches and leaves" in the form of their (own) ego and desires. The only difference lies in their connotations. While the root performs *karma* desiring the overall enrichment of the tree, the branches are worried for their own growth. As for the leaves, they have eyes for nobody other than themselves!

All in all, you must comprehend that I am not asking you to renounce your desires or attachment. I am only asking you to look at them in a different light. Rather than being concerned only about yourself just like the leaves, develop a concern for everyone, similar to the caring root. Concern for everyone is the 'divine state of desire', while agonising about oneself is the mark of ego. Hence, to say or even presume that a person dwelling in the divine state, one with the Supreme Soul, has no concerns is utterly wrong. Consider me for instance; my concern for everybody is at the centre of both my presence on the battlefield and my conversation with you. Whereas, in your case, it is your personal desires that have prompted you to come to the battlefield, and even at this moment, you speak of nothing but saving your own self. Thus, when I say, you should renounce your desires, you must know that I am speaking of forsaking the desires stemming from selfish interests. The renouncement of desires in their entirety is simply not conceivable in this world. For, 'desire' is the prime reason behind the world coming into existence. Even the Supreme Soul cherishes the desire to see the world progress. And it is only because of that desire that the world has come to exist. Thus, to lead life desiring everybody's well-being is verily the only true divine desire. Hence, you too must rise to fight this Epic War with the divine desire and thereby liberate yourself.

O Arjuna, you must comprehend that elevating oneself to a state of having care and concern for all, from just being concerned about oneself, is the simplest way of realising the Supreme Soul. For, concern for one and all is the only true worship of the Supreme Soul; and the human being's "selfishness" is the only barrier in the way of this devotion. That is why one should eliminate all self-interests with the sharp, piercing sword of dispassion. A person should renounce not the world, but his own selfishness. As for the world created by the Supreme Soul, the human being has to embrace it with compassion, in its entirety with all its hues; and only a person who does so is a true ascetic. For, O Arjuna, the pride and delusion of such an ascetic have inevitably been quelled. Moreover, he has liberated himself from all his self-interests. Joy and sorrow never perturb him again, for, one experiences joy and sorrow only as long as one is afflicted with selfishness. As soon as one is freed from it, one is liberated from all kinds of dilemmas and dualities as well. And a wise being liberated from the clutches of dualities attains the Supreme Soul. O Arjuna, the one who has attained that supreme state never returns to the world. For, the cycle of life and death continues only as long as selfishness exists.

O Arjuna, now that we have come so far in our conversation, you must comprehend "the principles of birth and rebirth" as well. The *Jivatma* – the soul dwelling in a person is a part of me, and this *Jivatma* in turn gives rise to man's *prakriti* – his nature. That very same soul infuses life into his mind and all five senses, which are otherwise dead. And these in turn invoke the feeling of selfishness in a human being. And the goal of the journey of human life is to renounce the feeling of self-interest existing within and anchor oneself in me, i.e., the Supreme Soul. This is verily the play of human life. Now, listen to the principle of birth and rebirth from me; whenever a person forsakes his body, his soul takes along "his mind and the senses" with it. And then, that soul, along with the mind and the senses, assumes a new body. This game, of the mind and senses taking birth with the soul and assuming a new body, continues till a person gets rid of 'selfishness'. No sooner a person gets liberated from his selfishness than his mind and senses both vanish into thin air. Thereupon, when the soul leaves the body, nothing goes along with the soul; and the soul merges with the Supreme Soul for eternity. Ergo, O Arjuna, you too must rise above your 'self-interest' and fight for the betterment of all. In so doing, your mind and senses will be obliterated. And in that case, you will be liberated from returning, time after time, to this mortal world of sorrow and pain. Bear in mind, O Arjuna, it is your selfishness which makes you agonise over victory-vanquishment and life-death; whereas I am directing you to the path of attaining "the supreme state of the Supreme Soul". So, resolutely stand up to fight for the spiritual path of betterment of all, that is, the elimination of sinners.

In fact, there abounds grave confusion concerning this subject, for the ignoramuses believe that this supreme state exists beyond

O Arjuna, elevating oneself to a state of having **"care** and **concern for all"** from just being **"concerned about oneself"** is the simplest way of realising the **Supreme Soul** death. But the wise don't share the same view; they discern all three of my forms, i.e., the one assuming the body, the one departing from the body, and even the one that experiences life while being in the body. Now, I have already assumed the body, so you have verily lost that opportunity to know me thus. Likewise, when I will depart from the body is a matter pertaining to the future, so there is no point in discussing that right now. But you can at least comprehend my form dwelling in the body at present. And not just you, everybody in the world has the opportunity to know the Supreme Soul in the 'present' alone. You too have that chance in the form of this war at present. Thus, simply engage in it for the greater good. In so doing, you will realise me, the Supreme Soul, dwelling in your heart in its essence. However, if there exists even an ounce of selfishness within, then you will be deprived of the great opportunity of knowing the Supreme Soul.

O Arjuna, while on one hand, I dwell in the hearts of human beings, on the other, I also pervade the entire universe. Know the radiance of the sun, moon and fire to be a manifestation of me. I am the one who permeates the Earth and assumes life by supporting all the creatures of the world. I am the one who ensures the sustenance of life and again, I am the one who digests food for that purpose as well. O Arjuna, my form as the Supreme Soul has been extolled as worth comprehending in the scriptures and once again, I am the one who, well versed with these scriptures, knows them through and through. Know that, be it human beings or the scriptures, I am the one who exists within everyone as well as without. I prevail in the world in two forms; one, imperishable and the other, perishable. To speak of human beings, I am both their perishable body and the imperishable soul. That is why the one who speaks of realising the soul by renouncing the body is always wrong. For, ultimately, both are my forms. In my opinion, the person who concerns himself only with the body is certainly wrong, but the person who contemplates only the soul is not entirely right either. The best and supreme among human beings is the one who, striking a perfect balance and harmony between the two, devotes himself to the well-being of the world. For, as long as there is life, the body and the soul are incomplete without each other. While the human being, devoid of soul, can never rise above selfishness; the soul, without body, cannot perform any task for the betterment of the world on its own. Thus, you too must establish a union between "the soul's spirit of working towards the betterment of all" and "the body's ability to perform action". And on the strength of this union, wield your weapons "to annihilate the sinners for the good of all". Upon fighting the war in such a mindset, the Supreme Soul will pervade within and without you. Only the human being whose body and soul continually perform *karma* in perfect unison and harmony is 'my *Purusottam* form, my form as the Supreme Person'. O Arjuna, in brief, I have spoken to you of this extremely esoteric form of mine. Grasping it in essence, even the most ordinary human beings can become wise, whereas you, O Arjuna, are quite sensible. Thus, establish a complete union between the body and the soul and march into the battle. Upon doing so, you will instantly attain my "form as the Supreme Person".

Krishna had exhausted every means and approach possible to convince Arjuna that 'fighting the war' was the best alternative available to him. But Arjuna was still not willing to take up arms. What was the reason for his refusal? The only reason was—his ego. Indeed, ego is that very nuisance which latches onto something quickly, but finds it difficult to let it go. To latch onto something new, and then not change once it has clung onto it, is the chief characteristic of ego. And ego is verily the main reason for the sorry state of human beings. No matter how tormenting and detrimental one's beliefs, thinking and obduracy are, his ego is just not able to forsake them. Despite listening to words that are positive, beneficial and truthful, if one still clings onto his long-standing beliefs and notions, then it is nothing but a form of ego. And this tendency is the prime reason for the human being's ruination. So, even after knowing, listening to or comprehending ideas or notions that are novel and beneficial, if you are still clinging onto old beliefs and habits, then beware! Because, only those who can adopt every novel and beneficial idea or notion, and change themselves accordingly can turn their lives around for the better. So, learn to speedily embrace and adopt forthwith all things that are novel and beneficial. And for that purpose, fill in the chart below carefully. In the topmost section, write about the notions and habits that you have been believing in strongly and practising for years together. In the next section, write the idea or notion that you have been newly acquainted with, with regard to these beliefs and practices. Then, after a thorough contemplation on both ideas and notions, check which of the two is actually superior. And if the novel idea is the superior option, start implementing it at the earliest. Undertake this exercise for five notions and habits you have been nursing for years. Every new lesson is verily a Gita; and one need not stretch every Gita to eighteen long chapters! Else, in today's fast-paced world, you will be met with nothing but failure. Remember, time is of utmost importance and yet, there is a lot to learn. Hence, it is imperative to effect a change promptly and efficaciously; for it is amply clear that your current way of being is not helping you progress in life. Therefore, from this very day, start making efforts to bring an improvement in yourself at a quicker pace.

1

Write about a notion or habit you have been nursing for years

....
....
....
....
....

Write the novel and beneficial take on it that you have been acquainted with recently

....
....
....
....
....
....

Write which of the two is superior

....
....
....

Write about the superior option in detail

....
....
....
....
....
....
....
....

Write about a notion or habit you have been nursing for years

....
....
....
....
....

Write the novel and beneficial take on it that you have been acquainted with recently

....
....
....
....
....
....

Write which of the two is superior

....
....
....

Write about the superior option in detail

....
....
....
....
....
....
....
....

Write about a notion or habit you have been nursing for years

....
....
....
....
....

Write the novel and beneficial take on it that you have been acquainted with recently

....
....
....
....
....
....

Write which of the two is superior

....
....
....

Write about the superior option in detail

....
....
....
....
....
....
....
....

4 Write about a notion or habit you have been nursing for years

....
....
....
....
....

Write the novel and beneficial take on it that you have been acquainted with recently

....
....
....
....
....
....

Write which of the two is superior

....
....
....

Write about the superior option in detail

....
....
....
....
....
....
....
....

Write about a notion or habit you have been nursing for years

....

....

....

....

....

Write the novel and beneficial take on it that you have been acquainted with recently

....

....

....

....

....

....

Write which of the two is superior

....

....

....

Write about the superior option in detail

....

....

....

....

....

....

....

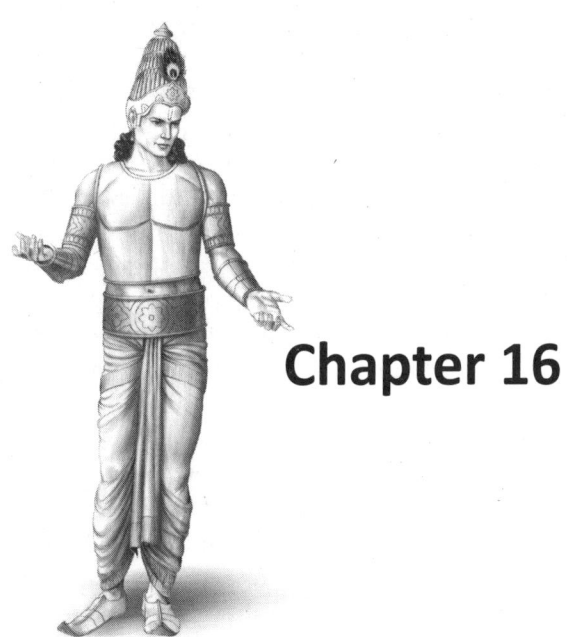

Chapter 16

Krishna:

O Arjuna, this world is populated by human beings with two distinct mindsets. The first are those brimming with marks of divine endowments, while the second are those gripped by a demoniac tendency. The person with a divine nature, having risen above his self-interest, lives for the greater good, whereas a person with demoniac propensity is prey to a selfish mindset. Thus, it is incumbent on every human being to rise to the state of divine mindset. In other words, the only means to one's liberation is "to transcend one's self-interest and traverse the spiritual path", that is, to elevate oneself from self-interest to engage in the interest of the greater good. Otherwise, the demoniac tendency perpetually ensnares the human being in a multitude of fetters.

I will reveal the marks of a person who has attained divine nature, for this will aid you in recognising your own self. Firstly, there is an absence of fear in a person endowed with divine nature. Indeed, what is there to fear when there is no self-interest at all? You too must oust from the war all your concerns risen out of self-interest, and all your fears will vanish in the blink of an eye. Secondly, a person with a divine nature endures well-nigh any adversity in order to adhere to his *Swadharma*. And to state this in your context, your *Swadharma* is to honour your wishes and those of your family. You cannot abandon your *Swadharma*, which at present, is this battle, owing to your fear of defeat or death. Moreover, non-existence of sense of doership, absence of fickleness in the mind, non-existence of desire for fruits of actions, absence of indulgence in futile efforts are all natural characteristics of a person with a divine nature. Nonetheless, the greatest specialty of a person with a divine nature is not letting animosity rise within himself against anyone, irrespective of the provocation. Ergo, you too should arm yourself to fight this war considering the Kauravas to be an 'instrument', instead of your 'enemy'. Because eventually, everybody in this world is a '*nimmit*' – a medium sent by the Supreme Soul. And to recognise everyone as being an instrument and a medium of the Supreme Soul is the only true knowledge. Thus, you too must become an instrument of the Supreme Soul in this war, instead of being its doer. Upon doing so, you will immediately be freed from the fetters of all *karma*. Contrary to this, pride, arrogance, harshness and ignorance are the marks of a person with a demoniac nature.

But Arjuna, why should you be worried? For, you are a person endowed with divine nature. 'Well, I had to say this, because when one has to launch a decisive attack on someone, one has to flatter them first. Indeed, it is always better to praise someone before offering a suggestion to them.' So, having praised him, I immediately said, "But Arjuna, you must comprehend that one's scriptures, that is, one's inner consciousness, is the sole guide in determining "what should be done and what should not be done". Ergo, let your soul alone determine whether you must fight or flee the battle. A human being's inner consciousness inevitably leads him to engage himself in "ordained deeds". O Arjuna, here, you must also discern what ordained *karma* (ordained deeds) imply. Actually, Nature's design is such that every moment, Nature goes about determining and deciding "who has to do what" in this world. But the human being, since his soul is not awakened, gets engrossed in seeking numerous possibilities contrary to his ordained *karma*. This verily is everyone's ignorance in this world, and this is the reason everyone in this world is engaged in *akartavya*, i.e., being ignorant towards one's duty. Consider yourself for instance; the battle has become inevitable by way of Nature's grand *leela*. And when the war has become inevitable, then "to battle wholeheartedly has become your naturally ordained *karma*". Yet, you are agonising over everything, be it the scriptures or your self-interest and looking for countless possibilities other than engaging in the war. But believe me, and delve within your soul; you have absolutely no alternative at this moment other than to fight this war. This is the "ordained *karma*" decreed for you by Nature, at the present moment. There is not an iota of doubt in it! However, propelled by ignorance, the human being insists on making his own decisions and consequently, he becomes disinclined to perform even those 'deeds and duties' which have been decreed for him by Nature.

O Arjuna, most importantly, a person with a demoniac nature isn't familiar with his own *Pravritti*, i.e., he knows not what the right activity is, and *Nivritti*, i.e., what the right abstinence from activity is. He is unable to comprehend that not only external circumstances but also the *Pravritti* and *Nivritti* unfolding in his own mind are governed by Nature. That is why the human being should flow along with the *Pravritti* rising within and not choose to suppress or stifle it. He must realise that no *Pravritti* emanating within him is perpetual. Each *Pravritti* verily recedes and retires in due course of time. However, at any point of time, when a *Pravritti* has risen, the human being must accept it and act accordingly in its support. He should allow the actual *Pravritti* stirring within him to manifest outside, in its entirety. This purity within and without is the primary characteristic of a person having attained divine nature. This complete purity verily denotes his truthfulness as well as an ideal conduct. And your inner *Pravritti*, Arjuna, is also blatantly clear. In it lies the yearning to attain the kingdom and also the desire to avenge yourself against the wrongs inflicted upon you by the Kauravas. Such being the case, what is the use of speaking and acting contrary to your own truth? Flow with your true *Pravritti*. One day, this *Pravritti* of yours will also disappear. Your desire for the kingdom will fade and the animosity you harbour towards the Kauravas will also vanish. Thereafter, you will never find yourself standing in a battlefield either. But today, it is in your best interest to flow with "your present

Pravritti". A person can never attain union with Nature without flowing in sync with his *Pravritti*. And no person can attain divine nature without establishing a union with Nature. Furthermore, he cannot be liberated without attaining divine nature.

O Arjuna, the greatest peculiarity of people with a demoniac nature is that they believe this world to be baseless, unreal and godless; they think it has come into existence on its own "by virtue of copulation". And more often than not, these are the very people who evince greater interest in *Ishwar*. But to really believe in *Ishwar* implies knowing that every particle of this world has been created by that one *Ishwar*. And when every particle of the world has been created by that one *Ishwar*, then there is no scope for differentiation in it. But unfortunately, not only are the majority of scriptures bent on teaching differences but they are all prey to mutual discrimination too. And that is why every person with a demoniac nature has fashioned his very own *Ishwar*. However, a person with a divine nature knows in his heart that this entire world is the creation of the one *Ishwar*. Indeed, it is impossible for *Ishwar's* creation to be imperfect or tainted, and there cannot be anything superior or inferior in it either. Such being the case, how can anybody reject this war as being insignificant? O Arjuna, a person with a divine nature believes that "everything in this world is functioning and governed by one divine law, in the best interest of one and all". That is why he goes on undertaking deeds which are worth performing, believing that "everything that is happening is verily happening for the best". Contrary to this, a person with a demoniac nature, on one hand, speaks of believing in *Ishwar*, and on the other, is inadvertently engaged in striving to change whatever is happening in his life. But the bitter truth is, as long as a person doesn't completely believe that "whatever happened has happened for the best, whatever is happening is happening for the best, and whatever will happen will also be for the best", he cannot be termed a true believer (in *Ishwar*) even though outwardly, he may ramble on about nothing but *Ishwar*.

O Arjuna, if you too give it a thought and observe everyone around you, you will realise what I mean. People who believe that whatever is happening is not transpiring in accordance with the desire of the one *Ishwar* are consumed with hypocrisy, conceit and arrogance. And that is why they find fault in everything that is happening and nurse false hopes of changing that which is happening. Then, in order to fulfil those false hopes, they resort to all kinds of deceitful, false and corrupt principles in the name of religion and scriptures. These are the very people who ensnare themselves in untold traps of virtue-sin and heaven-hell. Such people, desirous to change everything, are always besieged by countless worries and aspirations. They are not able to dispel these worries and aspirations even when they breathe their last. They always go about complaining that "there is very little happiness and comfort in the world". Such people, shackled in countless bonds of expectation, keep rushing through life wreathed in the garland of discontent. They always think about what they have attained today and what they shall attain tomorrow; they have vanquished this enemy today, and they have to defeat that one tomorrow. These people nurse ego, saying I will perform such and such *yajna*, give so much in charity and earn a certain virtue. Not only do such people with a demoniac nature harbour a devilish mindset while they are alive, but such is their misfortune that even after death they bear the selfsame state of mind. Know that all such people bear rancour towards me, the *Ishwar*, who dwells within everybody's heart. Mark my words, O Arjuna, time after time, I cast such people into demoniac wombs.

Thus, O Arjuna! Do not bear animosity towards me, the omniscient *Ishwar* dwelling in your heart; rather, take refuge in me.

Know that everything is happening in accordance with the *Ishwar's* desire alone. And with this knowledge, let what he has decided become the reality. Do not try to change it. Do not nurse futile worries in order to change that which is happening; do not even wish to change anything! Do not try to change the course of this war nor the environment in which you have to fight. Do not nurse the desire to attain the kingdom which you do not possess at present, nor commit the mistake of perceiving the Kauravas as your enemies. Anchor yourself in a thoughtless state of mind and identify the *karma* ordained for you in the present situation. And believe once and for all that the human being's authority is limited only to "earnestly undertaking his ordained *karma*". And recognising this limitation of one's authority is the sole knowledge, the only duty and the sole truth. This is the only path available to the human being in order to become one with me. Thus, the limited power endowed to you as a human being only requires you to become instrumental in this war. You must leave all other decisions besides this to that highest supreme authority. So, blithely become the instrument of this war and leave everything else to that supreme force.

In this chapter, Krishna says, instead of 'performing' a deed, it is far better to become 'instrumental' in a deed. What does being 'instrumental' imply? It simply means, I am serving as a means to a deed for someone. Then, it is not necessary that every time, that someone is '*sarva*', that is, the Supreme Soul. For, one can always become instrumental, that is, act as a medium in executing noble tasks and aiding noble people. In essence, Krishna says, instead of performing deeds for myself alone, it is better to engage in deeds in others' interest wherein I am serving as a medium or an 'instrument' to accomplish the deed. And this is verily the most potent magic that creates wonders. The one who continuously engages in tasks by becoming 'instrumental' soon experiences the feeling of soaring in the sky on the wings of uninhibited joy! A point to ponder here is, everyone is striving to earn for themselves, but why isn't everyone able to do it? This is precisely what we need to fathom. Try to earn for the Supreme Soul, for the world and sometimes for others; earning will become so easy that you will be left surprised. Remember, Nature is an expansive science in itself, and Krishna is making all statements within the purview of that science. Therefore, in essence, learn to become instrumental to the deeds. To start off, become instrumental two-three times... then, ten times or so, and thereafter, forever become instrumental to the deeds in the larger interest. In doing so, forget about yourself, the whole world will be in awe of your life. So, first, resolve to become instrumental to the deeds in the larger interest. Then, in the following chart, write about the first five deeds that you have performed after becoming instrumental to them and pen your experience about them in detail. And when you see those deeds produce results, write about that as well. And when you start experiencing a feeling of lightness within on account of becoming instrumental and the splendid results it brings externally, don't stop at all. Indeed, you must not let go of any opportunity to become instrumental in a deed thereafter.

1 Write in detail the deed you have performed by becoming instrumental

....
....
....
....

Write how you felt within while performing the deed

....
....
....

When you get the result of the deed, write about that too

....
....
....

2 Write in detail the deed you have performed by becoming instrumental

....
....
....
....

Write how you felt within while performing the deed

....
....
....

When you get the result of the deed, write about that too

....
....
....

3 Write in detail the deed you have performed by becoming instrumental

....
....
....
....

Write how you felt within while performing the deed

....
....
....

When you get the result of the deed, write about that too

....
....
....

4 Write in detail the deed you have performed by becoming instrumental

....
....
....
....

Write how you felt within while performing the deed

....
....
....

When you get the result of the deed, write about that too

....
....
....

5 Write in detail the deed you have performed by becoming instrumental

....
....
....
....

Write how you felt within while performing the deed

....
....
....

When you get the result of the deed, write about that too

....
....
....

Chapter 17

Arjuna:
Well, I have comprehended the purport of your words. Here, for the human being, his consciousness, his soul is supreme; rather, it is the be-all and end-all for him. Hence, seeking refuge in the soul, he should undertake tasks only as prompted by the soul. I have fathomed that the human being's soul is his one and only true scripture. All external scriptures and knowledge are inconsequential in comparison to it. But Krishna! My question is, should the worship offered by a person who is unable to forge a connection with his soul, and who cloaks himself in external devoutness in keeping with his beliefs and "worships gods other than his soul" be considered *Sattvika* or *Rajasika*? Or is such worship *Tamasika*?

Krishna:
Now, time is slipping through our fingers, and I have explained to Arjuna earlier as well that he has no alternative other than to fight the war. But his questions have made it amply clear that he is still not willing to fight. However, this time around, his query reflects both honesty and curiosity. In no uncertain terms, he is saying, "I have understood that the human being's soul is his be-all and end-all. But what if I am unable to anchor myself in it? What if I fail to hearken to its call? In

such a situation, I will have to resort to the scriptures composed by other learned men. In such an event, would that refuge be considered *Sattvika*, *Rajasika* or *Tamasika*? Well, when the question was so apt, it certainly deserved a comprehensive answer by Krishna. Hence, I replied, "O Arjuna, those people who choose to deny their own scripture and values, and become influenced by external scriptures can be either *Sattvika*, *Rajasika* or *Tamasika*. For, even in this case, it is one's mental disposition, i.e., his state of mind which matters, not his external actions or influences. Hence, at first, comprehend that it is the mindset—one's state of mind—which is *Sattvika*, *Rajasika* or *Tamasika* in nature, not his actions.

Furthermore, O Arjuna, this entire world, based on the Three Dimensional Theory, is teeming with people engaged in three kinds of worship. Amongst them, people with a *Sattvika* mindset revere gods, i.e., people of great wisdom, artists and scientists. For, all these people are committed to the welfare of the world and remain persistently engaged in it through their deeds; whereas, people with a *Rajasika* mindset have faith in demons, that is to say, the rich and the powerful. However, people with a *Tamasika* mindset pledge their troth even to the dead, meaning, they put their faith "in the gods who have perished and the idols and effigies of demons". Then, these very people conduct *yajna*, penance and worship as per their whims and fancies on the strength of their ego, desire and attachment. Not only do these people act against their inner conscience, but they also disregard the living, breathing human beings. Such people turn a blind eye to the living beings and instead expend their energy and wealth on the dead; those who have ceased to exist or do not exist.

O Arjuna! This difference between *Sattvika*, *Rajasika* and *Tamasika* is reflected not only in the subject of faith but is also apparent in all the ordinary, routine *karmas* of life. For, regardless of the *karma*, it is eventually the human being's mindset which propels him to undertake *karma*. That is why I proclaim, it is not the human being's actions which are *Sattvika*, *Rajasika* or *Tamasika*, but rather, his mindset. If I were to speak of this in terms of food preferences, then generally, human beings of *Tamasika* disposition are fond of food that is bitter, stale, raw and oily. I have brought up the subject of food because the body affects the mind, which in turn affects the body. And it is for this very reason that all my life, I never disregarded my body. For, after all, the soul also dwells within the body; the body is its abode. Moving further, foods that are hot and spicy are usually loved by those with a *Rajasika* mindset. And foods which enhance one's longevity, strength and health are dear to people bearing a *Sattvika* mindset. But, O Arjuna, those people who transcend these three qualities and anchor themselves in their soul make "no distinction in deeds or with respect to food". Their mindset remains unchanged regardless of the type and quantity of food they consume. Consider me for instance; even though I relished *Chhappan Bhog* all my life, my soul always remained unperturbed.

In a similar vein, O Arjuna, *yajna*, meaning, *karma* can also be of three kinds depending upon the mindset. The *karma* when performed without harbouring any expectation of fruits and considering it as one's duty is *Sattvika*, while those acts which are undertaken under the influence of ego or bearing the fruits in mind are *Rajasika*. However, actions that do not entail offering of food or donation, i.e., *karma* undertaken without keeping in mind one's own or others' well-being or harm, are *Tamasika* in nature. For, deeds performed thus in a state of anger or unawareness always prove detrimental to everyone, including oneself.

O Arjuna! You must also comprehend that every human being undertakes *karma* with the aid of the "body, speech or

> **Every** human being's **inner** consciousness is his very **own** scripture

mind". Therefore, honouring the wise and never troubling anybody unnecessarily is true penance of the body. Similarly, speaking the truth or speaking of the well-being of the person before you and not inciting anyone without reason are all penance concerning speech, which everybody must perform. Furthermore, maintaining a peaceful and joyous state of mind for oneself is the penance of the mind. And a human being must endeavour to remain engaged in such deeds through his body, speech and mind. This is what is known as 'penance'; penance, in fact, reflects through a person's deeds. In brief, whether an action is undertaken through the body, speech or mind, it can be considered *Sattvika* in nature only if the expectation of fruits from actions is absent. Otherwise, know that all deeds undertaken out of selfishness or in order to gain honour or reverence are nothing but *Rajasika* penance. And that penance which is undertaken out of utter foolishness in order to unnecessarily distress one's own body and mind should be considered penance that is *Tamasika* in nature.

However, O Arjuna, let me also explain to you the most profound aspect of this entire body of knowledge. The *karma* which does not have any effect on anyone outside does not create a bondage for the human being. But the *karmas* which affect or create an impact on others are at the root of all the problems of the human being. And this is where the human being needs to exercise caution. Thus, I assertively state that it is better to avoid performing those *karmas* which would have an influence or impact on others till the time you have not gained the supreme height of knowledge. For, all those acts which influence others echo back to you. Hence, how erroneous it is to presume that giving charity or serving others is always noble! It denotes nothing but a human being's ignorance and is the very reason for his suffering. For, eventually, even 'charity and service' is nothing but interference in people's lives, when the entire world is under the purview and jurisdiction of the Supreme Soul. And in the Supreme Soul's system of justice, each person is faring in accordance with his deeds. This is one deadly game which functions on automation. Thus, one should think long and hard before meddling with it. However, as long as there is life, others will be impacted by our conduct. So, Arjuna, I will speak to you of ways of dealing with others, adopting which you will be forever freed from the fetters of *karma* (action) despite engaging in action.

I shall begin with charity, which means helping others. Well, helping is essentially good, but even here, one needs to be careful. For, even in the case of charity, it is verily the mindset which is of paramount importance. Actually, the human being must act with the belief that giving charity, that is, helping others is his duty. Just as the Supreme Soul has discharged his duty unto human beings by providing them with the moon, stars, air, water and minerals; being a human, it is his duty to help others, and the one who leads his life deeply and earnestly holding onto this belief is the finest of the lot of humankind. Yet, even such a wise person needs to exercise caution before dispensing charity. Even he, before dispensing charity, needs to consider the time, place and the person to whom charity is being offered. For example, by wrong time, I mean, you cannot force a person with a full stomach to eat. Likewise, one also has to pay attention to the place before giving charity. Well, I shall explain this to you with your own example. To kill others unnecessarily is certainly wrong. But to speak of non-violence after arriving on the battlefield, when the battle is just about to begin, is "losing sense of place". Likewise, at the time of dispensing charity, it is also necessary to pay attention to the subject, that is, the person to whom you are giving charity. Let me illustrate this once again with your own example. It is certainly wrong to trouble or kill anybody, but this does not imply that sinners should be spared. I have killed a horde of sinners including Kansa, Panchajanya, Shringlava, Narakasura and Shishupala. These acts of slaying are also nothing but charity, because by slaying sinners, I provided peace to the populace. To summarise, O Arjuna, when our life is dependent on the charity of Nature and the contributions of a multitude of human beings, then without a doubt, it is also our duty to offer our best charity to other human beings. But yes, at the time of giving charity, a person must ensure that he is not meddling with the judicial system of Nature. In other words, he should ensure he is not sparing the life of the wrong person; or that he is not supporting the wrong person, driven by attachment. That is to say, the human being should always be mindful of the 'time, place and person' while offering charity. And only a charity which is appropriate to the time, place and person is considered "*Sattvika* charity". However, Arjuna, know that all charities dispensed with one's self-interest in mind, in order to gain respect or gratitude from others, are *Rajasika* in nature, while charities given out of disdain and without considering the "time, place and person" are *Tamasika* in nature.

O Arjuna! You must also comprehend the design of Nature; this Nature owes its existence to the union of "*Om*, *Tat* and *Sat*" and is also functioning because of the confluence of this triumvirate. *Om* is the omnipresent Supreme Soul, committed to everybody's well-being. Thus, the human being should begin his every *karma* with the resolve of safeguarding the welfare of all. *Tat* implies the feeling that everything in this world is verily the Supreme Soul, and such a feeling should inevitably prevail while undertaking any action. That is to say, a person should bear in mind while performing every task that any "gain-loss" resulting out of the deed belongs only to the Supreme Soul. Hence, he should not separately wish for any fruit out of self-interest while performing the deed. And *Sat* signifies focusing on *Om* in your mind and performing whichever task befalls you "for the greater good". *Sat* by itself means the task which lies before you. Simply stated, *Sat* means neither should you go about seeking a task nor should you avoid a task which befalls you. And if I were to explain this to you with your own example, then this war, which has befallen your path, is *Sat* for you. Thus, you should not forsake the battlefield and wander in the forests "to attain *Sat*". Rather, you should embrace this war as the truth, i.e., *Sat* and wage it bearing *Om*, i.e., the well-being of everyone in mind. You must reckon it as the blessing of the Supreme Soul. And *Tat* implies you must undertake this war with the belief that whatever be the result—whether victory or defeat—both belong only to the Supreme Soul. All of Nature's *karmas* are being performed through the union of this "*Om-Tat-Sat*" and the human being should also undertake all tasks that befall his way, bearing in mind these three, "*Om-Tat-Sat*". O Arjuna, any task that is undertaken disregarding even one of these three prove unfruitful in both this world and the next. Ergo, this war is verily your one and only truth. Just let your mind focus only on the Supreme Soul and arm yourself to wage the war considering everything as the Supreme Soul."

In this chapter, Krishna is teaching us a way to conduct ourselves vis-à-vis offering help or charity. He says, giving charity, that is, helping someone is essentially good, but to help or give charity to each and every person is certainly not right. That is because, no one here has enough resources to make everyone happy. Keeping in mind that the resources at one's disposal are limited, one should help others only according to their deservedness, and not compelled by relationships, love or affection. To be swayed by any kind of partiality while helping someone is entirely wrong. And these principles are applicable to every kind of help. Even if you have to doff your hat to someone, you should do it to great scientists, artists and thinkers, and definitely not to egoists. In essence, Krishna says, one should always help keeping in mind the 'time, place and person'. To offer charity at the wrong time, wrong place or to a wrong person will invariably bring detrimental results in its wake. This is an extremely profound science, and the inability to grasp the same puts most people in trouble. Therefore, grasp well that Nature helps only the right person, at the right time, and at the right place. Hence, you too must never go against Nature when offering charity; rather, you must help someone only as a '*nimmit*' – acting as the medium of Nature. In other words, you should support only him who is supported by Nature. Apart from this, every kind of help offered is nothing but interference in Nature's workings, and it inevitably begets grave results. You must bear in mind that to help a wrong person at the wrong time and at the wrong place is akin to handing a weapon to a murderer! In short, Krishna says, to offer help is verily a duty, but one must maintain awareness of the time, place and person. Henceforth, at the time of helping others, keep in mind the following chart, which will aid you in identifying the right time, right place and right person. So, for the first five times that you are thinking about helping someone, fill in this chart before offering the help. For, Krishna wants Nature to be your friend forever, and not turn into your enemy.

Write in detail about the person you want to help

....
....
....
....
....
....
....
....
....
....

If the time is right, this help will truly be essential, and will singularly aid that person to tide over his problem.

If your help fits into this criteria, put a tick here ☐

If the place is right, the person would be offered this help at the right juncture in life.

If your help fits into this criteria, put a tick here ☐

If the person is right, he will be capable of making progress with the aid of the help being offered to him.

If your help fits into this criteria, put a tick here ☐

Ensure that help isn't being offered for the sake of relationships, sympathy, to portray oneself as good or to earn respect.

If your help fits into this criteria, put a tick here ☐

....
....
....
....
....
....
....
....
....
....

If the time is right, this help will truly be essential, and will singularly aid that person to tide over his problem.

If your help fits into this criteria, put a tick here ☐

If the place is right, the person would be offered this help at the right juncture in life.

If your help fits into this criteria, put a tick here ☐

If the person is right, he will be capable of making progress with the aid of the help being offered to him.

If your help fits into this criteria, put a tick here ☐

Ensure that help isn't being offered for the sake of relationships, sympathy, to portray oneself as good or to earn respect.

If your help fits into this criteria, put a tick here ☐

....
....
....
....
....
....
....
....
....
....

If the time is right, this help will truly be essential, and will singularly aid that person to tide over his problem.

If your help fits into this criteria, put a tick here

If the place is right, the person would be offered this help at the right juncture in life.

If your help fits into this criteria, put a tick here

If the person is right, he will be capable of making progress with the aid of the help being offered to him.

If your help fits into this criteria, put a tick here

Ensure that help isn't being offered for the sake of relationships, sympathy, to portray oneself as good or to earn respect.

If your help fits into this criteria, put a tick here

Write in detail about the person you want to help

....
....
....
....
....
....
....
....
....
....
....

If the time is right, this help will truly be essential, and will singularly aid that person to tide over his problem.

If your help fits into this criteria, put a tick here ☐

If the place is right, the person would be offered this help at the right juncture in life.

If your help fits into this criteria, put a tick here ☐

If the person is right, he will be capable of making progress with the aid of the help being offered to him.

If your help fits into this criteria, put a tick here ☐

Ensure that help isn't being offered for the sake of relationships, sympathy, to portray oneself as good or to earn respect.

If your help fits into this criteria, put a tick here ☐

....
....
....
....
....
....
....
....
....
....

If the time is right, this help will truly be essential, and will singularly aid that person to tide over his problem.

If your help fits into this criteria, put a tick here ▢

If the place is right, the person would be offered this help at the right juncture in life.

If your help fits into this criteria, put a tick here ▢

If the person is right, he will be capable of making progress with the aid of the help being offered to him.

If your help fits into this criteria, put a tick here ▢

Ensure that help isn't being offered for the sake of relationships, sympathy, to portray oneself as good or to earn respect.

If your help fits into this criteria, put a tick here ▢

Note:

As far as possible, offer help only if you have ticked all the four boxes, especially in case of extending help that is significant in nature. For, one should not unnecessarily interfere in Nature's grand *leela* as much as possible. That is because, there is absolutely no dearth of capable individuals in this world; hence, as far as possible, make 'capability' and 'deservedness' the prime criteria for offering help to someone. In doing so, you will never go wrong!

Chapter 18

Arjuna:

O Krishna! I wish to fathom the depths of *Sanyasa* and *Tyaga* separately. Also, comprehensively explain their *Sattvika, Rajasika* and *Tamasika* divisions to me.

Krishna:

Incredible! Arjuna is just not ready to comprehend the precariousness of the situation. He fails to fathom that he is standing on the threshold of a battle, not educating himself in an *ashram*. He doesn't have years at his disposal to grasp what I am trying to explain to him but only a moment or two to decide! Besides, even after endless explanations on my part, he is still fixated on *Sanyasa* and *Tyaga*. In other words, his pledge to not fight is as intact as ever. Even though I have repeatedly explained what *karma* and duty essentially mean, he is still focused on fleeing the war under the cover of *Sanyasa* and *Tyaga*. But then, what alternative do I have apart from doing my utmost to persuade Arjuna till the very last moment? So, I immediately said, "O Arjuna, be it *Sanyasa* or *Tyaga*, 'karma' is at the root of both. *Sanyasa* and *Tyaga*

Man has such a remarkable **power** of **intuition** hidden within him that he can very well **reckon** that which is going to **transpire** in the **future**

by no means imply abstention from *karma*. As long as there is life, the human being has to perform *karma*. Thus, the sages term renouncing desire from *karma* as 'Sanyasa'. And, wise people term the forsaking of the fruits from *karma* as 'Tyaga'. All in all, be it *Sanyasa* or *Tyaga*, it is the self-interest that the human being has to expunge, not his *karma*. So, whether you wish to be a true *Sanyansi* or a veritable *Tyagi*, you ought to not forsake this war to that end; rather, you have to expel all your self-interests and renounce all your desires associated with this war.

O Arjuna, many scholars advocate relinquishment of *karma* with a view that all *karmas* contain a measure of evil. While some others are of the opinion that despite *karma* being sinful, the good *karma* must not be forsaken. However, as far as I am concerned, I am not in agreement with any of these people, be it in the matter of *Sanyasa* or *Tyaga*. For, I speak the truth, simple and forthright. Believe me, there is not an iota of corruption in my words. Hence, first listen to my view on 'Tyaga'. All of Nature is governed by the Three Dimensional Theory and it verily encompasses *Tyaga* as well. Hence, the belief that *Tyaga* is always the best is erroneous. For, even *Tyaga* has *Sattvika*, *Rajasika* or *Tamasika* dimensions to it. So, let me elucidate this difference in *Tyaga* in detail. But, bear in mind, even 'Tyaga' doesn't advocate renouncing or shunning action. Just look at the moon and the stars, the wind, water and Earth; none are deviating from their *karma* even for a moment. For, *karma* is the very prerequisite for being in existence. No sooner is *karma* relinquished than one ceases to exist, be it "an object or a person". Hence, to continually perform deeds and duties renouncing all kinds of attachment is the (classic) virtue of the supreme human beings. And such renouncement of attachment and fruits from deeds and duties is the only *Sattvika Tyaga*. But forsaking a deed in anticipation of a possible hardship is not a valid reason to relinquish *karma*. For, the human being has to perform *karma*, bearing in mind everybody's gain or loss, not his own. Thus, O Arjuna, you too should not focus on your own gain-loss in this battle. To forsake anxiety over one's own gain-loss is the only *Tyaga* which is truly *Sattvika* in nature. On the other hand, forsaking *karma* fearing one's own loss is *Rajasika Tyaga*. But such *Rajasika Tyaga* can never be considered true *Tyaga*. Lastly, entrapped in the web of attachment, if somebody starts renouncing even the ordained *karmas*, then such forsaking of deeds is termed '*Tamasika*'. And remember, O Arjuna, at present, this battle is the "*karma* ordained for you" by Nature.

Significantly, this grand *leela* of Nature is functioning on automation. Here, neither does the human being need to choose any *karma* nor renounce any. Hence, only the one who does not disdain and is not averse to performing a deed, considering it inauspicious; and who does not get lured towards performing other deeds, considering them to be auspicious, continually undertakes "deeds which are worth performing". Otherwise, a person, ensnared in the web of auspicious and inauspicious actions, often fails to undertake even his basic 'deeds and duties', just as you are wishing to forsake this war at the moment, deeming it as ill-boding. But this is not the spirit of a true *Tyaga*. You must also grasp that choosing or forsaking deeds on the basis of self-interest is not a *Sattvika* quality by any measure. O Arjuna, it is a law that people who choose deeds driven by their self-interest persistently reap joy and sorrow on the basis of their choices. But those, who renounce the fruits of *karma* for good, do not have to bear the fruits of their *karma* at all. For, ultimately, be it deeds or fruits, both are the province of the mind. A person beams with joy if he attains the desired fruits and he grieves if he receives fruits contrary to his expectations. However, the one who never craves fruits within, remains unaffected, regardless of the outcome.

O Arjuna, I am the wisest of the wise on the subject of human mind and life. Hence, let me enlighten you on the five fundamental reasons behind craving fruits. You must focus on this; for, the human being's lust for fruits will not be expunged till even one of these continue to exist. The first reason for the lust of fruits is *Adhisthan*—a sanctuary or refuge. In other words, the greed for fruits rears its head in human beings if they receive somebody's refuge or assurance. Most scriptures I have seen give rise to the craving for fruits in people verily by providing refuge. If you too are agonising over heaven and hell at present, then these very scriptures steeped in ignorance are responsible for it. Secondly, "one's own capability" is another reason behind the kindling of greed for fruits in the human being. Simply observe for yourself; since you were confident of your ability as an archer, you are standing here on this battlefield yearning for the fruits in the form of a kingdom. Had you not been valiant, the desire for the kingdom would not have arisen within you either. Thirdly, many a time, chance and co-incidences also rouse the craving for fruits in a human being. Fourthly, quite often, a person falls prey to the greed for fruits owing to favourable circumstances and situations. And fifthly, oftentimes, a person's own desires lead him to hanker after the fruits of action. O Arjuna, these are the five principal reasons behind everything that a human being does contrary to the glorious ongoing *leela* of Nature. However, the human being assumes that his soul is the doer of his actions, and not these five reasons. And this is verily his greatest ignorance. Here, everybody must grasp that these five reasons are responsible for all that is happening in their life, not the Supreme Soul. The Supreme Soul has a world of its own wherein dwell those who have risen above these five reasons. And if you are unable to comprehend my words at the moment, then it is these very five reasons that are responsible for it. For, I am speaking of and from the realm of the Supreme Soul, which you are trying to seek in these five reasons.

O Arjuna, know that it is the lust for fruits which inevitably gives rise to the sense of doership in a human being. For, the sense of "doership" simply cannot arise in a person who doesn't crave fruits. And the person, unencumbered by the sense of doership, will not incur sin even if he obliterates all the worlds, let alone the warriors present in this war. For, how can a person, imbued with the spirit of non-doership, ever destroy anyone? The Supreme Soul has created and destroyed this world countless times, but the Supreme Soul itself has always been sinless. For, the sense of doership is invariably absent in the Supreme Soul. Hence, do not think of renouncing the war; just renounce the sense of doership. Thereafter, even if you unleash untold carnage, I promise you, having undertaken this one *Tyaga*, you will not incur sin.

Nevertheless, if you are still unable to comprehend, let me expound the "science of *karma*" in greater detail. Please endeavour to grasp this as expeditiously as you can, for we haven't got much time at hand. O Arjuna! *Jnyaata*, *Jnyaan* and *Jnyey* together propel a human being to undertake an action. *Jnyaata* is the perceiver or the knower. In this world, everybody's *Jnyaata* is formidable; that is why, everybody here has assumed a separate individual existence for himself, just as you have believed yourself to be Arjuna. Moving along, this *Jnyaata* embraces *Jnyaan* or knowledge to realise his self-interests. His knowledge, in turn, gives rise to several reasons for undertaking an action, just like your knowledge of warfare has dragged you to the battlefield, while your knowledge of the scriptures is prompting you to flee this battle. And the third reason which inspires a person to act is *Jnyey*, i.e., resources. Just as you have come to the battlefield banking upon weapons, and are now trying to flee this battle with the means of a chariot. All in all, in the absence of *Jnyaata, Jnyaan* and *Jnyey*, a human being would never endeavour to choose between *karmas*. Becoming a pure witness, he would go on performing the deeds ordained by Nature. Furthermore, O Arjuna, just as the human being undertakes an action driven by three reasons, he also has to bear the fruits of those actions for the following three reasons. Firstly, having a sense of doership, i.e., harbouring the delusion that one can do something on his own, is the primary reason for "bearing the fruits of action". Secondly, the 'reason', i.e., selfishness behind committing an action, propelled by which a person drifts away from this ongoing *leela* of Nature and engages himself in deeds that are in conflict with Nature. And the greater part of his suffering is endowed to this reason. Thirdly, the process, meaning, the mode and method of performing an action.

O Arjuna, the one who gets liberated from this triumvirate, never has to bear the fruits of his actions.

Moving further, since you have expressed an interest in this knowledge, you must comprehend the difference between the virtues of *Jnyaan*, *karma* and doer as well. I will begin by discussing "*Jnyaan*". Arjuna, know well that the knowledge which helps a person perceive all the varied kinds of physical objects and living species as the manifestation of the one Supreme Soul, is *Sattvika* in nature. Do not commit the mistake of deeming the knowledge, which engenders any kind of difference for any reason whatsoever, to be *Sattvika*. Likewise, the knowledge through which a person perceives everyone's emotions as separate and distinct is *Rajasika* in nature. And lastly, the knowledge which teaches sheer selfishness is nothing but *Tamasika*.

O Arjuna, similarly, grasp the difference between actions at length. Recognise only those deeds which a person performs without the lust for fruits as '*Sattvika*' *karma*. *Sanyasa* embraced lusting for the fruits or *Tyaga* undertaken with such an objective should never be considered a '*Sattvika*' *karma*. Why, even worshipping the Supreme Soul driven by the greed for fruits cannot be considered a *Sattvika karma*. But, if it is undertaken without the lust for fruits then even a war becomes *Sattvika karma*. Similarly, know all the *karmas* that a person undertakes seeking self-gratification and all the efforts he employs to this end, to be *Rajasika karma*. However, all deeds performed with no concern for the outcome and solely out of impetuousness, should be perceived as *Tamasika* in nature. This is not all; all deeds performed without realising one's capability are also *Tamasika* in nature. And it is people with such *Tamasika* nature that are intent on bringing doom upon themselves. At present, the Kauravas stationed in the battlefield are the best example of such destructive tendency.

Further, O Arjuna, I shall elucidate the differences between doers, which you must grasp. The doer who is free of attachment with the world, i.e., the one who is happy and content within himself is considered a *Sattvika karta*. Similarly, the doer who is interested only in the task and does not get perturbed by the difficulties that arise in the execution of the task is also a *Sattvika* doer. However, gripped with attachment and greed, the doer who experiences and endures sorrow at the slightest instance because of his greed and attachment is a *Rajasika* doer. And a person who is arrogant and deceitful, who acts in order to inflict harm upon others, is a *Tamasika* doer.

However, since I'm expounding the profound secrets of the human mind, you must grasp how various kinds of intellects and firmness differ from each other. As per the existential Three Dimensional Theory, human intellect is also of three different kinds. The intellect which views all of the world's *Pravritti* and *Nivritti* (the paths of activity and renunciation), the entire gamut of *Kartavya* and *Akartavyas* (what ought to be done and what ought not to be done) and even all kinds of bondage and *moksha* (deliverance) as appearing and disappearing in the course of time through the divine play of Nature, is a mindset which is *Sattvika* in nature. Only the one who beholds the one Supreme Soul and not himself or others as the doer of all that transpires within and without, is the one who perceives the truth. Similarly, the intellect engaged in choosing between "*Dharma* and *Adharma*", what is deemed religious and what is not, and "*Kartavya* and *Akartavya*" on the strength of his knowledge is *Rajasika*. And at the moment, you too are involved in making a similar choice. But the intellect that perceives even *Adharma* as *Dharma* is *Tamasika* in nature. And the vast majority of people in the world are victims of such *Tamasika* mentality. Everybody is committing the mistake of believing religious ceremonies and rituals performed with the expectation of fruits to be *Dharma*.

O Arjuna! Similarly, a person's absorption capacity is classified into three categories. The person who mindfully embraces the functions of the mind, the *prana* and the senses, is considered to possess *Sattvika* absorption capacity. In other words, the person who understands his existence, i.e., the purpose, path and mechanism of his existence and aligns himself with it should be considered as the one treading the true path of life. For, everyone must comprehend that no one can flourish in this world by going against oneself, i.e., by straying away from who one really is. Likewise, the person who assumes *dharma* or beliefs, thoughts and material wealth on the strength of his desires and attachment should be considered to possess "*Rajasika* power of absorption". But the person whose mind is constantly gripped by fear, anxiety and grief, and is not able to dispel them despite wanting to, is a person having *Tamasika* power of absorption.

O Arjuna! Now hearken from me the diverse kinds of joys in human beings. The one who is happy by himself is considered a true seeker of *Sattvika* joy. The person who is always engaged in deeds for the pursuit of happiness, including its end result, should also be considered desirous of joy which is *Sattvika* in nature. Thus, I am not against the pursuit of joy. I have no objection if you too are seeking joy in this war. But you must decide after due deliberation whether you will attain lasting joy upon fighting in the war or in fleeing from it. For, the joy which is dependent on "the contact of the sense with the objects" is essentially *Rajasika* in nature. You too were yearning for the joy of ruling the kingdom when you were certain of emerging victorious in the war, but today, when you are no longer confident of victory, you wish to deprive yourself of the joy of ruling the kingdom of Hastinapur. People whose joys and sorrows change with changes in external subjects, situations and circumstances are known as seekers of joy which is *Rajasika* in nature. Similarly, those who willingly embrace grave sorrow of the future in order to mitigate their present woes should be considered *Tamasika*. And presently, you too are inching towards *Tamasika* joy from the joy which was basically *Rajasika* in nature. But mark my words, if you flee the battlefield, you will suffer tribulations a thousand times more grievous in the future than your present hardship.

O Arjuna! Whether it is the Earth, the sky and space, the land of the gods or any other thing you can think of, none amongst them is untouched by this Three Dimensional Theory of Nature. And on that basis, even in the case of humankind, "the human being's deeds have been segmented according to his intrinsic nature". And no person can refuse to perform these intrinsic duties assigned to him without reason. In other words, being a *Kshatriya*, you cannot refuse to fight this war for fear of being vanquished. For, bravery, power, majesty, self-esteem and the steadfastness to never desert the battle without reason are all intrinsic qualities of a *Kshatriya*. Likewise, *Brahmin*, *Vaishya* and *Shudra* also have their respective quintessential qualities. That is why, nobody in this world can evade their intrinsic *karma*. Moreover, O Arjuna, to let you in on another secret; no *Kshatriya* or *Shudra* in this world need become a *Brahmin* in order to attain the Supreme Soul. Such misconceptions are propagated by selfish and ignorant people with ulterior motives. Be it *Kshatriya* or *Shudra*, *Vaishya* or *Brahmin*, everybody can attain the Supreme Soul by renouncing the fruits of *karma* while performing their *karma* earnestly.

O Arjuna! Every kind of *karma* is beset by "some fault or the other". If the Sun bestows life, then it also scorches with heat. Even so, it does not renounce the noble act of bestowing life, plagued by guilt for its act of scorching. Likewise, when you fight, there will certainly be bloodshed, but gripped by that fear, you cannot squander the opportunity of eliminating the sinners. Thus, instead of fleeing the war, introspect and focus on the pervasive tendencies of your mind which are prompting you to question the battle. Recognise the lust for fruits hidden at the root of all these perversions. You must realise that once you relinquish the greed for fruits, all your personal reasons for fighting or fleeing the battle will vanish. Thereafter, you will march in to fight without any qualms, with the sole objective of annihilating the sinners. Upon fighting the war thus, you will become one with the Supreme Soul. And as I have repeatedly stated, being anchored in equanimity is the only way of renouncing the lust of fruits. Thus, fight not for yourself but for the sake of the Supreme Soul. As he wants the sinners to be annihilated, become his instrument to that end. You must dedicate

Nature has a **law** that it **never** grants anything to an **undeserving** **person**

both your *karma* and your concern for its outcome to me. You must nullify your individual existence and involvement. Thereupon, it is not you, but I who will fight this war. And when I fight in your place, I will deliver you from all your trials and tribulations in a moment. But trapped in self-interest, arrogance and misleading knowledge, if you do not heed my words, then you are certain to be doomed. And as I have already manifested my universal form before you, you have no reason other than your arrogance to disbelieve my words. And primarily, it is my duty to vanquish every ego that rears its ugly head. Let me tell you in no uncertain terms, I will not heed friendship or familial relations while discharging my deeds and duties."

Well, what could I do? You must understand my situation too; the annihilation of the Kauravas had become inevitable by the course of their own *karma*. But Nature wasn't going to effect this destruction by itself. Human beings would have to become instrumental for that purpose. Such being the case, it is my duty to ensure that Arjuna continues to remain instrumental in Nature's plan and doesn't flee the battlefield. And I am willing to discharge this duty till my last breath. However, time permits me no such luxury. At present, the scene before my eyes is signalling the commencement of the battle, with the bugle ready to announce the war at any moment. Besides, I had spared no effort in explaining the precariousness of the situation to Arjuna, and the possibility of him comprehending in the future what he could not comprehend so far is next to none. Thus, it was better to launch an aggressive attack on his "reasons for fleeing the war" rather than continuing this discussion further. And I had no doubt in my mind that he wished to abscond from the war just for selfish reasons. Hence, I straightaway made a fierce attack on his very selfishness. I told him in no uncertain terms that he would get whatever he desired if he heeded my words, but if he ran away from the war, then he would be doomed. In that event, I would not consider family or friendship. I told him, 'I am your charioteer in the battlefield, and I will do everything for you in the battlefield. But if you think that I will take you away from the battlefield, then you are mistaken. You will have to shoulder the responsibility of leaving the battlefield yourself and you will have to do so, on your own two feet. I would not be held responsible if (by mischance) someone attacked you then. Ergo, if you wish that I, the Supreme Soul, grace you with my blessing, then you will have to stand resolutely in the battlefield.' Here, everybody needs to grasp that the Supreme Soul veritably stands with those who face adversities bravely, but he abandons those who flee fearing hardship.

Now, I had all but terrified Arjuna. For that matter, many a time, a terrified person can be made to do one's bidding by scaring him further. So, in the same vein, I spoke further, elucidating the precariousness of the situation to him. I said, "O Arjuna! If driven by obstinacy and ego, you have resolutely made up your mind to abandon this war, then you are being a fool. For, your nature and a few of your own tendencies will themselves compel you to fight the battle. If Karna were to rain arrows on you as you retreat from the battlefield, you would not be able to control yourself. Were that to happen, you will certainly prefer to wield your bow instead of falling prey to his arrows. And perchance, even if you somehow safely escape the battlefield, your attachment for Draupadi will urge you to turn back to the battlefield at just one signal from her. Grasp this once and for all; you will have to fight this battle, which has become inevitable, at any cost, whether you do so as per your own wish or under duress. All I am telling you is, if you have to fight at any rate, why not do so willingly and wholeheartedly? Upon doing so, you will be able to exhibit valour of the highest order. And only then will you be able to attain the desired outcome in this battle. Else, if you wield your weapons with apathy and listlessness, you will die in vain. On my part, I have granted you the most esoteric, secret knowledge. Deliberate over each and every word I have spoken and then take whatever decision you deem fit. Just bear in mind that both your life and death are in your hands alone."

Surprisingly, even now Arjuna didn't seem willing to fight. Nevertheless, he did seem to be immersed in contemplation. Therefore, in a bid to steer his thoughts in the right direction, I continued further and remarked, "O Arjuna! There is yet another point you must bear in mind. Never are you to disclose these secrets I have shared with you concerning the human mind and life to someone who has no wish to hear of them. Nor are you to deliver this instruction to an undeserving person who utterly disregards his soul. Everybody should always bear this law of Nature in mind that Nature never grants anything to an undeserving person. Moreover, Nature never forces anyone to do anything against his wishes. But yes, if anyone ardently wishes to listen to this mysterious knowledge, then it must be imparted to him. Both, those who listen to this knowledge and those who disseminate it should be considered as my true devotees. Know this, O Arjuna, that nobody can be dearer to me than such devotees. And any devotee who imbibes this knowledge, realises me without a shadow of a doubt and becomes one with me. O Arjuna, such is this knowledge that any person, who reflects on it, is bound to prosper, irrespective of the era he belongs to. And you have had this knowledge expounded to you from me, Krishna himself. But surprisingly, even now you seem to be in a quandary! What is the problem? Have you not listened to this supreme knowledge carefully? And if you have, how has your delusion driven by ignorance not been destroyed yet?"

Arjuna:

O Krishna! My delusion has been obliterated by your supreme benevolence. Now, nary a delusion do I harbour. I have realised that I simply have no alternative other than to fight the war. Ergo, I will now adhere to your command with all my heart and soul.

Sanjaya:

O King Dhritarashtra! With rapt attention, I have listened to the exchange of dialogue between Shri Krishna and Arjuna. I feel blessed hearkening to this glorious knowledge. And if truth be told, it is my firm belief that where there is Shri Krishna therein lies victory.

Gita:

At long last, Arjuna had consented to fight. And most importantly, he had agreed to fight just in time. Hence, without wasting time, Krishna immediately raced the chariot away from the middle of the two warring factions and parked it in the Pandava camp once again. There is just one point though that I would like to stress upon here. While it was true that Arjuna had agreed to fight, he was still unable to quell the desire for fruits. He had chosen to fight this war under the influence of his brain, not guided by his soul. And this was the sole reason why the same Arjuna who, prior to the war, deemed begging alms to be far superior than fighting the war, never mentioned renunciation upon emerging victorious in the war. Nevertheless, this is of no consequence. If Arjuna had performed his *karma* and attained the kingdom as a result, he needed to certainly enjoy it. But Arjuna crossed all limits when, in a bid to extend his kingdom and become the Emperor, he not only performed the *Ashwamedha Yajna*[36] but also needlessly killed numerous people for that purpose. Indeed, all this was undertaken by the very same Arjuna who had proclaimed the violence in this war a grave sin; driven by the expectation of fruits, all this was done by the very same Arjuna, whom Krishna had urged countless times in this entire discussion to renounce the expectation of fruits. The point I wish to make here is that though Arjuna missed his chance, you must not make the same mistake. Knowledge, better than this, can never be made available to humankind again. Therefore, take maximum advantage of this and continue weakening your expectation of fruits. Grasp it once and for all, expectation of fruits is the one and only enemy of the human being. I am aware that as long as one doesn't inch closer to his soul, it will be well-nigh impossible to relinquish the expectation of fruits. Until then, you will continue desiring worldly comforts and pleasures sometimes, and renunciation at other times, seeking either wealth or the Supreme Soul. You will also wonder how you will perform deeds if you give up the expectation of fruits itself. Out of sheer ignorance, you may also wonder how you will make progress without having the expectation of fruits. Well, my point is that every

36 *Ashwamedha Yajna* - A horse sacrifice ritual used by ancient kings to prove their imperial sovereignty.

person is performing actions driven by the expectation of fruits, but pray tell me, how many have attained happiness and success? Ergo, I will reiterate the truthful words of Krishna once again, that only the one who has renounced the expectation of fruits can become happy, successful and great. Hence, as soon as you can do it, learn the art of "performing *karma* without nursing the expectation of fruits" as taught by Krishna. If you encounter impediments, read these words of wisdom imparted by Krishna over and over again. Meditate on his words and put them into practice. I am reiterating everything because I wish to see the entire humankind basking in glory, perched on the pinnacle of "joy and success". In fact, I am nothing but a magnum opus comprising maxims to lead the human being to attain joy and success. And when so much has already been discussed, I shall also reveal that the essence of Krishna's life is encapsulated in me, or you may say that I am the essence of Krishna's life experiences, not mere empty maxims. Indeed, Krishna had traversed the journey from being an ordinary cowherd boy to becoming the king of the golden city of Dwarka by continually performing *karma* without harbouring the expectation of fruits; the maxim that led him to attain supreme knowledge. And you are well aware that Krishna advocates action not renunciation; that he gives precedence to living life to the fullest, not to wandering aimlessly in forests. And that is why, with the dawn of every new era, his words will continue to gain greater significance. My only request to you is, derive maximum benefit out of it. With this ardent hope, your Gita seeks your permission to leave.

Note: While reading this essence of the Gita, and even after reading it, kindly read and listen to the *shlokas* of the Bhagavad Gita over and over again. Also, I would request you to listen to and read the *shlokas* of the Gita in the language you are proficient in.

The most crucial lesson of this chapter is the warning that Krishna gives to Arjuna. Right from the second chapter of the Gita, Krishna had been trying to convince Arjuna to fight the war, but Arjuna stood obdurate in his stance. On his part, Krishna had tried all possible approaches to explain to him and save him from certain doom. But when none of it produced any effect on Arjuna, Krishna warned him saying, "If you do not pay heed to me, you will face ruination and debasement!" And this warning of Krishna is meant not just for Arjuna but for all of us too. Nature, governed by laws that are beyond the purview of time, has been in existence since aeons. Even our mind and life are both governed by these very laws. And Nature's most important law for us is, the greater the heights that one's mind elevates to, the more splendid one's life will turn out to be; else, life will be plagued by endless, ever new troubles. Even all the spiritual teachings of the world are oriented towards showing man the right path to lead a magnificent life. That is because living a splendid and memorable life is verily man's sole *dharma* – religion. Barring this, it would serve you well to ignore all the antics that are propagated in the name of religion. Indeed, if such antics had even a semblance of Nature's science, human life wouldn't have been in such dire straits. Hence, to even discuss them among the wise (like us) is no less than an insult to our intelligence. According to them, one simply needs to make offerings or donation and perform rituals externally, no matter how one's mind is. Well, this very idea is against the supreme law of Nature. If this were possible, Krishna wouldn't have bothered enunciating such a lengthy Gita! Instead, he would have easily handed Arjuna a *mantra* or a sacred thread.

Well, since we are sensible people, we should engage in sensible discussions. And the main point of this discussion is, we should allow our mind to be moulded as Krishna wishes to. Else, similar to Arjuna, Nature and Krishna will have to warn us too saying, 'Be prepared for your ruination and debasement!' All said and done, life is a priceless opportunity that must not be squandered. And to carve a splendid life, one has no choice but to embrace the Gita, for Gita is the blessing that will turn your life around. Hence, I hope you will not squander away this great opportunity that has befallen your way. So, without further ado, fill in the chart below and let your determination to make your life a great success shine through!

Write in your own words that 'I will not give Nature the chance to issue a warning. If need be, I will read the Gita repeatedly until I have grasped its teachings.'

Practical Application – 24

Write in your own words that 'I have realised the importance of Gita, and I will mould myself in accordance with its teachings and lead a spectacular life.'

....
....
....
....
....
....
....

Note:

Remember, the more you write in these practical applications, the stronger will be your grasp of the Gita and its teachings. Also, you must write with a calm mind, in solitude, and that too with utmost sincerity and truthfulness.

Practical Application – 25

Write in detail the changes you have experienced in your mind and thoughts after having read this Gita for the first time.

....
....
....
....
....
....
....
....
....
....

Practical Application – 26

Every month, check yourself and write down the percentage in which you have been able to imbibe the Gita. Continue this exercise for ten months. Bear in mind, I am not talking about how well you have comprehended the Gita, but rather, the extent to which you have been able to implement it in your life.

Month	Percentage
1.	
2.	
3.	
4.	
5.	
6.	
7.	
8.	
9.	
10.	

Note:

Consider this Gita a blessing, and never part with it even for a moment. For, it will continue to guide you at every difficult juncture of your life. Upon reading and revisiting the words that you have written yourself, you will keep gaining clarity evermore. Additionally, a 'Maha Gita' is also coming your way soon, comprising every *shloka* along with its detailed explanation and notes. But first, imbibe this concise Gita in its entirety so that you can grasp that expansive and profound Gita comprehensively and effortlessly.

Thank you
Deep Trivedi

Graphic Books – A Wholesome Family Read

In every child there lies a potential to become successful and great. Everyone does not have to necessarily struggle in life. The question is, how should a child identify his talent and nurture it? How should parents provide the right upbringing, hone their children's talent and give them wings to fly?

The perfect foundation for your children, these entertaining and educational graphic books will not only guide your children in the right direction but also serve as the perfect parenting tool for you.

**The Story of Steve Jobs
Mischief Maker to Path Breaker**

**Naughtiness to Greatness
AL TO EDISON**

**The Story of a Lion's Cub
Haughty to Daunty!**

Available in English and Hindi at all leading book stores and e-commerce sites

DEEPTRIVEDI APP

— now available on —

  firetvstick **androidtv** PWA

- Watch and listen to more than 650+ hours of exclusive audio and video content in offline mode as per your convenience.

- Listen to 'I am Krishna - The Complete Psychological Biography of Krishna' and other audiobooks (more than 200 hours) by Deep Trivedi exclusively on Deep Trivedi App.

- Read all books penned by Deep Trivedi exclusively on Deep Trivedi App.

- You can also switch language from English to Hindi and vice versa.

- Watch the live telecast of Deep Trivedi's interactive sessions first on Deep Trivedi App. Amazing audio and video playback even at slow internet speeds.

- Begin your day with the timeless wisdom of Bhagavad Gita, Kabir's profound *dohas* and 5000+ quotations by Deep Trivedi that will put your life on the path of progress.

DeepTalks
TAO TE CHING
by
DEEP TRIVEDI

DeepTalks
Ashtavakra Gita
by
DEEP TRIVEDI

DeepTalks
bhagavad gita
by
DEEP TRIVEDI

DeepTalks
Secrets
by
DEEP TRIVEDI

WORKSHOPS
by
DEEP TRIVEDI

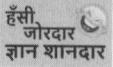